MW01092644

Shadows of the Messiah in the Torah

Volume Two
Revised Edition

And beginning with Moses and all the prophets, He explained what was said in all the scriptures concerning Himself.
Luke 24:27

Hebrew Roots Teachings for Home Studies
By
Dan and Brenda Cathcart

Scripture references used in this volume are from the following:

The New International Version, Copyright © 1973, 1978, 1984 by International Bible Society.

The New King James Version, Copyright © 1982 by Thomas Nelson, Inc.

MKJV - Scripture taken from the Modern King James Version of the Holy Bible
Copyright © 1962 - 1998
By Jay P. Green, Sr.
Used by permission of the copyright holder

Other Bible scripture versions as noted in the text.

Number references in the text, i.e. #1234, are from the Strong's Concordance, Copyright © 1890 James Strong, Madison, NJ

Copyright © 2009/2017 Moed Ministries, LLC Dan & Brenda Cathcart.

All rights reserved, including the right to copy this book in its entirety in any form whatsoever. Permission is granted for the end user to copy only the student notes, discussion question sections of each lesson and the appendices for the purpose of distributing to participants in your home or small study group.

Cover Design: Dan Cathcart

A Note From the authors:

With a great love for God's word and a desire to see the Hebraic nature of the scripters taught to the Nations, this volume has been compiled from studies conducted in our home over the last several years. It is our sincere prayer that this study volume will enrich your life and those who attend your home study or small group. May the LORD bless you and your family.

Dan & Brenda Cathcart

Published by Moed Publishing, Auburn, WA

Visit us on the web at www.moedministries.com

Table of Contents

Preface

Brenda and I started our home Bible study back in 2008. We titled the study series, "Shadows of the Messiah in the Torah." We meet twice each month on the "Erev Shabbat," the evening of the Sabbath. Each meeting begins with lighting the Sabbath candles and saying the blessings over the bread and wine. We then share a meal (pot luck), a time of fellowship and then a study of God's word. As we've learned more about Torah, the Books of Moses, the Sabbath has become more important to us. That's why we've started out this volume of with a lesson on the Sabbath which, not surprisingly, points to Messiah. If you choose to start observing the Sabbath in a more formal manner, there are many Messianic resources available on the web where you can find a formal liturgy for the Sabbath. We have chosen to write our own simple liturgy as a way to introduce our guests to the beauty and richness of Messiah in the Torah. The Hebrew blessings we use are the traditional blessings said in a Jewish home. A copy of it is included in this volume. Please feel free to use it and change it to suit your situation.

Observing the Sabbath or any other ritual or liturgy will not bring salvation. The only path to eternal life is the through faith that Yeshua is the Messiah, the Son of God and that He came to make atonement for all who will believe in Him. Observing the Sabbath is meaningless without faith. We are however to move beyond the salvation message. Paul tells the Corinthians (1 Cor. 3) that they are still babies in the Word needing milk and not solid food. The writer of Hebrews (Heb. 5) instructs his readers to move beyond milk to the meat of the Word. This is what we are striving to do. It is our desire that those who participate in these studies begin or continue to see the incredible depth and riches that God has hidden for us to discover in His Word.

We've chosen to focus on the revelation of Messiah in the scriptures particularly the Torah. We are to be disciples of Yeshua and to make more disciples of Yeshua. What better way is there to begin than with the revelation of Yeshua Himself? Our theme verse is Luke 24:27 "And beginning with Moses and all the prophets, He explained to them what was written in all the scriptures concerning Himself." We joke that each of our lessons start in Genesis, touch on the Feasts of the LORD, and end in Revelation. While this is not strictly true, each study does meld the Tenakh, the Old Testament, with the Gospels and Apostolic Writings or the New Testament. By the way, we touch on where the labels Old Testament and New Testament come from in the study "I Am the LORD Who Brought You Out."

Each lesson in this volume is independent of the others so they can be done in any order and newcomers can start at any time. There are a few lessons that go together, however. There are two on David and three that center on Abraham or Abram as he was called in the setting of these lessons. The lesson "The Queen Who Saved Her People" is about the book of Esther which establishes the Jewish feast of Purim. We've chosen to finish this volume with an in depth study of the first verse in Genesis, "The End is Declared From the Beginning." We examine the meaning of each word in the original Hebrew as well as the Hebrew picture language as we journey through the Feast of Firstfruits and conclude in

Isaiah 65, a companion passage to Revelation 21. Don't worry, though, Revelation is not neglected in this lesson!

This volume has four appendices. The first is the Hebrew alphabet. It contains background on the Hebrew letters as well as a chart with the original pictographs, the modern letters and the meaning and numerical value of each letter. You will want to have copies of this for all the lessons because almost all the lessons include some Hebrew. The second appendix is a summary of the Biblical calendar. You will find this helpful for all the lessons but especially "The tabernacle and Creation" and "The Commandment to Read the Torah before the Assembly." The third appendix is a copy of the Sabbath blessings that we use. Again, feel free to use it as you wish. The last appendix is a chart of the thirteen attributes of God used in the lesson "I am the LORD who brought you out." They can also be used independently to show the character of God.

Much of the materials in this volume have been developed from topics studied at El Shaddai Ministries' weekly Sabbath Torah Portion or from the weekly Torah Club Bible study. At home, we get out our Sabbath notes, our Torah Club notes, other books, Strong's Concordance and several translations of the Bible and then start digging. Many times one study will beget another, hence multiple studies in this volume on David and Abraham. A good Study Bible that helps to link verses is a must! One tool that has been of immense value is Power Bible available at www.powerbible.com. We'd like to acknowledge the inspiration Mark Biltz pastor of El Shaddai Ministries, First Fruits of Zion the publishers of the Torah Club, and Daniel Gruber author of The Separation of Church & Faith.

The best way to start a Home Bible study is to jump in and start!

1. Choose a day and time. It can be weekly, monthly or bi-monthly. You won't be able to please everyone so just choose what works best for you. As I stated, we chose to meet on first and third Fridays for the Sabbath. Allow about an hour and a half for each meeting. The study materials can be covered in about an hour. Extra time is good for questions, discussion and just getting to know each other.

2. Invite friends, neighbors, family members. You might encourage them to bring a friend also. The materials included here are not sequential so new people can start any time. Be enthusiastic and positive. Let your excitement show; it's contagious.

3. Leaders should read through all the material before teaching. It is especially helpful for the leader to be familiar with the contexts of the scriptures, so take some time and look up the scriptures and read the passages the scriptures are taken from. Leaders should also look up the Hebrew and/or Greek words and be familiar with their use in the scriptures.

4. Study for yourself. This is very important. Look up and read related scriptures using your study Bible. You might find something interesting that we didn't include in the material.

5. Pray! It's amazing how God opens our eyes and ears to see and understand when we ask Him. Pray before preparing and pray before teaching.

Preface for the Revised Edition

As we began to prepare this volume of <u>Shadows of Messiah in the Torah</u> for publishing in our new format, the first thing we did was to review each lesson in this volume. Since we are always learning more in God's Torah, we found many places where we could add new insight, depth, or additional connections. Our God is an awesome God faithful to bring us broader and deeper of understanding of Him through His Word!

Some lessons remain essentially the same with only minor revisions; adding or changing scripture or commentary to emphasize a point that we felt we hadn't completely communicated in the original. A few lessons have more significant changes. The lesson on the Sabbath underwent an entire re-write as we learned and experienced more of God's heart for the Sabbath. Most of the original lesson still exists in the form of the discussion questions but the focus of the lesson on the Sabbath has become the purpose of the Sabbath. Our own celebration of the Sabbath has evolved along the same path. The Sabbath Blessings that we currently use reflect that change and are included in the appendix on the Sabbath Blessings. Other lessons with significant changes are The Tabernacle and Creation, Eternity: In Heaven or on Earth?, David's Reign and Yeshua's Second Coming, and The Commandment to Read the Torah Before the Assembly.

We've added discussion questions to each lesson that allow for more diversity in presenting the material and promote more interaction with the material and between the participants. We didn't want the questions to just rehash the material in the lessons, so we've tried to pose questions that lead to deeper thinking and putting that understanding into words. We've included questions that extend beyond the lesson itself. Some questions connect the lessons together. Other questions ask the participant to apply concepts to their own lives. We have also added an appendix listing some additional resources.

The Student notes, discussion questions and other general handout materials in PDF format are available for FREE download on our website at MoedMinistries.com/bookstore.html. The download links are located on this pages.

As always, our prayer for you is that God will draw you into a deeper relationship with Him as you learn more about His character and great love for you. In the words of Peter as he closes his second epistle, "(May you) grow in the grace and knowledge of our Lord and Savior Jesus Christ. To Him be the glory both now and forever, amen. (2Pet. 3:18)

Shalom and be blessed,
Dan and Brenda Cathcart
Moed Ministries International

How to use these materials:

1. Each lesson contains two parts. One part is a detailed guide for the use of the leader. We've found it easier to teach if all the scriptures are written out in the notes so we've written out all the scriptures. The second part consists of note pages for students. Make copies of the student notes and discussion questions for each participant. With the addition of discussion questions, each lesson can easily be extended to two sessions if desired.

2. There are general handouts for all study participants included in the Appendices. The Hebrew Alphabet and Alphabet Chart should be available for all the sessions since most lessons have references to the Hebrew language or alphabet. The original Hebrew was written in pictographs. Each letter comes from a picture and retains the meaning of the picture. Many words make compelling "word pictures." Those are included in a separate text block. They may be used where they are inserted in the page or at the beginning or end of the lesson. The glossary is also useful especially for participants who drop in occasionally for a lesson.

3. Most of the lessons contain references to the original Hebrew or Greek. The number associated with the word is its reference in the Strong's Concordance and Dictionary. We use different versions of the Bible in our lessons; the version is noted in parentheses at the end of each scripture passage. We use the New King James (NKJV) and Modern King James (MKJV) versions most often followed by the New International Version (NIV) and the King James Version (KJV). Other versions include the Young's Literal Translation (YLT) and the New American Standard Bible (NASB).

4. Some people have each person in the study purchase their own copy of the book and read through the lessons together using the student notes to record their own thoughts or insights as they go through each lesson. The discussion questions will make this method of using the materials both easier and more meaningful.

The Sabbath

A. The Sabbath is one of the Feasts of the LORD; it is one of God's appointed times.

> Le 23:1-3 And the LORD spake unto Moses, saying, 2 Speak unto the children of Israel, and say unto them, Concerning the feasts of the LORD, which ye shall proclaim to be holy convocations, even these are my feasts. 3 Six days shall work be done: but the seventh day is the sabbath of rest, an holy convocation; ye shall do no work therein: it is the sabbath of the LORD in all your dwellings. (KJV)

The word "feasts" is not the best translation of the Hebrew word "moedim" in this passage. When we think of the word feast, we think primarily of food and partying. Although these activities play a role in moedim, that is not the primary purpose of moedim. Moedim, plural of moed, means appointed times.

Feast: #4150. מוֹעֵד mow'ed, mo-ade' properly, an appointment, i.e. a fixed time or season.

As we look at the Hebrew words from which we get "holy convocation," we will see the purpose of these appointed times. The word translated "holy" is the Hebrew word kadosh defined in Strong's Lexicon as sacred or hallowed.

Holy: #6944. קֹדֶשׁ ko'-desh a sacred place or thing; rarely abstract, sanctity:--consecrated (thing), dedicated (thing), hallowed

This definition is filled with "church" words. We know what they mean in the cultural context of church. But what do the words mean in English? Dictionary.com tells us the words sacred, sanctify, and hallow all mean to set apart.

The word translated "convocation" is the Hebrew word migrah meaning a public meeting or rehearsal.

Convocation: #4744. מִקְרָא miqra', mik-raw' from 7121; something called out, i.e. a public meeting also a rehearsal:--assembly.

These feasts are days that God establishes as His days. These are His appointed times that we are to set apart to assemble together and rehearse what He has done and what He will do! Of these appointed times, the Sabbath is the first one established and observed on its own fifty two times a year. This is in addition to the specific days within the other appointed times that are observed as Sabbaths! God is showing us the importance of the Sabbath. So, what is special about this appointed time? What are we rehearsing that God wants us to remember each and every week? Moses' words to the children of Israel right before they enter the Promised Land answer this question.

> De 5:15 And remember that you were a slave in the land of Egypt, and the LORD your God brought you out from there by a mighty hand and by an outstretched arm;

therefore the LORD your God commanded you to keep the Sabbath day. (NKJV)

As we dig into the observance of the Sabbath, we see that it is the remembrance and rehearsal of God's grace and redemption.

B. We are to remember and rehearse that God completed creation in six days and on the seventh day, He rested.

> Ge 2:1-3 Thus the heavens and the earth were finished, and all the host of them. 2 And on the seventh day God ended his work which he had made; and he rested on the seventh day from all his work which he had made. 3 And God blessed the seventh day, and sanctified it: because that in it he had rested from all his work which God created and made. (KJV)

We read twice in this passage that God finished or ended his work. After finishing everything He created, He blessed and set apart the seventh day and rested. What does it mean to "bless" something? The Hebrew word is barakh which means to kneel before, to adore or praise.

Bless: #1288. בְרַךְ barak, baw-rak' a primitive root; to kneel; by implication to bless God (as an act of adoration), bless, congratulate, kneel (down), praise, salute.

God kneels down, adores and praises the Sabbath! There must truly be something special in this day! He said He did this because He completed His work. What work did He complete? Everything! This includes His redemption plan. He knew from the beginning that redemption would be necessary and what it would entail. God accomplished it from the beginning of creation. Isaiah tells us He declared the end from the beginning and will accomplish all that He has declared.

> Is 46:10 Declaring the end from the beginning, and from ancient times the things that are not yet done, saying, My counsel shall stand, and I will do all my pleasure: (KJV)

Peter tells us that Yeshua was chosen from the foundation of the world, and the Book of the Revelation of Yeshua tells us that He was slain from the foundation of the world.

> 1 Pe 1:20 He indeed was foreordained before the foundation of the world, but was manifest in these last times for you (NKJV)

> Re 13:8 All who dwell on the earth will worship him, whose names have not been written in the Book of Life of the Lamb slain from the foundation of the world. (NKJV)

The Sabbath is an appointed time to remember and rehearse that God has purposed our redemption from the very beginning. He alone is king and creator of the universe and has created everything that has been created through His son Yeshua, including redemption!

C. After the establishment of the Sabbath in Genesis at creation, the scriptures are silent about the Sabbath until God redeems the children of Israel from Egypt. There in the wilderness, God provided manna for them but in such a way as to test if they would follow His Torah.

> Ex 16:4-5 Then the LORD said to Moses, "Behold, I will rain bread from heaven for you. And the people shall go out and gather a certain quota every day, that I may test them, whether they will walk in My law (Torah) or not. 5 "And it shall be on the sixth day that they shall prepare what they bring in, and it shall be twice as much as they gather daily." (NKJV)

They were to gather enough manna on the sixth day to provide enough food for the seventh day as well. They were not to gather manna on the Sabbath. But some went out to gather manna anyway.

> Ex 16:28-30 And the LORD said to Moses, "How long do you refuse to keep My commandments and My laws (Torah)? 29 "See! For the LORD has given you the Sabbath; therefore He gives you on the sixth day bread for two days. Let every man remain in his place; let no man go out of his place on the seventh day." 30 So the people rested on the seventh day. (NKJV)

Many people use this verse to say that everyone should stay home on the Sabbath and rest there. The word place in verse 29 is the Hebrew word maqowm meaning a standing, a spot or a locality.

#4725. מקום maqowm, maw-kome' from 6965; properly, a standing, i.e. a spot; but used widely of a locality

Their place on the Sabbath was to be at rest from their work and routine daily activities. In Leviticus, we read that they were to hold a holy convocation. When they later set up the Tabernacle, special offerings were to be brought before the LORD on the Sabbath. Their place on the Sabbath was the place they were to assemble together and rehearse God's grace and redemption. The writer of Hebrews says that we, who enter God's rest, cease from our own works.

> He 4:10 For he that is entered into his rest, he also hath ceased from his own works, as God did from his. (KJV)

The commandment is to rest on the Sabbath yet the test was whether they would walk in Torah. To walk implies action. So, when we rest on the Sabbath, we actively follow God's Torah, His instruction. This is consistent with Yeshua's teachings.

> Mat 11:28-30 "Come to Me, all you who labor and are heavy laden, and I will give you rest. 29 "Take My yoke upon you and learn from Me, for I am gentle and lowly in heart, and you will find rest for your souls. 30 "For My yoke is easy and My burden is light." (NKJV)

The word translated "labor" means to be fatigued.

#2872. κοπιαω kopiao, kop-ee-ah'-o from a derivative of 2873; to feel fatigue

Yeshua is referring to those who are fatigued from carrying the heavy legal burden imposed by the Pharisees. These same words are used in Yeshua's condemnation of extra burdens imposed by so-called experts in the Torah.

> Lu 11:46 And He said, "Woe to you also, lawyers! For you load men with burdens hard to bear, and you yourselves do not touch the burdens with one of your fingers. (NKJV)

The Pharisees burdened the people with a legalistic approach to God. They taught that the people must do certain actions in certain ways in order to earn God's favor or grace making the observance of the Sabbath, in particular, and the Torah, in general, burdensome. And, unlike Yeshua, they did nothing to help carry the load. In contrast, Yeshua said to walk in His ways, to join Him by putting on His yoke, and thus, find rest. Yeshua quoted Jeremiah in Matthew 11:29.

> Jer 6:16 Thus says the LORD: "Stand in the ways and see, And ask for the old paths, where the good way is, And walk in it; Then you will find rest for your souls. But they said, 'We will not walk in it.' (NKJV)

When we put on the yoke of Yeshua, we walk the way He walked and we find that He is the one carrying the load.

The writer of Hebrews also writes of a time when the children of Israel chose not to walk in God's ways. He writes of the rebellion in the wilderness when they refused to believe that God could bring them into the Promised Land and so refused to go up to battle against the Canaanites. God was angry with that generation and swore they would not enter His rest because of their unbelief.

> He 3:18-19 And to whom did He swear that they would not enter His rest, but to those who did not obey? 19 So we see that they could not enter in because of unbelief. (NKJV)

The writer goes on to say that the promise of God's rest is still there for those who believe the gospel.

> He 4:1-2 Therefore, since a promise remains of entering His rest, let us fear lest any of you seem to have come short of it. 2 For indeed the gospel was preached to us as well as to them; but the word which they heard did not profit them, not being mixed with faith in those who heard it. (NKJV)

So, entering into God's Sabbath, His rest, is to receive the promise of salvation. Every time we observe the Sabbath, we are proclaiming God's power to save. He brings us up out of the slavery to sin and death and into His Promised Land. And all this was accomplished from the creation.

> He 4:3 For we who have believed do enter that rest, as He has said: "So I swore in My wrath, 'They shall not enter My rest,'" although the works were finished from the foundation of the world. (NKJV)

We cease from our own work and rest in the completed work of Messiah Yeshua. But the writer of Hebrews goes on to admonish his readers to work diligently to enter that rest.

> He 4:11-13 Let us therefore be diligent to enter that rest, lest anyone fall according to the same example of disobedience. 12 For the word of God is living and powerful, and sharper than any two-edged sword, piercing even to the division of soul and spirit, and of joints and marrow, and is a discerner of the thoughts and intents of the heart. 13 And there is no creature hidden from His sight, but all things are naked and open to the eyes of Him to whom we must give account. (NKJV)

God's rest was available to the generation of the children of Israel who came out of Egypt, but they failed to enter that rest because of disobedience. God equates their disobedience with lack of faith. When we obey God, we are proclaiming our faith in Him.

D. It is only after we have entered into God's rest that we can start back to work. But we don't return to our work; we return to the work God has for us. After the children of Israel received atonement for the sin of building and worshipping the golden calf, God instructed them through Moses to observe a Sabbath.

> Ex 35:1-2 Then Moses gathered all the congregation of the children of Israel together, and said to them, "These are the words which the LORD has commanded you to do: 2 "Work shall be done for six days, but the seventh day shall be a holy day for you, a Sabbath of rest to the LORD. Whoever does any work on it shall be put to death. (NKJV)

After the observance of the Sabbath, God commanded that a voluntary offering be received for the building of the Tabernacle, the furnishings and the priestly garments.

> Ex 35:5 'Take from among you an offering to the LORD. Whoever is of a willing heart, let him bring it as an offering to the LORD: (NKJV)

In Hebrews 4:11-13, we read that the living word of God discerns our thoughts and the intent of our hearts. If we have truly entered into God's rest, the intent of our hearts is willingness toward God. Paul writes of this same progression of events in his letter to the Ephesians. First comes grace through faith as we enter into His Sabbath of rest. Then comes works of God outlined in His Torah that we complete with a willing heart.

> Eph 2:8-10 For by grace you have been saved through faith, and that not of yourselves; it is the gift of God, 9 not of works, lest anyone should boast. 10 For

we are His workmanship, created in Christ Jesus for good works, which God prepared beforehand that we should walk in them. (NKJV)

It is only after we have entered His rest, His grace and redemption, that we can offer our gifts and build His house. Paul goes on to say that we who have received God's redemption are no longer strangers and foreigners but part of the household of God.

> Eph 2:20-22 … having been built on the foundation of the apostles and prophets, Jesus Christ Himself being the chief cornerstone, 21 in whom the whole building, being joined together, grows into a holy temple in the Lord, 22 in whom you also are being built together for a dwelling place of God in the Spirit. (NKJV)

The offerings of our hearts go towards building the holy temple of our lives as a dwelling place for the Holy Spirit. The good works God has prepared beforehand are defined for us in His Torah. Will God find us obedient to walk in His ways?

E. How did Yeshua observe the Sabbath? Does He bring the message of salvation in His observance of the Sabbath? Yeshua taught on the Sabbath both in the synagogues and homes. He cast out demons and healed the sick.

At the time of Yeshua, there was disagreement among the Jewish leaders on how to observe the Sabbath. Early in Yeshua's ministry, a group of Pharisees question Him on how He and His disciples observe the Sabbath.

> Mat 12:1-8 At that time Jesus went through the grainfields on the Sabbath. His disciples were hungry and began to pick some heads of grain and eat them. 2 When the Pharisees saw this, they said to him, "Look! Your disciples are doing what is unlawful on the Sabbath." 3 He answered, "Haven't you read what David did when he and his companions were hungry? 4 He entered the house of God, and he and his companions ate the consecrated bread-- which was not lawful for them to do, but only for the priests. 5 Or haven't you read in the Law that on the Sabbath the priests in the temple desecrate the day and yet are innocent? 6 I tell you that one greater than the temple is here. 7 If you had known what these words mean, 'I desire mercy, not sacrifice,' you would not have condemned the innocent. 8 For the Son of Man is Lord of the Sabbath." (NIV)

The Pharisees accuse the disciples of breaking the Sabbath, but Yeshua does not answer them directly. If we skip ahead to verse seven, He says they would not have condemned the guiltless. So, Yeshua declares that His disciples are guiltless; they did not break the Sabbath. Further, the Pharisees would know this if they understood the concept of mercy. What was Yeshua talking about?

Before He declares His disciples' innocence, Yeshua cites two examples that clearly break the Sabbath. In the first, David and his men are fleeing from Saul and stopped at the Tabernacle of the LORD to ask for food. The only food available is the show bread which had been removed from the Tabernacle with fresh bread put in its place.

> 1 Samuel 21:6 So the priest gave him holy bread; for there was no bread there but the showbread which had been taken from before the LORD, in order to put hot bread in its place on the day when it was taken away. (NKJV)

This implies that David's request was on the very day the showbread was removed which is a Sabbath. Apparently David's need as he fled from Saul took precedence over the commandment reserving the showbread for the priests and to rest on the Sabbath.

In the second example, Yeshua cites that the priests serving in the temple always break the Sabbath. But since their service is ordained in the same scriptures that sanctify the Sabbath, serving in the temple must be a higher command than that of resting on the Sabbath. Yeshua even hints that serving Him is an even higher command than serving in the temple, hinting that He is more than just a man.

Later in the day, Yeshua heals a man's withered arm comparing the act with rescuing a sheep on the Sabbath.

> Mat. 12:12 "Of how much more value then is a man than a sheep? Therefore it is lawful to do good on the Sabbath." (NKJV)

He concludes that it is lawful to do good on the Sabbath. So preserving a life, David's life, and serving God is doing good and, thus, lawful on the Sabbath.

Yeshua went on to chide the Pharisees in their understanding of the verse from Hosea 6:6 that God desires mercy and not sacrifice.

> Hos 6:6 For I desire mercy and not sacrifice, And the knowledge of God more than burnt offerings. (NKJV)

The Hebrew word translated as mercy is chesed which is frequently translated as loving kindness. It has the connotation of right conduct toward one's fellow man or towards God.

#2617. חסד checed, kheh'-sed from 2616; kindness; by implication (towards God) piety: good deed(-liness, -ness), kindly, (loving-)kindness

The context of this verse in Hosea is the faithlessness of Ephraim and Judah. Sacrifices and observances are in vain, if their actions don't match their lip service.

> Ho 6:4 "O Ephraim, what shall I do to you? O Judah, what shall I do to you? For your faithfulness (chesed) is like a morning cloud, And like the early dew it goes away. (NKJV)

The word faithfulness here is the same word, chesed, which is translated as mercy in Hosea 6:6. Other versions translate this word here in verse four as goodness, kindness or mercy. Their right conduct, goodness, mercy, and kindness toward God and man is fleeting. The prophet Amos, a contemporary of Hosea, also prophesied about their lack of chesed.

Am 5:22-24 Though you offer Me burnt offerings and your grain offerings, I will not accept them, Nor will I regard your fattened peace offerings. 23 Take away from Me the noise of your songs, For I will not hear the melody of your stringed instruments. 24 But let justice run down like water, And righteousness like a mighty stream. (NKJV)

Isaiah says that the practice of justice and righteousness is the proper way to observe the Sabbath. True Chesed, mercy, loving kindness, and goodness, is exhibited through justice and righteousness.

Is 56:1-2 Thus says the LORD: "Keep justice, and do righteousness, For My salvation is about to come, And My righteousness to be revealed. 2 Blessed is the man who does this, And the son of man who lays hold on it; Who keeps from defiling the Sabbath, And keeps his hand from doing any evil." (NKJV)

Yeshua says that these Pharisees don't understand the concept of chesed or mercy. They are instead practicing a type of self-denial in terms of their observance of the Sabbath. Their rituals and sacrifices were all about them and not about what God requires. Hedged about with man made laws, they have lost the meaning of the Sabbath. They have defiled the Sabbath by failing to keep justice and righteousness. All their sacrifices are in vain. Mark's version of Yeshua's encounter with the Pharisees records Yeshua's words straightening them out.

Mar 2:27-28 And He said to them, "The Sabbath was made for man, and not man for the Sabbath. 28 "Therefore the Son of Man is also Lord of the Sabbath." (NKJV)

Isaiah goes on to tell us that those who observe His Sabbaths, walk in His way and keep His covenant, receive an everlasting name and their sacrifices will be accepted.

Is 56:4-7 For thus says the LORD: "To the eunuchs who keep My Sabbaths, And choose what pleases Me, And hold fast My covenant, 5 Even to them I will give in My house And within My walls a place and a name Better than that of sons and daughters; I will give them an everlasting name That shall not be cut off. 6 "Also the sons of the foreigner Who join themselves to the LORD, to serve Him, And to love the name of the LORD, to be His servants-Everyone who keeps from defiling the Sabbath, And holds fast My covenant- 7 Even them I will bring to My holy mountain, And make them joyful in My house of prayer. Their burnt offerings and their sacrifices Will be accepted on My altar; For My house shall be called a house of prayer for all nations." (NKJV)

How is the Son of Man Lord of the Sabbath? He is the higher authority who shows us the true way to observe the Sabbath; living out God's words, delighting in the Sabbath, and doing God's will as spoken through the prophet Isaiah.

Is 58:13-14 "If you turn away your foot from the Sabbath, From doing your pleasure on My holy day, And call the Sabbath a delight, The holy day of the LORD honorable, And shall honor Him, not doing your own ways, Nor finding your own pleasure, Nor speaking your own words, 14 Then you shall delight yourself in the LORD; And I will cause you to ride on the high hills of the earth, And feed you with the heritage of Jacob your father. The mouth of the LORD has spoken." (NKJV)

F. When the children of Israel reached Mt. Sinai, God spoke the ten words, or commandments, outlining His plan for how they were to live and govern their lives including the commandment to remember and keep the Sabbath. Moses then went up Mt. Sinai where God again spoke the words to Moses giving more details about His plan.

Ex 31:16-17 Wherefore the children of Israel shall keep the sabbath, to observe the sabbath throughout their generations, for a perpetual covenant. 17 It is a sign between me and the children of Israel for ever: for in six days the LORD made heaven and earth, and on the seventh day he rested, and was refreshed. (KJV)

The Sabbath is a sign between God and the children of Israel. The word sign is owth.

#226. אות 'owth, oth (in the sense of appearing); a signal

Hebrew word picture:

Sign: Owth: אות

Aleph: א: ox, strength, leader, abbreviation for God's title Elohim

Vav: ו: nail, connects

Tav: ת: Sign, cross, to covenant, to seal

Sign: Leader nailed to the cross. God is firmly fixed or connected to the covenant.

In the Hebrew word picture for sign, we see that God is committed to His covenant and that He will carry it out by the death of His Son Yeshua on the cross. The observance of the Sabbath is the sign or signal of these things. How does the observance of the Sabbath signal Yeshua's death and resurrection? We find the answer in the last phrase of verse 17. God not only rested but He was refreshed. Why did God need rest and refreshing? Was He tired out? God establishes the pattern for us to follow. We are to observe the Sabbath in rest because God rested. In the plain meaning of the text we also are refreshed by our observance of the Sabbath. But there is a deeper meaning as well. The word refresh is the word naphash meaning to breathe.

#5314. נפש naphash, naw-fash' a primitive root; to breathe

When God created man, He breathed into his nostrils and man became a living soul.

Ge 2:7 And the LORD God formed man of the dust of the ground, and breathed into his nostrils the breath of life; and man became a living soul. (KJV)

This word for living soul is nephesh from the root naphash.

#5315. נֶפֶשׁ nephesh, neh'-fesh from 5314; properly, a breathing creature

When we enter into the rest of the Sabbath, it is as if God breathes into our nostrils once again and we become a living soul. We receive the life that Adam received before he sinned. We receive eternal life; we are refreshed.

On another level, we know that Yeshua died just as the High Sabbath of the Feast of Unleavened Bread began and rose from the dead at the end of the weekly Sabbath three days later. He rested in the earth and was refreshed. Because Yeshua rested in the earth and was refreshed, we are redeemed from the slavery of sin and death. We observe the Sabbath to remember that Yeshua is our redeemer.

Finally, we see that the Sabbath is a sign of Yeshua's second return. It is a sign or signal that in six days God created the heavens and the earth and on the seventh day, He rested. A Psalm of Moses records that a thousand years is like a day.

Ps 90:4 For a thousand years in Your sight Are like yesterday when it is past, And like a watch in the night. (NKJV)

Peter tells us that a day with God is like a thousand years when he writes of Yeshua's certain return.

2 Pe 3:8 But, beloved, be not ignorant of this one thing, that one day is with the Lord as a thousand years, and a thousand years as one day. (KJV)

As we approach the six thousandth year since Adam's creation, we look forward to the Sabbath of the seventh millennium corresponding to the reign of Yeshua.

Re 20:6 Blessed and holy is he who has part in the first resurrection. Over such the second death has no power, but they shall be priests of God and of Christ, and shall reign with Him a thousand years. (NKJV)

In the Sabbatical reign of Yeshua, it is lawful to do good works. Yeshua will reign according to the word delivered by Isaiah and Jeremiah with justice and righteousness.

Jer 23:5 "Behold, the days are coming," says the LORD, "That I will raise to David a Branch of righteousness; A King shall reign and prosper, And execute judgment and righteousness in the earth. (NKJV)

Student Notes for the Sabbath

A. The Sabbath is one of the Feasts of the LORD; it is one of God's appointed times.

> Lev. 23:1-3 And the LORD spake unto Moses, saying, 2 Speak unto the children of Israel, and say unto them, Concerning the feasts of the LORD, which ye shall proclaim to be holy convocations, even these are my feasts. 3 Six days shall work be done: but the seventh day is the sabbath of rest, an holy convocation; ye shall do no work therein: it is the sabbath of the LORD in all your dwellings. (KJV)

Feast: #4150. מועד mow'ed, mo-ade' properly, an appointment, i.e. a fixed time or season.

Holy: #6944. קדש ko'-desh a sacred place or thing; rarely abstract, sanctity:--consecrated (thing), dedicated (thing), hallowed

Convocation: #4744. מקרא miqra', mik-raw' from 7121; something called out, i.e. a public meeting also a rehearsal:--assembly.

These feasts are days that God establishes as His days. These are His appointed times that we are to set apart to assemble together and rehearse what He has done and what He will do! What are we rehearsing that God wants us to remember each and every week? (Deu. 5:15)

B. We are to remember and rehearse that God completed creation in six days and on the seventh day, He rested. (Gen. 2:1-3, Isa. 46:10, 1Pet. 1:20, Rev. 13:8)

Bless: #1288. ברך barak, baw-rak' a primitive root; to kneel; by implication to bless God (as an act of adoration), bless, congratulate, kneel (down), praise, salute.

The Sabbath is an appointed time to remember and rehearse that God has purposed our redemption from the very beginning. He alone is king and creator of the universe and has created everything that has been created through His son Yeshua, including redemption!

C. There in the wilderness, God provides manna for them but in such a way as to test if they will follow His Torah. (Ex. 16:4-5, Ex. 16:28-30, Heb. 4:10)

Place: #4725. מָקוֹם maqowm, maw-kome' from 6965; properly, a standing, i.e. a spot; but used widely of a locality

When we rest on the Sabbath, we actively follow God's Torah, His instruction. (Mat. 11:28-30, Lu. 11:46, Jer. 6:16, Heb. 3:18-19, Heb. 4:1-2)

Labor: #2872. κοπιαω kopiao, kop-ee-ah'-o from a derivative of 2873; to feel fatigue

So, entering into God's Sabbath, His rest, is to receive the promise of salvation. (Heb. 4:3, Heb. 4:11-13)

When we obey God, we are proclaiming our faith in Him.

D. It is only after we have entered into God's rest that we can start back to work. (Ex. 35:1-2, Ex. 35:5, Eph. 2:8-10, Eph. 2:20-22)

The offerings of our hearts go towards building the holy temple of our lives as a dwelling place for the Holy Spirit.

E. How did Yeshua observe the Sabbath? (Mat. 12:1-8, 1Sam. 21:6, Mat. 12:12, Hos. 6:6, Hos. 6:4, Amos 5:22-24)

Isaiah says that the practice of justice and righteousness is the proper way to observe the Sabbath. (Isa. 56:1-2, Mark 2:27-28, Isa. 56:4-7)

How is the Son of Man Lord of the Sabbath? He is the higher authority who shows us the true way to observe the Sabbath living out God's words spoken through the prophet Isaiah. (Isa. 58:13-14)

F. The Sabbath is a sign. (Ex. 31:16-17)

Sign: #226. אות 'owth, (in the sense of appearing); a signal

Hebrew word picture:
Sign: Owth: אות
Aleph: א: ox, strength, leader, abbreviation for God's title Elohim
Vav: ו: nail, connects
Tav: ת: Sign, cross, to covenant, to seal

Sign: Leader nailed to the cross. God is firmly fixed or connected to the covenant.

We are to observe the Sabbath in rest because God rested. In the plain meaning of the text we also are refreshed by our observance of the Sabbath. But there is a deeper meaning as well. (Gen. 2:7)

Refresh: #5314. נָפַשׁ naphash, naw-fash' a primitive root; to breathe

Soul: #5315. נֶפֶשׁ nephesh, neh'-fesh from 5314; properly, a breathing creature

When we enter into the rest of the Sabbath, it is as if God breathes into our nostrils once again and we become a living soul.

On another level, we observe the Sabbath to remember that Yeshua is our redeemer.

Finally, we see that the Sabbath is a sign of Yeshua's second return. (Ps. 90:4, 2Pet. 3:8, Rev. 20:6, Jer. 23:5)

Discussion Questions for the Sabbath

1. We observe the Sabbath to remember that God created everything He created in six days. Read Psalm 95. How can we put God on the throne in our lives? How is this a rehearsal of the millennial reign of Messiah?

2. The Sabbath is also a promise of provision. Read Exodus 16:4-5, 22-30. How does Yeshua reiterate that promise of provision in Matthew 6:25-34?

3. God views the Sabbath as a delight. Isaiah 58:13-14 tells us that if we delight in the Sabbath, then we delight ourselves in the LORD. Delight is more than an emotion or feeling. Read Psalm 37:3-7. How can we delight in the Sabbath, and thus, in the LORD?

4. Yeshua's statement that the Sabbath was made for man in Mark 2:27-28 can be read that the Sabbath is our gift from God. In contrast, many people ask if we have to observe the Sabbath. Discuss the differences in these viewpoints.

5. Yeshua said that He was greater than the temple in Matthew 12:6. What does this mean about our observance of the Sabbath?

6. We are commanded to rest and be refreshed on the Sabbath. How is this rest and refreshment a rehearsal of our resurrection? Read Revelation 21:1-5 and Revelation 22:1-5. How is this rest and refreshment a rehearsal of the new heavens and earth?

The Tabernacle and Creation

A. Moses' completion of the Tabernacle parallels God's finished work of creation. The steps of erecting the Tabernacle mirror the six days of creation. As we examine the parallels, we will see that setting up the Tabernacle is like a new creation.

Day	Creation	Tabernacle
1	God separated the light from the darkness. (Gen.1:4)	Moses separated the area of the Tabernacle from the common area. (Ex. 40:18-19)
2	God set apart the heavens from the earth. (Gen. 1:8)	Moses set apart the ark of the Testimony. (Ex. 40:20-21)
3	God brought forth plants from the earth. (Gen. 1:11)	Moses set the bread on the table before the LORD. (Ex. 40:22-23)
4	God placed the lights in the heavens, naming the sun, moon and stars. (Gen. 1:14-18)	Moses placed the lampstand in the Tabernacle. (Ex. 40:26-28)
5	God created the creatures in the sea and birds of the air. (Gen. 1:20)	Moses set up the altar and burned incense on it with the fragrance going up to heaven. (Ex. 40:26-27)
6	God created the animals on the land. He formed Adam and breathed life into his nostrils. (Gen 1:24-26, Gen. 2:7) The LORD God planted a garden eastward in Eden, and there He put the man whom He had formed. (Gen 2:8)	Moses offered burnt offerings on the altar and set up the laver for washing. He washed Aaron and Aaron's sons' feet. (Ex. 40:29-32) Moses set up the courtyard. (Ex. 40:33)
7	God ended His work. (Gen. 2:2)	So Moses finished the work. (Ex. 40:33)

1. When each had ended their work, they examined it and pronounced it good.

> Ge 1:31-2:3: Then God saw everything that He had made, and indeed it was very good. So the evening and the morning were the sixth day. 2:1 Thus the heavens and the earth, and all the host of them, were finished. 2 And on the seventh day God ended His work which He had done, and He rested on the seventh day from all His work which He had done. 3 Then God blessed the seventh day and sanctified it, because in it He rested from all His work which God had created and made. (NKJV)

In Moses' case it was done "as the LORD commanded."

> Ex 39:42-43: According to all that the LORD had commanded Moses, so the children of Israel did all the work. 43 Then Moses looked over all the work, and indeed they had done it; as the LORD had commanded, just so they had done it. And Moses blessed them. (NKJV)

Ex 40:33 And he raised up the court all around the tabernacle and the altar, and hung up the screen of the court gate. So Moses finished the work. (NKJV)

We have an interesting play on the word "good" as we compare the creation with the setting up of the Tabernacle. The word "good" throughout the creation story is the Hebrew word "tov."

#2896. טוֹב towb, tobe, to from 2895; good

When Moses was born, his mother described him as a goodly child. The Hebrew word for goodly is again "tov."

Ex 2:2 And the woman conceived, and bare a son: and when she saw him that he was a goodly child, she hid him three months. (KJV)

Using the Hebrew convention that a child is named for a descriptive word about him from birth, we can deduce that Moses' Hebrew name was most likely a form of the word "tov" perhaps Tovia. So, the man described as good finishes the work on the Tabernacle as the LORD commanded. And God pronounced each day of creation as good.

2. God blessed the seventh day and Moses blessed the people who had completed the work. God finished His work with a Sabbath Day while Moses began the work with a Sabbath Day.

Ex 35:1-2 Then Moses gathered all the congregation of the children of Israel together, and said to them, "These are the words which the LORD has commanded you to do: 2 "Work shall be done for six days, but the seventh day shall be a holy day for you, a Sabbath of rest to the LORD. Whoever does any work on it shall be put to death. (NKJV)

The work building the Tabernacle started after a Sabbath and after a reminder to observe the Sabbath. Even work on the Tabernacle of God was to cease on the Sabbath.

After Moses finished the Tabernacle, there was a full week or "seven" for the ordination of Aaron and his sons and the dedication of the Tabernacle. We will see that seven is the number for spiritual completion.

Le 8:1-3: And the LORD spoke to Moses, saying: 2 "Take Aaron and his sons with him, and the garments, the anointing oil, a bull as the sin offering, two rams, and a basket of unleavened bread; 3 "and gather all the congregation together at the door of the tabernacle of meeting."

Le 8:33-34, 36: "And you shall not go outside the door of the tabernacle of meeting for seven days, until the days of your consecration are ended. For seven days he shall consecrate you. 34 "As he has done this day, so the LORD has commanded to do, to make atonement for you. 36 So Aaron and his sons did all the things that the LORD had commanded by the hand of Moses. (NKJV)

Aaron and his sons spent the seven days of dedication outside the door of the Tabernacle. It wasn't until the eighth day that they made sacrifices and entered the Tabernacle for the first time. It was also on the eighth day that the LORD appeared to all the people.

Le 9:1-2: It came to pass on the eighth day that Moses called Aaron and his sons and the elders of Israel. 2 And he said to Aaron, "Take for yourself a young bull as a sin offering and a ram as a burnt offering, without blemish, and offer them before the LORD. (NKJV)

Le 9:23-24 And Moses and Aaron went into the tabernacle of meeting, and came out and blessed the people. Then the glory of the LORD appeared to all the people, 24 and fire came out from before the LORD and consumed the burnt offering and the fat on the altar. When all the people saw it, they shouted and fell on their faces. (NKJV)

God took up His residence in the Tabernacle.

B. Like Eden, the Tabernacle was the place where God dwelt. The Garden of Eden was created as a place where God could dwell with man. The Tabernacle was created so God could once again dwell with man.

Ge 3:8 And they heard the sound of the LORD God walking in the garden in the cool of the day, and Adam and his wife hid themselves from the presence of the LORD God among the trees of the garden. (NKJV)

Ex 25:8 "And let them make Me a sanctuary, that I may dwell among them. (NKJV)

God Himself planted the Garden of Eden and put Adam into it. It is a special place, set aside from the rest of creation.

Ge 2:8 And the LORD God planted a garden eastward in Eden; and there he put the man whom he had formed. (KJV)

Similarly, the Tabernacle was a special place set apart from the rest of the camp of Israel. The Tabernacle, like the Garden of Eden, was a place where man could meet with God and live. Moses, a man to whom God spoke clearly, built the Tabernacle from specific instructions from God.

Ex 25:9 According to all that I shew thee, after the pattern of the tabernacle, and the pattern of all the instruments thereof, even so shall ye make it. (KJV)

The writer of Hebrews says the Tabernacle was based on the heavenly Tabernacle.

> Heb 8:5 (The earthly priests) serve the example and shadow of heavenly things, as Moses was warned of God when he was about to make the tabernacle. For, He says "See that you make all things according to the pattern shown to you in the mountain." (MKJV)

C. Man served in both the garden and the Tabernacle. Adam's role in the Garden was similar to Aaron's in the Tabernacle.

Adam's job was to take care of God's garden.

> Ge 2:15 Then the LORD God took the man and put him in the garden of Eden to tend and keep it. (NKJV)

The word translated tend in the New King James Version of the Bible is the Hebrew word "abad" meaning to work or serve. The Hebrew word "ebed" meaning servant comes from this root word.

#5647. עבד `abad, aw-bad' a primitive root; to work (in any sense); by implication, to serve, till

The word translated keep is the Hebrew word shamar meaning to guard.

#8104. שמר shamar, shaw-mar' a primitive root; properly, to hedge about (as with thorns), i.e. guard; generally, to protect, attend to.

We can see that Adam is God's servant given the task of guarding, protecting, and tending God's garden. Although he tended and protected the garden, His service was to God, not the garden. Similarly, Aaron and his sons have the role of ministering to God in the Tabernacle.

> Ex 30:30 "And you shall anoint Aaron and his sons, and consecrate them, that they may minister to Me as priests. (NKJV)

> Ex 28:1 "Now take Aaron your brother, and his sons with him, from among the children of Israel, that he may minister to Me as priest, Aaron and Aaron's sons: Nadab, Abihu, Eleazar, and Ithamar. (NKJV)

The role of Aaron and his sons was to minister **to God** as priests by tending God's people. Both Adam and Aaron's service was to God not to man.

God's dwelling place, the Holy of Holies was to remain holy so only Aaron and the high priests after him could enter. But when he did enter, he represented all Israel by wearing the breastplate of judgment.

> Ex 28:29-30 "So Aaron shall bear the names of the sons of Israel on the breastplate of judgment over his heart, when he goes into the holy place, as a memorial before the LORD continually. 30 "And you shall put in the breastplate of judgment the Urim and the Thummim, and they shall be over Aaron's heart when he goes in before the LORD. So Aaron shall bear the judgment of the children of Israel over his heart before the LORD continually. (NKJV)

Even Aaron could only enter the Holy of Holies once a year. The impurities of just being at the center of the camp permeated the Tabernacle so that even the Holy of Holies needed to be cleansed once a year on the Day of Atonement.

> Le 16:16 "So he shall make atonement for the Holy Place, because of the uncleanness of the children of Israel, and because of their transgressions, for all their sins; and so he shall do for the tabernacle of meeting which remains among them in the midst of their uncleanness. (NKJV)

We can see that the Tabernacle is only a temporary fix for the problem of sin and God's desire to live with and have fellowship with man. Although only a temporary fix, it points to God's ultimate solution.

D. There is a similarity of dates for the creation of the garden and the erecting of the Tabernacle. According to Jewish tradition, Adam was created on the first of Tishrei. This date is in the fall and is celebrated as the Jewish New Year.

When God brought the Israelites out of Egypt, He told them to count the months beginning with Nisan instead of Tishrei. While Tishrei remained the month at which the calendar year changed, Nisan was given status as month number one. It is the month of new birth and redemption.

> Ex 12:1-2 Now the LORD spoke to Moses and Aaron in the land of Egypt, saying, 2 "This month shall be your beginning of months; it shall be the first month of the year to you. (NKJV)

God's presence entered the Tabernacle on the first of Nisan.

> Ex 40:1-2, 33-34 Then the LORD spoke to Moses, saying; 2"On the first day of the first month you shall set up the tabernacle of the tent of meeting… 33 And he raised up the court all around the tabernacle and the altar, and hung up the screen of the court gate. So Moses finished the work. 34 Then the cloud covered the tabernacle of meeting, and the glory of the LORD filled the tabernacle. (NKJV)

The following chart shows the sequence of the Biblical Calendar. Notice that Tishrei is the first month in the civil sequence and the seventh month in the redemption sequence. The reverse is true for Nisan.

Biblical Calendar

Hebrew Name	Civil sequence #	Redemption sequence #	Gregorian equivalent
Tishrei	1	7	Sept-Oct
Chesvan	2	8	Oct-Nov
Kislev	3	9	Nov-Dec
Tevet	4	10	Dec-Jan
Shevat	5	11	Jan-Feb
Adar (I and II)	6	12	Feb-Mar
Nisan	7	1	Mar-April
Iyyar	8	2	April-May
Sivan	9	3	May-June
Tammuz	10	4	June-July
Av	11	5	July-Aug
Elul	12	6	Aug-Sept

In the Calendar, we see the progression in the civil sequence from creation in month 1 (Tishrei) to redemption in month seven (Nisan). Then, in the redemption sequence, we see the progression from redemption in month one (Nisan) to triumphant return and spiritual completion in month seven (Tishrei). And, thus, the cycle is complete.

> **Tishrei 1**: The creation of man. God dwelt with man in the Garden of Eden.
> **Nisan 1**: The month of deliverance or redemption. The Tabernacle was set up and God again dwelt with man.
> **Tishrei 1**: In the redemption sequence, Tishrei becomes the seventh month. Seven is the number of spiritual perfection.

Let's look in detail at the number seven. The Hebrew word for seven is "shevah."

Seven: #7651 שֶׁבַע sheba`, sheh'-bah or (masculine) shibrah {shib-aw'}; from 7650; a primitive cardinal number; seven (as the sacred full one); also (adverbially) seven times; by implication, a week; by extension, an indefinite number

The word "savah" is the Hebrew root word for shevah. It is spelled the same but has different vowel sounds.

#7646 שָׂבַע saba`, saw-bah' or sabeay {saw-bay'-ah}; a primitive root; to sate, i.e. fill to satisfaction (literally or figuratively):--have enough, fill (full, self, with), be (to the) full (of), have plenty of, be satiate, satisfy (with), suffice, be weary of.

A "seven," whether seven days, seven weeks, seven months, seven years, or seven millennia represents satisfaction or fullness.

Tishrei is the month that concludes the Feasts of the LORD cycle each year. In it we see a triple "seven." The seventh Feast, the Feast of Tabernacles, occurs in the seventh month and lasts for seven days. It is celebrated in the third week or seven of the month again pointing to three sevens. Its purpose is to remember the time in the wilderness when God dwelt with man and to celebrate the end of the harvest. It is a time of great rejoicing.

> De 16:13-14 "You shall observe the Feast of Tabernacles seven days, when you have gathered from your threshing floor and from your winepress. 14 "And you shall rejoice in your feast, you and your son and your daughter, your male servant and your female servant and the Levite, the stranger and the fatherless and the widow, who are within your gates. (NKJV)

Because the Feast of Tabernacles occurs at the end of the harvest, it is the end of the agricultural year and, of course, the beginning of the new agricultural year. Tishrei is, therefore, both a beginning and an end. When talking about the Feast of Tabernacles, Deuteronomy refers to it as occurring at the end of the year. Specifically, Sabbath years which are observed every seventh year begin and end at the Feast of Tabernacles.

> De 31:10 And Moses commanded them, saying: "At the end of every seven years, at the appointed time in the year of release, at the Feast of Tabernacles, (NKJV)

Another new year observed in the seventh month is the Year of Jubilee. The year of Jubilee occurs every fiftieth year after seven Sabbatical years.

> Le 25:9-10 'Then you shall cause the trumpet of the Jubilee to sound on the tenth day of the seventh month; on the Day of Atonement you shall make the trumpet to sound throughout all your land. 10 'And you shall consecrate the fiftieth year, and proclaim liberty throughout all the land to all its inhabitants. It shall be a Jubilee for you; and each of you shall return to his possession, and each of you shall return to his family. (NKJV)

Ezekiel refers to Tishrei 1 as the beginning of the year in his vision of the restored temple. The phrase "beginning of the year" is "Rosh Hashannah" in Hebrew. Literally, this is the "head of the Year" referring to the Jewish New Year of the Civil calendar which is on the first of Tishrei. In fact, the first 21 days of Tishrei, three sevens of days, are considered as the end of one year and the beginning of the next. Again, we see three sevens.

> Eze 40:1 In the twenty-fifth year of our captivity, at the beginning of the year, on the tenth day of the month, in the fourteenth year after the city was captured, on the very same day the hand of the LORD was upon me; and He took me there. (NKJV)

Specifically, the day of this vision is the tenth of Tishrei which is Yom Kippur, the Day of Atonement. Ezekiel goes on to describe the returning of the glory of God to the third temple.

> Eze 43:1-5 Afterward he brought me to the gate, the gate that faces toward the east. 2 And behold, the glory of the God of Israel came from the way of the east. His voice was like the sound of many waters; and the earth shone with His glory. 3 It

was like the appearance of the vision which I saw-like the vision which I saw when I came to destroy the city. The visions were like the vision which I saw by the River Chebar; and I fell on my face. 4 And the glory of the LORD came into the temple by way of the gate which faces toward the east. 5 The Spirit lifted me up and brought me into the inner court; and behold, the glory of the LORD filled the temple. (NKJV)

In this month of Tishrei, we come full circle. The heavens and earth will be recreated and God will finally and forever dwell with man.

Re 21:1-3: Now I saw a new heaven and a new earth, for the first heaven and the first earth had passed away. Also there was no more sea. 2 Then I, John, saw the holy city, New Jerusalem, coming down out of heaven from God, prepared as a bride adorned for her husband. 3 And I heard a loud voice from heaven saying, "Behold, the tabernacle of God is with men, and He will dwell with them, and they shall be His people. God Himself will be with them and be their God. (NKJV)

E. Because of their sin, Adam and Eve were exiled from the Garden of Eden and God no longer dwelt with man. Because of the sin of Israel, they were exiled from the land and God's presence left the temple.

Eze 10:18-19 Then the glory of the LORD departed from the threshold of the temple and stood over the cherubim. 19 And the cherubim lifted their wings and mounted up from the earth in my sight. When they went out, the wheels were beside them; and they stood at the door of the east gate of the LORD'S house, and the glory of the God of Israel was above them. (NKJV)

So God sent His son to dwell with man.

Joh 1:14 And the Word became flesh and dwelt among us, and we beheld His glory, the glory as of the only begotten of the Father, full of grace and truth. (NKJV)

When Yeshua ascended to the Father, He sent His Spirit to dwell with man.

Ac 1:8 "But you shall receive power when the Holy Spirit has come upon you; and you shall be witnesses to Me in Jerusalem, and in all Judea and Samaria, and to the end of the earth." (NKJV)

The Spirit of God dwells in us individually and collectively. Together, we are the temple of God built upon the foundation of Yeshua our Messiah. Like the Tabernacle, we are to be holy.

1Co 3:9-17 For we are God's fellow workers; you are God's field, you are God's building. 10 According to the grace of God which was given to me, as a wise master builder I have laid the foundation, and another builds on it. But let each one take heed how he builds on it. 11 For no other foundation can anyone lay than that which is laid, which is Jesus Christ. 12 Now if anyone builds on this foundation with gold, silver, precious stones, wood, hay, straw, 13 each one's work will become clear; for the Day will declare it, because it will be revealed by fire; and the fire will test each one's work, of what sort it is. 14 If anyone's work which he has built on it endures, he will receive a reward. 15 If anyone's work is burned, he will suffer loss; but he himself will be saved, yet so as through fire. 16 Do you not know that you are the temple of God and that the Spirit of God dwells in you? 17 If anyone defiles the temple of God, God will destroy him. For the temple of God is holy, which temple you are. (NKJV)

We are God's temple. But unlike Moses' Tabernacle, we are not yet finished. The work is ongoing. Like the builders of the Tabernacle, our work will be examined. Was it done "as the LORD had commanded?"

In the parable of the talents, Yeshua tells the story of a master coming home after a long time and rewarding his faithful servants. Will you be one who is rewarded?

Mt 25:21 "His lord said to him, 'Well done, good and faithful servant; you were faithful over a few things, I will make you ruler over many things. Enter into the joy of your lord.' (NKJV)

At the end of the book of Revelation, God examines the work and pronounces judgment.

Re 20:11-12 Then I saw a great white throne and Him who sat on it, from whose face the earth and the heaven fled away. And there was found no place for them. 12 And I saw the dead, small and great, standing before God, and books were opened. And another book was opened, which is the Book of Life. And the dead were judged according to their works, by the things which were written in the books. (NKJV)

When God recreates the heaven and the earth, the New Jerusalem will be our dwelling place. And, like Adam before us, we will dwell there with God and serve Him.

Re 22:3 And there shall be no more curse: but the throne of God and of the Lamb shall be in it; and his servants shall serve him: (KJV)

Student Notes for the Tabernacle and Creation

A. Moses' completion of the Tabernacle parallels God's finished work of creation.

Day	Creation	Tabernacle
1	God separated the light from the darkness. (Gen.1:4)	Moses separated the area of the Tabernacle from the common area. (Ex. 40:18-19)
2	God set apart the heavens from the earth. (Gen 1:8)	Moses set apart the ark of the Testimony. (Ex. 40:20-21)
3	God brought forth plants from the earth. (Gen 1:11)	Moses set the bread on the table before the LORD. (Ex. 40:22-23)
4	God placed the lights in the heavens, naming the sun, moon and stars. (Gen 1:14-18)	Moses placed the lampstand in the Tabernacle. (Ex. 40:26-28)
5	God created the creatures in the sea and birds of the air. (Gen. 1:20)	Moses set up the altar and burned incense on it with the fragrance going up to heaven. (Ex. 40:26-27)
6	God created the animals on the land. He formed Adam and breathed life into his nostrils. (Gen 1:24-26, Gen. 2:7) The LORD God planted a garden eastward in Eden, and there He put the man whom He had formed. (Gen 2:8)	Moses offered burnt offerings on the altar and set up the laver for washing. He washed Aaron and his sons' feet. (Ex. 40:29-32) Moses set up the courtyard. (Ex. 40:33)
7	God ended His work. (Gen. 2:2)	So Moses finished the work. (Ex. 40:33)

    1. The inspection (Gen. 1:31-2:3, Ex. 39:42-43, Ex. 40:33, Ex. 2:2)

    2. Beginning and ending. (Ex. 35:1-2, Lev. 8:1-3, Lev. 8:33-34, 36, Lev. 9:1-2, Lev. 9:23-24)

B. Like Eden, the Tabernacle was the place where God dwelt. (Gen. 3:8, Ex. 25:8, Gen. 2:8. Ex. 25:9, Heb. 8:5)

C. Man served in both the garden and the Tabernacle. (Gen. 2:15, Ex. 30:30, Ex. 28:1)

God's dwelling place was to remain set apart. (Ex. 28:29-30, Lev. 16:16)

D. The dates of constructing the Tabernacle and of the creation (Ex. 12:1-2, Ex. 40:1-2, 33, 34)

Biblical Calendar

Hebrew Name	Civil sequence #	Redemption sequence #	Gregorian equivalent
Tishrei	1	7	Sept-Oct
Chesvan	2	8	Oct-Nov
Kislev	3	9	Nov-Dec
Tevet	4	10	Dec-Jan
Shevat	5	11	Jan-Feb
Adar (I and II)	6	12	Feb-Mar
Nisan	7	1	Mar-April
Iyyar	8	2	April-May
Sivan	9	3	May-June
Tammuz	10	4	June-July
Av	11	5	July-Aug
Elul	12	6	Aug-Sept

Tishrei 1:

Nisan 1:

Tishrei 1:

Seven: #7651 שבע sheba`, sheh'-bah or (masculine) shibrah {shib-aw'}; from 7650; a primitive cardinal number; seven (as the sacred full one); also (adverbially) seven times; by implication, a week; by extension, an indefinite number

Savah: #7646 שבע saba`, saw-bah' or sabeay {saw-bay'-ah}; a primitive root; to sate, i.e. fill to satisfaction (literally or figuratively):--have enough, fill (full, self, with), be (to the) full (of), have plenty of, be satiate, satisfy (with), suffice, be weary of.

The beginning and the end (Deu. 16:13-14, Deu. 31:10, Lev. 25:9-10, Eze. 40:1, Eze. 43:1-5, Rev. 21:1-3)

E. The presence of God: (Eze. 10:18-19, John 1:14, Acts 1:8)

Together, we are the temple of God. (1 Cor. 3:9-17)

Was it done "as the LORD had commanded?" (Mat. 25:21, Rev. 20:11-12, Rev. 22:3)

Discussion Questions for the Tabernacle and Creation

1. The Tabernacle is the dwelling place of God. Paul describes us as God's temple. Hebrews 3:6 says that we are the house He is building. Finally, Revelation 21:1-3 says that the New Jerusalem is the bride of Messiah. How are all these saying the same thing?

2. In our role as priests, the writer of Hebrews assures us that we have full access to the Holy of Holies (Hebrews 10:19-22). Read Leviticus 16 and Exodus 28:29-30. Using Aaron's role as a pattern, what is our purpose as we go into the Holy of Holies in prayer?

3. The number seven comes from a Hebrew word to fill or satisfy giving the number seven the symbolic meaning of spiritual completion. What are some other sevens in scripture? How do these represent satisfaction, fullness or spiritual completion?

4. God struck down Aaron's sons Nadab and Abihu when they brought strange fire before the LORD thus defiling the Tabernacle (Leviticus 10:1-3). Hebrews 11:26-30 warns us not to trample on the blood of Yeshua. How, then, should we treat our physical and spiritual bodies?

5. Those who brought offerings to build the Tabernacle were to do so with a willing heart. Paul calls us God's fellow workers on the Temple (1 Cor. 3:9-17). How are we to regard our work on the temple?

6. Paul calls us a new creation (2 Cor. 5:17). How do we as new creations go through each of the steps of creation and setting up the Tabernacle? Try to support your answers with scripture.

Eternity: In heaven or on Earth?

Everyone knows that after we die, we will go to heaven and be with Yeshua. We will spend eternity there in the presence of Yeshua and God. Or will we? What do the scriptures say? Yeshua Himself tells us that we will be with Him.

> Joh 14:3 And if I go and prepare a place for you, I will come again, and receive you unto myself; that where I am, there ye may be also. (KJV)

Yeshua says He is coming again to receive us. The apostle Paul assures us that we will always be with Yeshua.

> 1 The 4:17 Then we which are alive and remain shall be caught up together with them in the clouds, to meet the Lord in the air: and so shall we ever be with the Lord. (KJV)

We will definitely be with Yeshua. The questions remain, where is the place Yeshua is preparing for us and where will He be? In order to answer these two questions, we need to go back to the beginning.

A. In the beginning, God created Adam to dwell on the earth, specifically in the Garden of Eden. God gave Adam dominion over every living thing on the earth. Adam had the title or deed to the earth.

> Ge 1:27-28 So God created man in His own image; in the image of God He created him; male and female He created them. 28 Then God blessed them, and God said to them, "Be fruitful and multiply; fill the earth and subdue it; have dominion over the fish of the sea, over the birds of the air, and over every living thing that moves on the earth." (NKJV)

But Adam didn't have the ultimate authority, God did. Adam was to rule in submission and in service to God.

> Ge 2:15-17 Then the LORD God took the man and put him in the garden of Eden to tend and keep it. 16 And the LORD God commanded the man, saying, "Of every tree of the garden you may freely eat; 17 "but of the tree of the knowledge of good and evil you shall not eat, for in the day that you eat of it you shall surely die." (NKJV)

Adam was to tend the garden and protect it. He was also to submit himself to God and obey His command not to eat of the tree of the knowledge of good and evil.

1. Because of his sin, Adam forfeited his authority over the earth to Satan until the time of the end. Satan flaunts this transfer of authority during the temptation of Yeshua by tempting Him with the power to rule over all the earth.

> Mt 4:8-10 Again, the devil took Him up on an exceedingly high mountain, and showed Him all the kingdoms of the world and their glory. 9 And he said to Him, "All these things I will give You if You will fall down and worship me."10 Then Jesus said to him, "Away with you, Satan! For it is written, 'You shall worship the LORD your God, and Him only you shall serve.'" (NKJV)

Yeshua verifies that Satan is indeed the "ruler of this world" as He readies His disciples for His crucifixion.

> Joh 14:30 "I will no longer talk much with you, for the ruler of this world is coming, and he has nothing in Me. (NKJV)

In Revelation, Satan is referred to as the great dragon who deceives the whole world.

> Re 12:9 So the great dragon was cast out, that serpent of old, called the Devil and Satan, who deceives the whole world; he was cast to the earth, and his angels were cast out with him. (NKJV)

Paul refers to Satan as the "prince of the power of the air."

> Eph 2:1-2 And you He made alive, who were dead in trespasses and sins, 2 in which you once walked according to the course of this world, according to the prince of the power of the air, the spirit who now works in the sons of disobedience, (NKJV)

So, in the beginning, God created Adam to rule over all the earth and everything in it but under the authority of God. Adam was also to tend and protect the special part of God's creation which is the Garden of Eden. But Adam forfeited that authority to Satan.

B. Who can reclaim the deed to the earth and the authority that goes with it? The Psalmist tells us that the Messiah is the one who inherits the earth.

> Ps 2:6-8 `And I--I have anointed My King, Upon Zion--My holy hill.' 7 I declare concerning a statute: Jehovah said unto me, `My Son Thou art, I to-day have brought thee forth. 8 Ask of Me and I give nations--thy inheritance, And thy possession--the ends of earth. (YLT)

Paul tells us Yeshua's qualifications to be the ruler over all God's creation.

> Ro 1:1-4 Paul, a bondservant of Jesus Christ, called to be an apostle, separated to the gospel of God 2 which He promised before through His prophets in the Holy Scriptures, 3 concerning His Son Jesus Christ our Lord, who was born of the seed of David according to the flesh, 4 and declared to be the Son of God with power according to the Spirit of holiness, by the resurrection from the dead. (NKJV)

Yeshua was to be the seed of David and the Son of God imbued with the power of the Holy Spirit. He was declared to be the Son of God by His resurrection from the dead.

1. He is the seed of David, the Seed of Eve.

Ge 3:15 And I will put enmity Between you and the woman, And between your seed and her Seed; He shall bruise your head, And you shall bruise His heel." (NKJV)

A promise was made to David that one of His descendants would sit on his throne and rule forever.

1Ch 17:11-14 "And it shall be, when your days are fulfilled, when you must go to be with your fathers, that I will set up your seed after you, who will be of your sons; and I will establish his kingdom. 12 "He shall build Me a house, and I will establish his throne forever. 13 "I will be his Father, and he shall be My son; and I will not take My mercy away from him, as I took it from him who was before you. 14 "And I will establish him in My house and in My kingdom forever; and his throne shall be established forever."'" (NKJV)

Psalm 89 talks about God's covenant with David.

Ps 89:28-36 My mercy I will keep for him forever, And My covenant shall stand firm with him. 29 His seed also I will make to endure forever, And his throne as the days of heaven. 30 "If his sons forsake My law And do not walk in My judgments, 31 If they break My statutes And do not keep My commandments, 32 Then I will punish their transgression with the rod, And their iniquity with stripes. 33 Nevertheless My lovingkindness I will not utterly take from him, Nor allow My faithfulness to fail. 34 My covenant I will not break, Nor alter the word that has gone out of My lips. 35 Once I have sworn by My holiness; I will not lie to David: 36 His seed shall endure forever, And his throne as the sun before Me; (NKJV)

Psalms 89 makes a clear reference to the Messiah and His divine nature. Twice we read that David's seed endures forever. In verse 32, the transgression of the kings following David who don't keep God's commands will be punished with the rod, their iniquity punished with stripes. Yeshua received the punishment of those kings. Isaiah also speaks of the suffering of Messiah.

Is 53:4-5 Surely He has borne our griefs And carried our sorrows; Yet we esteemed Him stricken, Smitten by God, and afflicted. 5 But He was wounded for our transgressions, He was bruised for our iniquities; The chastisement for our peace was upon Him, And by His stripes we are healed. (NKJV)

The angel Gabriel promised Mary that her son Yeshua would inherit David's throne and the promise to rule on it forever.

Lu 1:30-33 Then the angel said to her, "Do not be afraid, Mary, for you have found favor with God. 31 "And behold, you will conceive in your womb and bring forth a Son, and shall call His name JESUS. 32 "He will be great, and will be called the Son of the Highest; and the Lord God will give Him the throne of His father David. 33 "And He will reign over the house of Jacob forever, and of His kingdom there will be no end." (NKJV)

2. Yeshua is not only the seed of David; He is the seed of God begotten by the Holy Spirit. The Holy Spirit spoke to Joseph, Yeshua's earthly father, about Yeshua's true Father and His role as God's salvation.

Mat 1:20-21 But while he thought about these things, behold, an angel of the Lord appeared to him in a dream, saying, "Joseph, son of David, do not be afraid to take to you Mary your wife, for that which is conceived in her is of the Holy Spirit. 21 "And she will bring forth a Son, and you shall call His name JESUS, for He will save His people from their sins." (NKJV)

Peter testified in Acts of Yeshua's resurrection and of the power of the Holy Spirit promised by Yeshua.

Ac 2:32-33 "This Jesus God has raised up, of which we are all witnesses. 33 "Therefore being exalted to the right hand of God, and having received from the Father the promise of the Holy Spirit, He poured out this which you now see and hear. (NKJV)

Notice Peter says that it is Yeshua who pours out the Holy Spirit. Yeshua is the only one who can reclaim that which was lost.

C. When Yeshua died and rose again, He actually reclaimed the deed to the earth. In the last hours before His arrest and death on the cross, Yeshua tells His disciples that He has overcome the world.

Joh 16:33 "These things I have spoken to you, that in Me you may have peace. In the world you will have tribulation; but be of good cheer, I have overcome the world." (NKJV)

Yeshua testifies again in the vision to John that He is the one with authority.

Re 1:18 "I am He who lives, and was dead, and behold, I am alive forevermore. Amen. And I have the keys of Hades and of Death. (NKJV)

Even though Yeshua already has the authority over all the earth, He has not yet exercised that authority over all of creation.

Heb 2:7-8 You have made him a little lower than the angels; You have crowned him with glory and honor, And set him over the works of Your hands. 8 You have put all things in subjection under his feet." For in that He put all in subjection under him, He left nothing that is not put under him. **But now we do not yet see all things put under him.** (NKJV)

When Yeshua comes again, His first task is to assert that authority and reign over all the earth.

> 1Co 15:24-28 Then comes the end, when He delivers the kingdom to God the Father, when He puts an end to all rule and all authority and power. 25 For He must reign till He has put all enemies under His feet. 26 The last enemy that will be destroyed is death. 27 For "He has put all things under His feet." But when He says "all things are put under Him," it is evident that He who put all things under Him is excepted. 28 Now when all things are made subject to Him, then the Son Himself will also be subject to Him who put all things under Him, that God may be all in all. (NKJV)

He is to rule until all His enemies are under His feet. The chief of these enemies is Satan whom Yeshua binds at the beginning of the one thousand year reign and releases for a final battle after the one thousand years are completed. Back in Genesis 1:28 when God gave Adam dominion over all living creatures, the Hebrew word translated dominion is "radah" which literally means to tread down.

Dominion: #7287. רדה radah, raw-daw' a primitive root; to tread down, i.e. subjugate; specifically, to crumble off:--(come to, make to) have dominion.

Adam had the authority to tread the serpent under his feet; indeed he had the responsibility as the guardian of the Garden of Eden to do so; but instead he chose to listen to the serpent and eat from the tree of the knowledge of good and evil. So Yeshua reclaims the authority that Adam lost and, in the process, treads the serpent under His feet.

D. Yeshua, then, is Eve's seed who crushes the serpent's head and the king on David's throne. Where is the seat of His government? Here are just a few of the scriptures from the writings, the prophets and the Brit Chadashah that tell us the location of Yeshua's throne as well as His title.

> Ps 48:2 Beautiful in elevation, The joy of the whole earth, Is Mount Zion on the sides of the north, The city of the great King. (NKJV)

> Is 24:23 Then the moon will be disgraced And the sun ashamed; For the LORD of hosts will reign On Mount Zion and in Jerusalem And before His elders, gloriously. (NKJV)

> Mic 4:7 I will make the lame a remnant, And the outcast a strong nation; So the LORD will reign over them in Mount Zion From now on, even forever. (NKJV)

> Zep 3:15 The LORD has taken away your judgments, He has cast out your enemy. The King of Israel, the LORD, is in your midst; You shall see disaster no more. (NKJV)

> Joh 1:49 Nathanael answered and said to Him, "Rabbi, You are the Son of God! You are the King of Israel!" (NKJV)

> Joh 12:12 The next day a great multitude that had come to the feast, when they heard that Jesus was coming to Jerusalem, 13 took branches of palm trees and went out to meet Him, and cried out: "Hosanna! 'Blessed is He who comes in the name of the LORD!' The King of Israel!" (NKJV)

Yeshua will rule from Jerusalem and He will be the great king, the LORD of hosts, and the King of Israel.

E. Adam dwelled in the Garden of Eden and had authority over all living things on the earth. Yeshua will dwell in and reign from Jerusalem. What will be the extent of Yeshua's kingdom?

> Zec 14:9, 17 And the LORD shall be King over all the earth. In that day it shall be- "The LORD is one," And His name one... 17 And it shall be that whichever of the families of the earth do not come up to Jerusalem to worship the King, the LORD of hosts, on them there will be no rain. (NKJV)

> Re 11:15 Then the seventh angel sounded: And there were loud voices in heaven, saying, "The kingdoms of this world have become the kingdoms of our Lord and of His Christ, and He shall reign forever and ever!" (NKJV)

> Ps 47:2-8 For the LORD Most High is awesome; He is a great King over all the earth. 3 He will subdue the peoples under us, And the nations under our feet. 4 He will choose our inheritance for us, The excellence of Jacob whom He loves. Selah 5 God has gone up with a shout, The LORD with the sound of a trumpet. 6 Sing praises to God, sing praises! Sing praises to our King, sing praises! 7 For God is the King of all the earth; Sing praises with understanding. 8 God reigns over the nations; God sits on His holy throne. (NKJV)

Yeshua reigns as the King of Israel from Jerusalem and His kingdom, like Adam's kingdom, is the entire earth.

F. How long will Yeshua's reign last? Everyone knows that Yeshua will rule over the whole earth during the millennium then we all go to heaven, right? Isn't that what the book of Revelation says?

> Re 20:4 And I saw thrones, and they sat on them, and judgment was committed to them. Then I saw the souls of those who had been beheaded for their witness to Jesus and for the word of God, who had not worshiped the beast or his image, and had not

received his mark on their foreheads or on their hands. And they lived and reigned with Christ for a thousand years. (NKJV)

What about after the millennium? Does Yeshua cease to reign after the one thousand years? The promise to David was that His seed would reign forever.

> 2Sa 7:16-17 "And your house and your kingdom shall be established forever before you. Your throne shall be established forever."'" 17 According to all these words and according to all this vision, so Nathan spoke to David. (NKJV)

In the book of Daniel, we read of two visions that reveal that Messiah will reign forever. The first is in Daniel's interpretation of Nebuchadnezzar's dream.

> Da 2:44 "And in the days of these kings the God of heaven will set up a kingdom which shall never be destroyed; and the kingdom shall not be left to other people; it shall break in pieces and consume all these kingdoms, and it shall stand forever. (NKJV)

The second is in Daniel's dream and the interpretation the angel gave to him in a vision.

> Da 7:14 Then to Him was given dominion and glory and a kingdom, That all peoples, nations, and languages should serve Him. His dominion is an everlasting dominion, Which shall not pass away, And His kingdom the one Which shall not be destroyed. (NKJV)

Messiah's reign is an everlasting reign. At the end of the millennium, God releases Satan to test those born during the millennial reign. Will they follow Him or the lies of Satan? There is one last battle and Yeshua defeats Satan.

> Re 20:14-15 And death and hell were cast into the lake of fire. This is the second death. 15 And whosoever was not found written in the book of life was cast into the lake of fire. (KJV)

The final judgment and the final death take place. We will see the realization of the promise that all things will be under His feet. Yeshua defeats the last enemy, death itself, as Paul wrote in 1 Corinthians 15.

G. Surely, now we all go to heaven to be with Yeshua, right? After all, that is where our treasure is stored. Yes, we store our treasure in heaven for now.

> Mat 19:20-21 The young man said to Him, "All these things I have kept from my youth. What do I still lack?" 21 Jesus said to him, "If you want to be perfect, go, sell what you have and give to the poor, and you will have treasure in heaven; and come, follow Me." (NKJV)

Mat 6:19-21 "Do not lay up for yourselves treasures on earth, where moth and rust destroy and where thieves break in and steal; 20 "but lay up for yourselves treasures in heaven, where neither moth nor rust destroys and where thieves do not break in and steal. 21 "For where your treasure is, there your heart will be also. (NKJV)

Our treasure in heaven is our eternal reward. Right now, our heart is there, too, because Yeshua is in heaven with God. When we die, our spirits are with Yeshua in heaven. Yeshua told the thief on the cross that when he died, he would be with Yeshua in heaven.

Lu 23:43 And Jesus said to him, "Assuredly, I say to you, today you will be with Me in Paradise." (NKJV)

Paul tells us that when we are absent from our physical bodies, we are home with Christ.

2 Cor 5:6-8 Therefore we are always confident and know that as long as we are at home in the body we are away from the Lord. 7 We live by faith, not by sight. 8 We are confident, I say, and would prefer to be away from the body and at home with the Lord. (NIV)

But, when Messiah comes, those who are dead in Him come with Him and He brings His rewards with Him.

Re 19:14-16 The armies of heaven were following him, riding on white horses and dressed in fine linen, white and clean. 15 Out of his mouth comes a sharp sword with which to strike down the nations. "He will rule them with an iron scepter." He treads the winepress of the fury of the wrath of God Almighty. 16 On his robe and on his thigh he has this name written: KING OF KINGS AND LORD OF LORDS. (NIV)

Isa 40:10 Behold, the Lord GOD shall come with a strong hand, And His arm shall rule for Him; Behold, His reward is with Him, And His work before Him. (NKJV)

Isa 62:11 Indeed the LORD has proclaimed To the end of the world: "Say to the daughter of Zion, 'Surely your salvation is coming; Behold, His reward is with Him, And His work before Him.'" (NKJV)

Re 22:12 "And behold, I am coming quickly, and My reward is with Me, to give to every one according to his work. (NKJV)

H. After the millennium, Yeshua will rule over the new earth and God will dwell with man on the new earth. David describes the one who can dwell in God's Tabernacle in Jerusalem.

> Psalms 15:1-2 <<A Psalm of David.>> LORD, who shall abide in thy tabernacle? Who shall dwell in thy holy hill? 2 He that walketh uprightly, and worketh righteousness, and speaketh the truth in his heart. (KJV)

Yeshua promises that the one who overcomes and has his name written in the Book of Life will dwell in the New Jerusalem.

> Re 3:12 "He who overcomes, I will make him a pillar in the temple of My God, and he shall go out no more. And I will write on him the name of My God and the name of the city of My God, the New Jerusalem, which comes down out of heaven from My God. And I will write on him My new name. (NKJV)

The true tabernacle of God which is now in heaven will be with men on the new earth. The writer of Hebrews tells us Yeshua is even now in the true tabernacle in God's presence.

> Heb 9:24 For Christ has not entered the holy places made with hands, which are copies of the true, but into heaven itself, now to appear in the presence of God for us; (NKJV)

Isaiah also speaks of the new heavens and a new earth. Man will once again tend the garden and the earth will bring forth abundant fruit. When Yeshua told the thief on the cross that he would be with him in Paradise, the word Paradise means park or garden. The new earth will be a place of joy and peace. Life continues with the building of houses, planting and tending gardens, and having children. Isaiah's description of the new earth sounds very much like the Garden of Eden.

> Is 65:17-25 "For behold, **I create new heavens and a new earth**; And the former shall not be remembered or come to mind. 18 But be glad and rejoice forever in what I create; For behold, **I create Jerusalem as a rejoicing**, And her people a joy. 19 I will rejoice in Jerusalem, And joy in My people; The voice of weeping shall no longer be heard in her, Nor the voice of crying. 20 "No more shall an infant from there live but a few days, Nor an old man who has not fulfilled his days; For the child shall die one hundred years old, But the sinner being one hundred years old shall be accursed. 21 They shall build houses and inhabit them; **They shall plant vineyards and eat their fruit.** 22 They shall not build and another inhabit; They shall not plant and another eat; For as the days of a tree, so shall be the days of My people, And **My elect shall long enjoy the work of their hands.** 23 They shall not labor in vain, Nor bring forth children for trouble; For they shall be the descendants of the blessed of the LORD, And their offspring with them. 24 "It shall come to pass That before they call, I will answer; And while they are still speaking, I will hear. 25 The wolf and the lamb shall feed together, The lion shall eat straw like the ox, And dust shall be the serpent's food. They shall not hurt nor destroy in all My holy mountain," Says the LORD. (NKJV)

John describes the same scene in the Book of Revelation.

Re 21:1-4 Now I saw a **new heaven and a new earth,** for the first heaven and the first earth had passed away. Also there was no more sea. 2 **Then I, John, saw the holy city, New Jerusalem, coming down out of heaven from God,** prepared as a bride adorned for her husband. 3 And I heard a loud voice from heaven saying, **"Behold, the tabernacle of God is with men, and He will dwell with them, and they shall be His people. God Himself will be with them and be their God.** 4 "And God will wipe away every tear from their eyes; there shall be no more death, nor sorrow, nor crying. There shall be no more pain, for the former things have passed away." (NKJV)

The New Jerusalem comes down out of heaven. This is the new dwelling place and the tabernacle of God. But what is this New Jerusalem? It is more than just a city; it is all of her inhabitants. Who are the inhabitants of the New Jerusalem, the Tabernacle of God?

Re 19:6-8 And I heard as the sound of a great multitude, and as the sound of many waters, and as the sound of strong thunders, saying, Hallelujah! For the Lord God omnipotent reigns! 7 Let us be glad and rejoice and we will give glory to Him. For the marriage of the Lamb has come, and His wife has prepared herself. 8 And to her was granted that she should be arrayed in fine linen, clean and white. For the fine linen is the righteousness of the saints. (MKJV)

Re 21:9-11 Then one of the seven angels who had the seven bowls filled with the seven last plagues came to me and talked with me, saying, "Come, I will show you the bride, the Lamb's wife." 10 And he carried me away in the Spirit to a great and high mountain, and showed me the great city, the holy Jerusalem, descending out of heaven from God, 11 having the glory of God. Her light was like a most precious stone, like a jasper stone, clear as crystal. (NKJV)

We are the New Jerusalem! We are the inhabitants! The city is clothed in our righteous acts. Together we will worship God the Father and Yeshua the Son observing the beginning of each month and especially the Sabbaths!

Is 66:22-23 **"For as the new heavens and the new earth Which I will make shall remain before Me,"** says the LORD, "So shall your descendants and your name remain. 23 And it shall come to pass That from one New Moon to another, And from one Sabbath to another, All flesh shall come to worship before Me," says the LORD. (NKJV)

All men will worship God who reigns in righteousness from the Holy Jerusalem that descends from heaven. We will serve Him as Adam was meant to serve Him.

2Pe 3:13 Nevertheless we, according to His promise, **look for new heavens and a new earth in which righteousness dwells.** (NKJV)

Conclusion: What place is Yeshua preparing for us and where will He be? Where will we spend eternity with Him? Yeshua is preparing the New Jerusalem for us to dwell in with

Him on the New Earth. When the New Jerusalem is ready, the Father will announce, "It is time!" Yeshua will come for us, His bride, and we will serve God and Yeshua who will reign together in righteousness for ever and ever.

> Re 22:3b, 5b The throne of God and of the Lamb will be in the city, and his servants will serve him. 5b And they will reign for ever and ever. (NIV)

Student Notes: Eternity: In heaven or on Earth?

Everyone knows that after we die, we will go to heaven and be with Yeshua. We will spend eternity there in the presence of Yeshua and God. Or will we? What do the scriptures say? (John 14:3, 1The. 4:17)

A. In the beginning God gave dominion of the earth to Adam. (Gen. 1:27-28, Gen. 2:15-17)

    1. Because of Adam's sin, Satan was given dominion until the time of the end. During the temptation of Yeshua, Satan tempted Him with the power to rule over all the earth. (Mat. 4:8-10, John 14:30, Rev. 12:9, Eph. 2:1-2)

B. Who can reclaim the deed to the earth? (Ps. 2:6-8, Rom. 1:1-4)

    1. He is the seed of David, the Seed of Eve. (Gen. 3:15, 1 Chr. 17:11-14, Ps. 89:28-36, Isa. 53:4-5, Luke 1:30-33)

    2. He is the Seed of God. (Mat. 1:20-21, Ac. 2:32-33)

C. Yeshua reclaimed the deed to the earth. (John 16:33, Rev. 1:18, Heb. 2:7-8, 2Cor. 15:24-28)

#7287. רדה radah, raw-daw' a primitive root; to tread down, i.e. subjugate; specifically, to crumble off:--(come to, make to) have dominion.

D. Yeshua will rule from David's throne. Where will He rule? (Ps. 48:2, Isa. 24:23, Mic. 4:7, Zep. 3:15, John 1:49, John 12:13)

E. What is the extent of His kingdom? (Zec. 14:9, 17, Rev 11:15, Ps. 47:2-8)

F. How long will His reign last? (Rev. 20:4, 2Sam. 7:16-17, Dan. 2:44, Dan. 7:14, Rev. 20:14-15)

G. Our treasure is **stored** in heaven. (Mat. 19:20-21, Mat. 6:19-21, Lu. 23:43, 2Cor. 5:6-8)

When Messiah comes, He brings His reward with Him. (Rev. 19:14-16, Isa. 40:10, Isa. 62:11, Rev. 22:12)

H. After the millennium, Yeshua will rule over the new earth and God will dwell with man. (Ps. 15:1-2, Rev. 3:12, Heb. 9:24, Isa. 65:17-25, Rev. 21:1-4)

Who are the inhabitants of the New Jerusalem? (Rev. 19:6-8, Rev. 21:9-11, Isa. 66:22-23, 2Pet. 3:13)

Conclusion: Where will we spend eternity? We will spend eternity in the New Jerusalem on the New Earth serving God and Yeshua who will reign in righteousness for ever and ever.

> Rev. 22:3b, 5b The throne of God and of the Lamb will be in the city, and his servants will serve him… 5b And they will reign for ever and ever. (NIV

Discussion Questions for Eternity: In Heaven or on Earth?

1. In Hebrews 2:7-8, we read that we don't see all things subject to Yeshua yet. Read 2 Peter 3:1-9. Discuss the reasons for God's delay in sending Yeshua to put all things under His feet.

2. Read Yeshua's messages to the churches in Revelation 2 and 3 focusing on His words to the one who overcomes. How is each promise to the one who overcomes referring to dwelling in the New Jerusalem?

3. In part H, we looked at numerous scriptures describing life after God creates the new heavens and the new earth. Are we going to be sitting around on the clouds of heaven playing harps? Discuss life on the new earth.

4. Read Matthew 6:19-21 and Matthew 19:16-30. How do we store up treasure in heaven? What is that treasure?

5. Yeshua's title is the King of Israel. The name Israel means "Prince with God." Jacob received this name the night before he crossed into the Promised Land. Read the account of Jacob receiving his new name in Genesis 32:24-31. Why did Jacob receive that name? How must each of us face the same test before we can enter into the Promised Land?

6. Yeshua already has the authority over all the earth, but he has not yet exercised that authority. Read Revelation 5. Only Yeshua is found worthy to open the scroll. Discuss how this applies to and speaks to the authority of Yeshua.

David's Early Life and Yeshua's First Coming

God's covenant with David promises that his seed will sit upon his throne and the reign of the Son of David will be established forever.

> 1Ch 17:11-14 "And it shall be, when your days are fulfilled, when you must go to be with your fathers, that I will set up your seed after you, who will be of your sons; and I will establish his kingdom. 12 "He shall build Me a house, and I will establish his throne forever. 13 "I will be his Father, and he shall be My son; and I will not take My mercy away from him, as I took it from him who was before you. 14 "And I will establish him in My house and in My kingdom forever; and his throne shall be established forever."'" (NKJV)

The life of David himself shows many parallels with Yeshua. The early part of David's life from his first anointing by Samuel through his exile to the Philistines foreshadows Yeshua's first coming. David's return from exile and triumph over his enemies foreshadows Yeshua's second coming. This study will focus on the first part of David's life and the next study will focus on David's triumph.

A. Both David and Yeshua were from Bethlehem.

> 1Sa 16:4-5 So Samuel did what the LORD said, and went to Bethlehem. And the elders of the town trembled at his coming, and said, "Do you come peaceably?" 5 And he said, "Peaceably; I have come to sacrifice to the LORD. Sanctify yourselves, and come with me to the sacrifice." Then he consecrated Jesse and his sons, and invited them to the sacrifice. (NKJV)

> 1Sa 17:12 Now David was the son of that Ephrathite of Bethlehem Judah, whose name was Jesse, and who had eight sons. And the man was old, advanced in years, in the days of Saul. (NKJV)

The Name Bethlehem means House of Bread (Strong's reference #1035). It was in the region known as Ephratha meaning fruitful. Ephratha is from the Hebrew word Ephrath with Strong's reference #672. 'Ephraath, ef-rawth' or Ephrathah, ef-raw'-thaw; from 6509; fruitfulness. This recalls God's marvelous provision of manna or bread in the wilderness. When David was anointed, God said, "He would provide for Himself a king."

> 1Sa 16:1 Now the LORD said to Samuel, "How long will you mourn for Saul, seeing I have rejected him from reigning over Israel? Fill your horn with oil, and go; I am sending you to Jesse the Bethlehemite. For I have provided Myself a king among his sons." (NKJV)

God provided both the manna and the king, providing King David from the house of bread. Later, He provided Yeshua who is the bread (manna) of life and the eternal King.

B. David and Yeshua both received a special anointing of the Holy Spirit at the beginning of their ministry or service. David was anointed by Samuel and the Spirit of the LORD came on him.

> 1Sa 16:13 Then Samuel took the horn of oil, and anointed him in the midst of his brethren: and the Spirit of the LORD came upon David from that day forward. So Samuel rose up, and went to Ramah. (KJV)

Yeshua received His special anointing when He was baptized by John.

> Lu 3:21-22 Now when all the people were baptized, it came to pass, that Jesus also being baptized, and praying, the heaven was opened, 22 And the Holy Ghost descended in a bodily shape like a dove upon him, and a voice came from heaven, which said, Thou art my beloved Son; in thee I am well pleased. (KJV)

There were witnesses to both David and Yeshua's anointing by the Spirit. David's brothers were witnesses to David's anointing, and John's followers witnessed Yeshua's anointing.

C. Both David and Yeshua were shepherds and were given the responsibility to protect their fathers' flocks.

> 1Sa 17:34-35 But David said to Saul, "Your servant used to keep his father's sheep, and when a lion or a bear came and took a lamb out of the flock, 35 I went out after it and struck it, and delivered the lamb from its mouth; and when it arose against me, I caught it by its beard, and struck and killed it. (NKJV)

David fought to protect his father's sheep risking his life to fight the lion and the bear. He speaks of saving the lamb which was practically in the lion's mouth.

> Joh 10:11-15 "I am the good shepherd. The good shepherd gives His life for the sheep. 12 "But a hireling, he who is not the shepherd, one who does not own the sheep, sees the wolf coming and leaves the sheep and flees; and the wolf catches the sheep and scatters them 13 "The hireling flees because he is a hireling and does not care about the sheep. 14 "I am the good shepherd; and I know My sheep, and am known by My own. 15 "As the Father knows Me, even so I know the Father; and I lay down My life for the sheep. (NKJV)

Like David, Yeshua protects His flock. He gives His life so His sheep may live. Yeshua kept and continues to keep all those that the Father gave Him.

> Joh 17:12 While I was with them in the world, I kept them in thy name: those that thou gavest me I have kept, and none of them is lost, but the son of perdition; that the scripture might be fulfilled. (KJV)

Again like David, He protected and continues to protect us from the lion that seeks to destroy us.

1Pe 5:8 Be sober, be vigilant; because your adversary the devil, as a roaring lion, walketh about, seeking whom he may devour: (KJV)

The only one Yeshua lost was Judas Iscariot to fulfill the scripture that one of His closest companions would betray him. David himself was the prophet who recorded this prophecy.

Ps 41:9 Even my own familiar friend in whom I trusted, Who ate my bread, Has lifted up his heel against me. (NKJV)

Judas was lost when greed took hold of him and he allowed Satan, that roaring lion, to enter him.

Joh 13:26-27 Jesus answered, It is he to whom I shall give the morsel when I have dipped it. And dipping the morsel, He gave it to Judas Iscariot, the son of Simon. 27 And after the morsel, then Satan entered into him. Then Jesus said to him, What you do, do quickly. (MKJV)

D. Both David and Yeshua provoked the jealousy of those in authority. Saul was jealous of David and his victories over the Philistines. He was afraid that David would take his place as ruler over the kingdom.

1Sa 18:6-9 Now it had happened as they were coming home, when David was returning from the slaughter of the Philistine, that the women had come out of all the cities of Israel, singing and dancing, to meet King Saul, with tambourines, with joy, and with musical instruments. 7 So the women sang as they danced, and said: "Saul has slain his thousands, And David his ten thousands." 8 Then Saul was very angry, and the saying displeased him; and he said, "They have ascribed to David ten thousands, and to me they have ascribed only thousands. Now what more can he have but the kingdom?" 9 So Saul eyed David from that day forward. (NKJV)

The scribes and Pharisees were jealous of Yeshua's popularity with the people.

Mat 12:23-24 And all the multitudes were amazed and said, "Could this be the Son of David?" 24 Now when the Pharisees heard it they said, "This fellow does not cast out demons except by Beelzebub, the ruler of the demons." (NKJV)

The leaders of the Jewish people were also fearful of losing their office of authority given to them by the Romans.

Joh 11:45-48 Then many of the Jews who had come to Mary, and had seen the things Jesus did, believed in Him. 46 But some of them went away to the Pharisees and told them the things Jesus did. 47 Then the chief priests and the Pharisees gathered a council and said, "What shall we do? For this Man works many signs. 48 "If we let Him alone like this, everyone will believe in Him, and the Romans will come and take away both our place and nation." (NKJV)

Both with Saul and the leaders of Yeshua's time, God had already removed their authority and given it to David and Yeshua, respectively.

E. Not all of those in authority hated David and Yeshua. Saul's son Jonathan loved David and intervened on his behalf. Nicodemus and Joseph of Arimathea, members of the Jewish Council, were followers of Yeshua. Nicodemus intervenes on Yeshua's behalf at the Feast of Tabernacles. After Yeshua's death, Nicodemus and Joseph of Arimathea claimed Yeshua's body for burial even burying Him in Joseph's own tomb.

> 1Sa 19:2-4 but Jonathan, Saul's son, delighted greatly in David. So Jonathan told David, saying, "My father Saul seeks to kill you. Therefore please be on your guard until morning, and stay in a secret place and hide. 3 "And I will go out and stand beside my father in the field where you are, and I will speak with my father about you. Then what I observe, I will tell you." 4 Thus Jonathan spoke well of David to Saul his father, and said to him, "Let not the king sin against his servant, against David, because he has not sinned against you, and because his works have been very good toward you. (NKJV)

> Joh 7:45-51 Finally the temple guards went back to the chief priests and Pharisees, who asked them, "Why didn't you bring him in?" 46 "No one ever spoke the way this man does," the guards declared. 47 "You mean he has deceived you also?" the Pharisees retorted. 48 "Has any of the rulers or of the Pharisees believed in him? 49 No! But this mob that knows nothing of the law-- there is a curse on them." 50 Nicodemus, who had gone to Jesus earlier and who was one of their own number, asked, 51 "Does our law condemn anyone without first hearing him to find out what he is doing?" (NIV)

F. Neither David nor Yeshua countenanced harming those in authority. Quite the contrary, David had the opportunity twice to personally kill Saul when Saul was after him. David refused to harm him because Saul was God's anointed leader. He wouldn't let the men with him harm Saul either.

> 1Sa 24:2-6 Then Saul took three thousand chosen men from all Israel, and went to seek David and his men on the Rocks of the Wild Goats. 3 So he came to the sheepfolds by the road, where there was a cave; and Saul went in to attend to his needs. (David and his men were staying in the recesses of the cave.) 4 Then the men of David said to him, "This is the day of which the LORD said to you, 'Behold, I will deliver your enemy into your hand, that you may do to him as it seems good to you.'" And David arose and secretly cut off a corner of Saul's robe. 5 Now it happened afterward that David's heart troubled him because he had cut Saul's robe. 6 And he said to his men, "The LORD forbid that I should do this thing to my master, the LORD'S anointed, to stretch out my hand against him, seeing he is the anointed of the LORD." (NKJV)

The other incident is in 1 Samuel 26 shortly before David flees to the Philistines. David goes into Saul's camp and finds Saul and all his men sleeping. David takes Saul's spear which was stuck in the ground near Saul's head and Saul's water jug from beside his head, but he refuses to strike against the LORD's anointed.

Yeshua would not allow his disciples to harm those in authority either. When the high priest came with the temple guards to arrest Yeshua, Peter cut off the right ear of the high priest's servant. Yeshua immediately healed him.

> Joh 18:10 Then Simon Peter, who had a sword, drew it and struck the high priest's servant, cutting off his right ear. (The servant's name was Malchus.) (NIV)

Interestingly, the servant's name is given. Why? The name Malchus is the Greek form of the Hebrew name Melek which means king.

#3124.   Malchos, mal'-khos of Hebrew origin (4429); Malchus, an Israelite:--Malchus.
#4429.   מֶלֶך   Melek, meh'-lek the same as 4428; king; Melek, the name of two Israelites.

David would not allow anyone to harm King Saul. Yeshua would not allow the high priest's servant "King" to be harmed.

G. David and Yeshua both flee to the Gentiles. David leaves Israel and joins up with the Philistines. He lives with them for sixteen months conducting raids against various tribes of Canaanites. He continues to fight against the enemies of Israel even while in exile.

> 1Sa 27:7-8 Now the time that David dwelt in the country of the Philistines was one full year and four months. 8 And David and his men went up and raided the Geshurites, the Girzites, and the Amalekites. For those nations were the inhabitants of the land from of old, as you go to Shur, even as far as the land of Egypt. (NKJV)

After Yeshua's death and resurrection, His gospel was preached to the Jew first and then the Gentile. It was only after Yeshua was rejected by the Jews in authority such as the leaders of the Pharisees and the rulers of the synagogues, that belief in Yeshua became primarily a Gentile faith. Just like the Philistines benefited from David's presence, the Gentiles benefit from Yeshua's presence among us.

> Ro 10:21 But to Israel he says: "All day long I have stretched out My hands To a disobedient and contrary people." (NKJV)

> Ro 11:11-12 I say then, have they stumbled that they should fall? Certainly not! But through their fall, to provoke them to jealousy, salvation has come to the Gentiles. 12 Now if their fall is riches for the world, and their failure riches for the Gentiles, how much more their fullness! (NKJV)

> Ro 11:28-29 Concerning the gospel they are enemies for your sake, but concerning the election they are beloved for the sake of the fathers. 29 For the gifts and the calling of God are irrevocable. (NKJV)

Although Saul rejected David and sought to kill him, David had his faithful followers from among the Jews.

> 1Sa 27:2 Then David arose and went over with the **six hundred men who were with him** to Achish the son of Maoch, king of Gath. (NKJV)

Like David, Yeshua had and continues to have Jewish people who believe that He is indeed the Messiah and have become "obedient to the faith."

> Ac 6:7 Then the word of God spread, and the number of the disciples multiplied greatly in Jerusalem, and a great many of the priests were obedient to the faith. (NKJV)

> Ac 21:20 And when they heard it, they glorified the Lord. And they said to him, "You see, brother, how many myriads of Jews there are who have believed, and they are all zealous for the law; (NKJV)

H. When David later wrote of the time when he was being hunted by Saul, he compares it to going to the grave, to Sheol. Symbolically, David experienced a death of separation from his people over whom he had already been anointed by Samuel as the next king.

> 2Sa 22:5-7 "For the waves of death encompassed me; The torrents of destruction overwhelmed me; 6 The cords of Sheol surrounded me; The snares of death confronted me. 7 "In my distress I called upon the LORD, Yes, I cried to my God; And from His temple He heard my voice, And my cry for help came into His ears. (NASB)

At that time, David speaks as if God Himself had rejected him.

> Ps 22:1 (To the Chief Musician. Set to "The Deer of the Dawn." A Psalm of David.) My God, My God, why have You forsaken Me? Why are You so far from helping Me, And from the words of My groaning? (NKJV)

Yeshua experienced physical death—separation from both the people He was destined to rule and from God His Father. He speaks the very words prophesied by David in Psalm 22.

> Mat 27:46 And about the ninth hour Jesus cried out with a loud voice, saying, "Eli, Eli, lama sabachthani?" that is, "My God, My God, why have You forsaken Me?" (NKJV)

In 2 Samuel 22:7, David wrote that God did indeed hear his voice and answered. He also prophesies that God would save Yeshua from the grave as well.

> Ps 16:10 For You will not leave my soul in Sheol, Nor will You allow Your Holy One to see corruption. (NKJV)

I. David and Yeshua still have a heart for Israel. Even in his exile, David mourns the deaths of both Saul and Jonathan. David never ceased to care for the people of Israel.

> 2Sa 1:17 Then David lamented with this lamentation over Saul and over Jonathan his son, (NKJV)

Later, we read that David mourns the death of Abner, the general who advocated for making Saul's son Ish-Bosheth king of Israel instead of David.

> 2Sa 3:31 And David said to Joab, and to all the people that were with him, Rend your clothes, and gird you with sackcloth, and mourn before Abner. And king David himself followed the bier. (KJV)

David seeks out the descendants of Saul to make sure that they have been provided for.

> 2Sa 9:3 And the king said, Is there not yet any of the house of Saul, that I may shew the kindness of God unto him? And Ziba said unto the king, Jonathan hath yet a son, which is lame on his feet. (KJV)

Yeshua mourns the coming destruction of Jerusalem and the scattering of the people of Israel.

> Mat 23:37-38 "O Jerusalem, Jerusalem, the one who kills the prophets and stones those who are sent to her! How often I wanted to gather your children together, as a hen gathers her chicks under her wings, but you were not willing! 38 "See! Your house is left to you desolate; (NKJV)

At the cross, Yeshua intercedes with the Father to forgive those who put Him there.

> Luke 23:34a Then said Jesus, Father, forgive them; for they know not what they do. (KJV)

J. David was anointed king over Judah while in Hebron. His kingdom was not yet established. This is his second anointing.

> 2Sa 2:4 Then the men of Judah came, and there **they anointed David king over the house of Judah**. And they told David, saying, "The men of Jabesh Gilead were the ones who buried Saul." (NKJV)

Yeshua, was anointed king over Judah in a different manner. Yeshua died on the cross with the title "King of the Jews" inscribed over Him by the command of Pilate.

> Lu 23:3 Then Pilate asked Him, saying, "Are You the King of the Jews?" He answered him and said, "It is as you say." (NKJV)

Lu 23:38 And a superscription also was written over him in letters of Greek, and Latin, and Hebrew, THIS IS THE KING OF THE JEWS. (KJV)

David does not immediately reign over Israel, only the men of the tribe of Judah proclaim him king. He rules from Hebron in midst of the land of Judah.

2Sa 2:11 And the time that David was king in Hebron over the house of Judah was seven years and six months. (NKJV)

Yeshua does not immediately reign over Israel either. On the day of His ascension, the fortieth day after His resurrection, his disciples ask Him if He would throw out the Romans and reign as the King of Israel.

Ac 1:6-7 Therefore, when they had come together, they asked Him, saying, "Lord, will You at this time restore the kingdom to Israel?" 7 And He said to them, "It is not for you to know times or seasons which the Father has put in His own authority. (NKJV)

Yeshua waits at the right hand of the Father for the appointed time to arrive for establishing His earthly kingdom. There were many Jewish people who believed in Yeshua and followed like there were many people who believed David was the rightful king and followed him. The book of Acts records the explosive growth in the number of believers in Yeshua including many of the priests.

Right now, those of us who believe that Yeshua is Messiah and who have acknowledged Him as King, are separated from the majority of the Jewish people. At times there has been war between us but we will be united when Yeshua comes again. We will help to bring the people of Israel home to Israel.

Is 49:22 Thus says the Lord GOD: "Behold, I will lift My hand in an oath to the nations, And set up My standard for the peoples; They shall bring your sons in their arms, And your daughters shall be carried on their shoulders; (NKJV)

Student Notes for David's Early Life and Yeshua's First Coming

God's covenant with David promises that his seed will sit upon his throne. The reign of the Son of David will be established forever.

> 1Ch 17:11-14 "And it shall be, when your days are fulfilled, when you must go to be with your fathers, that I will set up your seed after you, who will be of your sons; and I will establish his kingdom. 12 "He shall build Me a house, and I will establish his throne forever. 13 "I will be his Father, and he shall be My son; and I will not take My mercy away from him, as I took it from him who was before you. 14 "And I will establish him in My house and in My kingdom forever; and his throne shall be established forever.""" (NKJV)

The life of David himself shows many parallels with Yeshua. The early part of David's life from his first anointing by Samuel through his exile to the Philistines foreshadows Yeshua's first coming. David's return from exile and triumph over his enemies foreshadows Yeshua's second coming. This study will focus on the first part of David's life and the next study will focus on David's triumph.

A. Both David and Yeshua were from Bethlehem. (1 Sam. 16:4-5, 1 Sam. 17:12, 1 Sam. 16:1)

Bethlehem: #1035 House of Bread
Ephratha: fruitful. from Ephrath #672. 'Ephraath, ef-rawth' or Ephrathah {ef-raw'-thaw}; from 6509; fruitfulness.

B. David and Yeshua both received a special anointing of the Holy Spirit (1Sam. 16:13, Lu. 3:21-22)

C. Both David and Yeshua were shepherds (1Sam. 17:34-35, John 10:11-15, John 17:12. 1Pet. 5:8, Ps. 41:7, John 13:26-27)

D. Both David and Yeshua provoked the jealousy of those in authority. (1Sam. 18:6-9, Mat. 12:23-24, John 11:45-48)

E. Not all of those in authority hated David and Yeshua. (1Sam. 19:2-4, John 7:45-51)

F. Neither David nor Yeshua countenanced harming those in authority. (1Sam. 24:2-6)

Yeshua didn't allow His disciples to harm those in authority. (John 18:10)

#3124.   Malchos, mal'-khos of Hebrew origin (4429); Malchus, an Israelite:--Malchus. #4429. מלך   Melek, meh'-lek the same as 4428; king; Melek, the name of two Israelites.

G. David and Yeshua both flee to the Gentiles. (1Sam. 27:7-8, Rom. 10:21, Rom. 11:11-12, Rom. 11:28-29, 1Sam. 27:2)

David and Yeshua both had faithful followers from among the Jews. (Acts 6:7, Acts 21:20)

H. Symbolically, David experienced a death of separation from his people (2Sam. 22:5-7, Ps. 22:1)

Yeshua experienced physical death—separation from both the people He was destined to rule and from God His Father. (Mat. 27:46)

.

Both were preserved. (Ps. 16:10)

I. David and Yeshua still have a heart for Israel. (2Sam. 1:17, 2Sam. 3:31, 2Sam. 9:3, Mat. 23:37-38, Lu. 23:34a)

J. Both received an anointing as king of Judah. (2Sam 2:4, Lu. 23:3, Lu. 23:38, Acts 2:29-33)

Their kingdoms were yet to come. (2Sam. 2:11, Acts 1:6-7, Isa. 49:22)

Discussion Questions for David's Early Life and Yeshua's First Coming

1. Yeshua entrusts Peter with the job of taking care of His sheep in His absence (John 21:15-17). Peter in turn passes that trust on. Read 1 Peter 5:1-10. What characteristics should the shepherd of God's people have? What is our defense against Satan, the roaring lion that seeks to destroy us?

2. The war between Judah and Israel is a pattern of the differences between believers, both Jew and Gentile, and non-believers. Read 1 Samuel 3:22-39 and Romans 12:17-18. Based on this pattern, how should we conduct ourselves with non-believers especially the Jewish people?

3. David reigned in Hebron before He was accepted as King over all Israel. His time in Hebron corresponds to the time from Yeshua's resurrection to the time He will be crowned king of all the earth. Hebron is also the location of the tomb of the patriarchs, Abraham, Isaac and Jacob. Hebron means "seat of association." David associated himself with the patriarchs when he chose Hebron as his capitol. How do we associate with the patriarchs as we wait for Yeshua's return?

4. We have the impression that all the Jews rejected Yeshua as their Messiah. Read Acts 2:40-47, Acts 4:32, Acts 5:12-16, Acts 6:1-7, Acts 8:5 and Acts 21:20. The word translated as "myriad" in Acts 21:20 means ten thousands, so to have myriads, plural, means tens of thousands! Discuss the spread of the gospel among the Jewish people in the first thirty years after Yeshua's resurrection.

5. Moses laid hands on Joshua to transfer his authority to Joshua (Num. 27:18-23). Read Matthew 21:23-27. How can we view Yeshua's baptism by John and the Holy Spirit as a transfer of authority or an ordination? What does this passage show us about the chief priests and the elders?

David's Reign and Yeshua's Second Coming

David was the king who first conquered and reigned from Jerusalem foreshadowing the eternal reign of Yeshua from Jerusalem. But David's reign began in Hebron not in Jerusalem. This period of time beginning with David's reign in Hebron and leading up to his reign in Jerusalem is a foreshadowing of the time from Yeshua's death and resurrection to His ultimate triumphant entry into Jerusalem as the conquering king.

David was first anointed king over Judah in Hebron after the death of Saul.

> 2Sa 2:4a Then the men of Judah came, and there they anointed David king over the house of Judah. (NKJV)

It looked like this anointing would lead to his anointing as king over all of Israel as prophesied by Samuel. Saul and his son Jonathan were dead at the hands of the Philistines and it seems as if David would be the obvious choice as the next king. The nation of Israel goes her own way, however, and chooses Saul's son Ishbosheth as their king.

In a similar way, when Yeshua entered Jerusalem just prior to that last Passover it seems as if he would be declared king of Israel. In fact, if we trace Yeshua's final journey to Jerusalem as related in the Gospel of Luke, we see a procession that begins months before His actual arrival in Jerusalem. After Yeshua's visit to Jerusalem for the Feast of Tabernacles recorded in John 7-9, Yeshua sends seventy messengers to go out before Him into all the cities of Judea that He will visit.

> Lu 10:1-2 After these things the Lord appointed seventy others also, and sent them two by two before His face into every city and place where He Himself was about to go. 2 Then He said to them, "The harvest truly is great, but the laborers are few; therefore pray the Lord of the harvest to send out laborers into His harvest. (NKJV)

He sent them out to begin the harvest. They report back that even the demons submit to them in His name. Along the way, He visits Mary and Martha in Bethany. This may have been at the Feast of Dedication when John records that Yeshua again went to Jerusalem. John records that after this Yeshua stayed for some time at the Jordan where John the Baptist baptized in his early ministry.

Later, we read that Yeshua is once again teaching throughout Judea. John gives the location as the mountains of Ephraim which is the heartland of Israel. As might be expected from sending out seventy messengers before Him, the crowds begin to gather.

> Lu 12:1 In the meantime, when an innumerable multitude of people had gathered together, so that they trampled one another, He began to say to His disciples first of all, "Beware of the leaven of the Pharisees, which is hypocrisy. (NKJV)

He teaches about the leaven of the Pharisees which indicates that the Passover and the Feast of Unleavened Bread may be approaching. Yeshua continues to teach as He slowly makes His way to Jerusalem.

> Lu 13:22 And He went through the cities and villages, teaching, and journeying toward Jerusalem. (NKJV)

As He journeyed, opposition began to grow. Some Pharisees brought word that Herod was out to kill Him. His reply prophesies about His death, resurrection and determination to go up to Jerusalem.

> Lu 13:32-33 And He said to them, "Go, tell that fox, 'Behold, I cast out demons and perform cures today and tomorrow, and the third day I shall be perfected.' 33 "Nevertheless I must journey today, tomorrow, and the day following; for it cannot be that a prophet should perish outside of Jerusalem. (NKJV)

He continues His journey and multitudes begin to travel with Him.

> Lu 14:25 NKJV 25 Now great multitudes went with Him. And He turned and said to them,

Imagine the scene as He travels on foot from place to place with thousands of people traveling with Him. No wonder Herod thought Yeshua wanted to take His place as King of Israel. We can see why the chief priests and Pharisees were nervous about the Roman authorities taking action against them. Was Yeshua coming up to Jerusalem to declare that He was king?

In Luke 17, Yeshua makes one last sweep through Galilee and Samaria.

> Lu 17:11 Now it happened as He went to Jerusalem that He passed through the midst of Samaria and Galilee. (NKJV)

In all this traveling, His ultimate goal was Jerusalem! As He approaches Jericho He takes His disciples aside and warns them of His coming death and resurrection.

> Lu 18:31-33 Then He took the twelve aside and said to them, "Behold, we are going up to Jerusalem, and all things that are written by the prophets concerning the Son of Man will be accomplished. 32 "For He will be delivered to the Gentiles and will be mocked and insulted and spit upon. 33 "They will scourge Him and kill Him. And the third day He will rise again." (NKJV)

They are nearly there, but He must first stop in Jericho. As He enters Jericho, the crowds are so thick that Zacchaeus must climb a tree in order to get a glimpse of Yeshua.

> Lu 19:1-3 Then Jesus entered and passed through Jericho. 2 Now behold, there was a man named Zacchaeus who was a chief tax collector, and he was rich. 3 And he

sought to see who Jesus was, but could not because of the crowd, for he was of short stature. (NKJV)

Yeshua stops to eat with Zacchaeus and tells a parable warning that the kingdom of God was not going to appear at once.

> Lu 19:11 Now as they heard these things, He spoke another parable, because He was near Jerusalem and because they thought the kingdom of God would appear immediately. (NKJV)

Imagine the expectation of the crowd, though. Thousands are now following Him and they know His destination is Jerusalem for the Feast of Passover. Jewish tradition holds that Nisan is the month of the New Year for kings. No matter when a Jewish king ascended the throne, the initial year of his reign concluded on Passover. Even though Yeshua warned that the kingdom of God would not appear immediately, the crowd was expectant.

As they approach Jerusalem, Yeshua sends out two of His disciples to bring the colt of a donkey so He can ride into Jerusalem.

> Mat 21:1-5 As they approached Jerusalem and came to Bethphage on the Mount of Olives, Jesus sent two disciples, 2 saying to them, "Go to the village ahead of you, and at once you will find a donkey tied there, with her colt by her. Untie them and bring them to me. 3 If anyone says anything to you, tell him that the Lord needs them, and he will send them right away." 4 This took place to fulfill what was spoken through the prophet: 5 "Say to the Daughter of Zion, 'See, your king comes to you, gentle and riding on a donkey, on a colt, the foal of a donkey.'" (NIV)

Yeshua entered Jerusalem riding on the colt of a donkey just like Zechariah prophesied.

> Zec 9:9 Rejoice greatly, O Daughter of Zion! Shout, Daughter of Jerusalem! See, your king comes to you, righteous and having salvation, gentle and riding on a donkey, on a colt, the foal of a donkey. (NIV)

When the crowd saw Yeshua approaching Jerusalem on the donkey, they could not contain their excitement!

> Lu 19:37-38 Then, as He was now drawing near the descent of the Mount of Olives, the whole multitude of the disciples began to rejoice and praise God with a loud voice for all the mighty works they had seen, 38 saying:" 'Blessed is the King who comes in the name of the LORD!' Peace in heaven and glory in the highest!" (NKJV)

Yeshua entered Jerusalem in apparent triumph to the shouts and acclamation of all the people. It looks like His reign as eternal King will begin at this time.

But this entrance ushered in His crucifixion a mere five days later. Imagine the despair and sorrow over the entire city at the crucifixion of the one they thought would deliver them from Rome and reign over Israel.

Again, at His resurrection, the disciples thought that surely now would be the start of His eternal reign. But when the disciples asked Yeshua after His resurrection if He would establish His kingdom at that time, Yeshua didn't give a direct answer. Instead He gave them their orders to be His witnesses throughout the world very much like He sent out the seventy to go before Him into all the cities He would visit.

> Ac 1:6-8 Therefore, when they had come together, they asked Him, saying, "Lord, will You at this time restore the kingdom to Israel?" 7 And He said to them, "It is not for you to know times or seasons which the Father has put in His own authority. 8 "But you shall receive power when the Holy Spirit has come upon you; and you shall be witnesses to Me in Jerusalem, and in all Judea and Samaria, and to the end of the earth." (NKJV)

When will His reign truly begin? David's time as king in exile sheds light on this question.

A. Both David and Yeshua were initially accepted as king by only part of Israel. While David was king over Judah in Hebron, David sent word to his fellow Israelites that he had been anointed king over Judah. The implication is that he should be accepted as king over all Israel.

> 2Sa 2:7-9 "Now therefore, let your hands be strengthened, and be valiant; for your master Saul is dead, and also the house of Judah has anointed me king over them." 8 But Abner the son of Ner, commander of Saul's army, took Ishbosheth the son of Saul and brought him over to Mahanaim; 9 and he made him king over Gilead, over the Ashurites, over Jezreel, over Ephraim, over Benjamin, and over all Israel. (NKJV)

Ishbostheth was king over Israel not by God's anointing but by the choice of man. Did the Israelites know that Samuel had anointed David as Israel's next king even before Saul's death (1Sam. 16:13)? It seems as if they did as evidenced by their own words when they finally anoint David king of all Israel seven and a half years after Judah proclaimed him king.

> 2Sa 5:2 "Also, in time past, when Saul was king over us, you were the one who led Israel out and brought them in; and the LORD said to you, 'You shall shepherd My people Israel, and be ruler over Israel.'" (NKJV)

If they did indeed know that David was to be ruler over all Israel, then they are deliberately going against what they know to be God's will. Although the rest of Israel had rejected him, David remained king over some of Israel, the tribe of Judah.

Yeshua, also, presented his credentials to Israel. He states that His authority is by the works He does in the Father's name and by the testimony of God the Father Himself.

> Joh 5:36-37 "But I have a greater witness than John's; for the works which the Father has given Me to finish--the very works that I do--bear witness of Me, that the Father has sent Me. 37 "And the Father Himself, who sent Me, has testified of Me. You have neither heard His voice at any time, nor seen His form. (NKJV)

> Joh 10:24-25 Then the Jews surrounded Him and said to Him, "How long do You keep us in doubt? If You are the Christ, tell us plainly." 25 Jesus answered them, "I told you, and you do not believe. The works that I do in My Father's name, they bear witness of Me. (NKJV)

But He was rejected by the leaders and they selected another king instead.

> Joh 19:12-15 From then on Pilate sought to release Him, but the Jews cried out, saying, "If you let this Man go, you are not Caesar's friend. Whoever makes himself a king speaks against Caesar." 13 When Pilate therefore heard that saying, he brought Jesus out and sat down in the judgment seat in a place that is called The Pavement, but in Hebrew, Gabbatha. 14 Now it was the Preparation Day of the Passover, and about the sixth hour. And he said to the Jews, "Behold your King!" 15 But they cried out, "Away with Him, away with Him! Crucify Him!" Pilate said to them, "Shall I crucify your King?" The chief priests answered, "We have no king but Caesar!" (NKJV)

Although rejected by most of Israel, Yeshua is still today the king over some of the Jews. The first believers were Jews as are many believers today.

> Ac 2:41 Then those who gladly received his word were baptized; and that day about three thousand souls were added to them. (NKJV)

> Ac 6:7 Then the word of God spread, and the number of the disciples multiplied greatly in Jerusalem, and a great many of the priests were obedient to the faith. (NKJV)

B. While David reigned in Hebron, there was conflict between his followers and the followers of Ishbosheth. During all this time, even when Saul was alive and sought to kill him, David did not condone harming Saul or any member of Saul's house. David continually refused to act against Saul, God's anointed king.

> 1Sa 26:9-11a And David said to Abishai, "Do not destroy him; for who can stretch out his hand against the LORD'S anointed, and be guiltless?" 10 David said furthermore, "
> As the LORD lives, the LORD shall strike him, or his day shall come to die, or he shall go out to battle and perish. 11 "The LORD forbid that I should stretch out my hand against the LORD'S anointed." (NKJV)

Even though the people of Israel, not God, selected Ishbosheth as king, David continued this policy of not harming any member of Saul's household into the reign of Ishbosheth. When the two men who murdered Ishbosheth came to David with the news, David commanded that they be executed just like he had done with the soldier who killed Saul.

> 2Sa 4:9-12 But David answered Rechab and Baanah his brother, the sons of Rimmon the Beerothite, and said to them, "As the LORD lives, who has redeemed my life from all adversity, 10 "when someone told me, saying, 'Look, Saul is dead,' thinking to have brought good news, I arrested him and had him executed in Ziklag-the one who thought I would give him a reward for his news. 11 "How much more, when wicked men have killed a righteous person in his own house on his bed? Therefore, shall I not now require his blood at your hand and remove you from the earth?" 12 So David commanded his young men, and they executed them, cut off their hands and feet, and hanged them by the pool in Hebron. But they took the head of Ishbosheth and buried it in the tomb of Abner in Hebron. (NKJV)

Even though there is conflict between the Jewish people and the Christians, Yeshua would not condone the killing of the Jewish people. The Church will have to answer to God for their sins against the Jewish people. Paul tells us that the calling of God is irrevocable.

> Ro 11:27-29 And this is my covenant with them when I take away their sins. 28 As far as the gospel is concerned, they are enemies on your account; but as far as election is concerned, they are loved on account of the patriarchs, 29 for God's gifts and his call are irrevocable. (NIV)

Paul is telling us that, like in the time of Ishbosheth when Israel chose their own way, the Jewish people may have chosen the wrong king to follow but they are still beloved of God and are his chosen people.

This is further illustrated by God's judgment on Assyria and Babylon. Assyria conquered the northern kingdom of Israel and threatened Jerusalem (2 Kings 18-19). Isaiah says that Assyria will be judged for that action.

> Is 10:5-7, 12 "Woe to the Assyrian, the rod of my anger, in whose hand is the club of my wrath! 6 I send him against a godless nation, I dispatch him against a people who anger me, to seize loot and snatch plunder, and to trample them down like mud in the streets. 7 But this is not what he intends, this is not what he has in mind; his purpose is to destroy, to put an end to many nations.12 When the Lord has finished all his work against Mount Zion and Jerusalem, he will say, "I will punish the king of Assyria for the willful pride of his heart and the haughty look in his eyes. (NIV)

Although God used Babylon to exact punishment against Judah, He in turn punished Babylon for coming against His people.

> Jer 25:11-13 'And this whole land shall be a desolation and an astonishment, and these nations shall serve the king of Babylon seventy years. 12 'Then it will come

to pass, when seventy years are completed, that I will punish the king of Babylon and that nation, the land of the Chaldeans, for their iniquity,' says the LORD; 'and I will make it a perpetual desolation. 13 'So I will bring on that land all My words which I have pronounced against it, all that is written in this book, which Jeremiah has prophesied concerning all the nations. (NKJV)

In Deuteronomy, God promised Abraham that through His seed the nations would be blessed. The rest of the promise is that God would curse those who cursed Abraham.

Ge 12:2-3 I will make you a great nation; I will bless you And make your name great; And you shall be a blessing. 3 I will bless those who bless you, And I will curse him who curses you; And in you all the families of the earth shall be blessed." (NKJV)

The promise is passed on to Jacob who is later given the name Israel.

Ge 27:29 Let peoples serve you, And nations bow down to you. Be master over your brethren, And let your mother's sons bow down to you. Cursed be everyone who curses you, And blessed be those who bless you!" (NKJV)

The promise is repeated, entirely against his will, by Balaam who tried to call down God's curses on Israel.

Nu 24:9 'He bows down, he lies down as a lion; And as a lion, who shall rouse him?' "Blessed is he who blesses you, And cursed is he who curses you." (NKJV)

God will punish the nations that come against Israel and His people.

C. David and Yeshua are anointed as king over all Israel. David waited for the elders to come to him. He did not force them to accept him as king.

2Sa 5:3 Therefore, all the elders of Israel came to the king at Hebron, and King David made a covenant with them at Hebron before the LORD. And they anointed David king over Israel. (NKJV)

He reigned in Hebron for seven and a half years before they came to him to make him king. Whenever we see a seven in scriptures, we look again to see if there is significance in the number. Seven is the number of spiritual completion, the number of fullness and completion. David's time as king over Judah in Hebron is complete. As king over all Israel, He will take charge of all the armies of Israel and drive the Philistines out of Israel. But David's reign in Hebron was not exactly seven years; it was seven and a half years. What if anything is the significance of the half year? Why is it even mentioned? There were certainly kings of Israel and Judah whose reigns did not last an exact number of years yet the scriptures don't record the additional number of months.

A possibility of the meaning of this goes back to the death of Saul. We read in the days before his death that Saul consulted a medium who called up the spirit of Samuel. Samuel confirmed that Saul would die and David would reign in his place. Saul collapses from anguish complicated by hunger since he had not eaten. The medium has compassion on Saul and feeds him.

> 1Sa 28:24-25 Now the woman had a fatted calf in the house, and she hastened to kill it. And she took flour and kneaded it, and baked unleavened bread from it. 25 So she brought it before Saul and his servants, and they ate. Then they rose and went away that night. (NKJV)

The woman prepares unleavened bread for Saul. This could be just because unleavened bread is quick to make, but the scriptures don't usually record what kind of bread a person makes or offers. Other than in reference to the Feast of Unleavened Bread and offerings to the LORD, there is only one other place that specifies unleavened bread. In Genesis, Lot is in Sodom and prepares unleavened bread for the angels of the LORD.

> Ge 19:3 But he insisted strongly; so they turned in to him and entered his house. Then he made them a feast, and baked unleavened bread, and they ate. (NKJV)

Jewish tradition says that because Lot served unleavened bread, the destruction of Sodom and Gomorrah as well as God's promise that Abraham would have a son at this same time the next year was at the Feast of Unleavened Bread. Using this same reasoning, the death of Saul most likely occurred at the Feast of Unleavened Bread.

David, then, is crowned king of Judah at the time of the Feast of Unleavened Bread. As mentioned earlier, this month is the New Year for a king's reign. In contrast, the coronation of God as King is on the first of Tishrei, the Feast of Trumpets. This is the day that God created Adam and thus is the appropriate time to proclaim God as King. The seven and a half years that David reigned in Hebron take us to Tishrei for the month that David is proclaimed king of all Israel.

Yeshua was first proclaimed King of the Jews as He entered Jerusalem five days before the beginning of the Feast of Unleavened Bread. When He returns with the trumpet blast of God on the Feast of Trumpets in the seventh month of the year as the seventh Sabbatical year concludes and the Year of Jubilee begins, He will receive the crown of the King of all Israel and the entire Earth. He is the King on David's throne and the King of all Creation.

It is interesting that although David reigns over Judah in Hebron for seven and a half years, his counterpart Ishbosheth only reigns over the rest of Israel for two years.

> 2Sa 2:10 Ishbosheth, Saul's son, was forty years old when he began to reign over Israel, and he reigned two years. Only the house of Judah followed David. (NKJV)

We see a similar division of five years and two years when Joseph reveals himself to his brothers two years into the seven year famine over Egypt and the surrounding countries.

> Ge 45:6 "For these two years the famine has been in the land, and there are still five years in which there will be neither plowing nor harvesting. (NKJV)

The scriptures are silent about what happens during the five years when Israel didn't have a king. We do know that God gave Israel over to the Philistines at Saul's death sparing only Judah under David. Samuel's words to Saul through the medium tell of the coming defeat by the Philistines.

> 1Sa 28:19 "Moreover the LORD will also deliver Israel with you into the hand of the Philistines. And tomorrow you and your sons will be with me. The LORD will also deliver the army of Israel into the hand of the Philistines." (NKJV)

The scriptures go on to record that the Philistines occupied all the cities of Israel.

> 1Sa 31:7 And when the men of Israel who were on the other side of the valley, and those who were on the other side of the Jordan, saw that the men of Israel had fled and that Saul and his sons were dead, they forsook the cities and fled; and the Philistines came and dwelt in them. (NKJV)

Could the five years that are unaccounted for be after Israel accepts David as king and before he relocates to Jerusalem? Or are the five years after Ishbosheth's death and before Israel accepts David as king? Will there be five years between the time that Israel accepts Yeshua as king and His triumphant return? What we do know is that even after Israel accepts David as king, they still have battles to fight to rid the land of the Philistines. It is not until after the Philistines are defeated that David makes his triumphant entry into Jerusalem.

D. At the time David is anointed as king over all Israel, Jerusalem is held by the Jebusites, a tribe of Canaanites. All of Israel goes up with him to conquer Jerusalem.

> 2Sa 5:6-7 And the king and his men went to Jerusalem against the Jebusites, the inhabitants of the land, who spoke to David, saying, "You shall not come in here; but the blind and the lame will repel you," thinking, "David cannot come in here." 7 Nevertheless David took the stronghold of Zion (that is, the City of David). (NKJV)

In all the years that Israel had been in the Promised Land, no one had been able to drive the Jebusites completely out of Jerusalem. Josephus records that the time from Joshua to David was 515 years. (Josephus, The Antiquities of the Jews, Book 7, Chapter 3; 68) So, why did David focus on Jerusalem and the Jebusites after all these years instead of focusing on the Philistines?

Whatever the reason, David's first task was to drive the Canannites out of Jerusalem. Will Yeshua's first task be to drive the Arabs out of Jerusalem? To accomplish the task of taking over Jerusalem, David begins to gather the people of Israel. When David is anointed king by all the elders, Josephus reports that David sent the elders out to gather the people.

So when he had feasted them, and treated them kindly, he sent them out to bring all the people to him. (Josephus, <u>The Antiquities of the Jews</u>, Book 7, Chapter 2; 54)

Josephus goes on to enumerate all the thousands of Israelites who came to David in Hebron to go with him to Jerusalem. Similarly, at the time of the end, God says the people will seek Him out, and then He will gather the people back to Jerusalem, the place from where they were taken captive.

Jer 29:14 I will be found by you, says the LORD, and I will bring you back from your captivity; I will gather you from all the nations and from all the places where I have driven you, says the LORD, and I will bring you to the place from which I cause you to be carried away captive. (NKJV)

Eze 37:21-22, 24-25 "Then say to them, 'Thus says the Lord GOD: "Surely I will take the children of Israel from among the nations, wherever they have gone, and will gather them from every side and bring them into their own land; 22 "and I will make them one nation in the land, on the mountains of Israel; and one king shall be king over them all; they shall no longer be two nations, nor shall they ever be divided into two kingdoms again... 24 "David My servant shall be king over them, and they shall all have one shepherd; they shall also walk in My judgments and observe My statutes, and do them. 25 "Then they shall dwell in the land that I have given to Jacob My servant, where your fathers dwelt; and they shall dwell there, they, their children, and their children's children, forever; and My servant David shall be their prince forever. (NKJV)

The division between believing Israel and the rest of Israel will be mended. The division between the Gentiles grafted into Israel and the Jewish people will be mended. Together, we will proclaim Yeshua as King!

D. The nations come against both David and Yeshua in Jerusalem. When the Philistines heard about David being anointed king over all Israel, they went up to Jerusalem to fight against him. David went out from Jerusalem after inquiring of the LORD, and fought against the nations in Israel. But Israel did not go alone, God went before them.

2Sa 5:17-19 Now when the Philistines heard that they had anointed David king over Israel, all the Philistines went up to search for David. And David heard of it and went down to the stronghold. 18 The Philistines also went and deployed themselves in the Valley of Rephaim. 19 So David inquired of the LORD, saying, "Shall I go up against the Philistines? Will You deliver them into my hand?" And the LORD said to David, "Go up, for I will doubtless deliver the Philistines into your hand." (NKJV)

1Ch 14:15 "And it shall be, when you hear a sound of marching in the tops of the mulberry trees, then you shall go out to battle, for God has gone out before you to strike the camp of the Philistines." (NKJV)

(The Valley of Rephaim is on the west and southwest of Jerusalem.)

Josephus says that it wasn't just the Philistines who came against Jerusalem; they were joined by the surrounding nations who also wanted to destroy Israel.

> "… but let him know that all Syria and Phoenicia, with many other nations also, came to their assistance, and had a share in this war; -- which thing was the only cause why, when they had been so often conquered, and had lost so many ten thousands of their men, they still came upon the Hebrews with greater armies. (Josephus, The Antiquities of the Jews, Book 7, Chapter 3; 74-75)

When Yeshua comes again, the nations, like the Philistines and her allies of David's time, will come against Jerusalem. God, through His Son Yeshua, will fight for Jerusalem. Yeshua will then defeat all the nations of the earth and establish His reign from Jerusalem. Ezekiel and Zechariah prophesy against those nations who come against Israel.

> Eze 39:3-6 "Then I will knock the bow out of your left hand, and cause the arrows to fall out of your right hand. 4 "You shall fall upon the mountains of Israel, you and all your troops and the peoples who are with you; I will give you to birds of prey of every sort and to the beasts of the field to be devoured. 5 "You shall fall on the open field; for I have spoken," says the Lord GOD. 6 "And I will send fire on Magog and on those who live in security in the coastlands. Then they shall know that I am the LORD. (NKJV)

> Zec 14:2-4 For I will gather all the nations to battle against Jerusalem; The city shall be taken, The houses rifled, And the women ravished. Half of the city shall go into captivity, But the remnant of the people shall not be cut off from the city. 3 Then the LORD will go forth And fight against those nations, As He fights in the day of battle. 4 And in that day His feet will stand on the Mount of Olives, Which faces Jerusalem on the east. And the Mount of Olives shall be split in two, From east to west, Making a very large valley; Half of the mountain shall move toward the north And half of it toward the south. (NKJV)

Yeshua will bring us into the Promised Land and be the king and shepherd over us all.

> Ps 45:6-7 Your throne, O God, is forever and ever; A scepter of righteousness is the scepter of Your kingdom. 7 You love righteousness and hate wickedness; Therefore God, Your God, has anointed You With the oil of gladness more than Your companions. (NKJV)

E. David and Yeshua rejoice in their triumphs. David brings the ark of the LORD into Jerusalem after his defeat of the Philistines. He dances and sings before the LORD. David wears the garments of a priest when he comes into Jerusalem foreshadowing Yeshua's coming as priest and king.

1Ch 15:25-28 So David, the elders of Israel, and the captains over thousands went to bring up the ark of the covenant of the LORD from the house of Obed-Edom with joy. 26 And so it was, when God helped the Levites who bore the ark of the covenant of the LORD, that they offered seven bulls and seven rams. 27 David was clothed with a **robe of fine linen, as were all the Levites** who bore the ark, the singers, and Chenaniah the music master with the singers. David also wore a **linen ephod**. 28 Thus all Israel brought up the ark of the covenant of the LORD with shouting and with the sound of the horn, with trumpets and with cymbals, making music with stringed instruments and harps. (NKJV)

2Sa 6:14 And David danced before the LORD with all his might; and David was girded with a linen ephod. (KJV)

Many people erroneously believe that David danced naked before the LORD. This is based on his wife Michal's reaction to seeing him dance before the LORD (2 Sam.6:20). She was Saul's daughter and, like Saul, was concerned with appearance (1 Sam. 15:10-30). She scornfully speaks of David putting himself on display using the Hebrew word #1540. גלה galah, gaw-law' a primitive root; to denude (especially in a disgraceful sense); by implication, to exile (captives being usually stripped); figuratively, to reveal, X shamelessly. The NIV version uses the word "disrobing." Since David wasn't captive and being forcibly stripped, the only meaning that makes sense in the context of Michal's scorn is to "reveal shamelessly." David was not naked; the previous verses describe his clothing. Further, this would not be honoring to God. In Exodus 20:26, the priests are commanded to use a ramp to approach the altar instead of steps so they would not show their nakedness. Michal scorns David because he shamelessly revealed himself before the people by dancing before the LORD (1 Chron. 15:29).

Yeshua acted as a prophet during His first coming. David also filled the role of prophet; many, if not all, of his Psalms speak of the coming Messiah. We, like David and his entourage, will enter Jerusalem with singing and rejoicing at the coming of our Prophet, Priest and King.

Is 51:11 Therefore the redeemed of the LORD shall return, and come with singing unto Zion; and everlasting joy shall be upon their head: they shall obtain gladness and joy; and sorrow and mourning shall flee away. (KJV)

Is 52:7-9 How beautiful upon the mountains Are the feet of him who brings good news, Who proclaims peace, Who brings glad tidings of good things, Who proclaims salvation, Who says to Zion, "Your God reigns!" 8 Your watchmen shall lift up their voices, With their voices they shall sing together; For they shall see eye to eye When the LORD brings back Zion. 9 Break forth into joy, sing together, You waste places of Jerusalem! For the LORD has comforted His people, He has redeemed Jerusalem. (NKJV)

Student Notes: David's Reign and Yeshua's Second Coming

Introduction: David was the king who first conquered and reigned from Jerusalem foreshadowing the eternal reign of Yeshua from Jerusalem. But David's reign began in Hebron not in Jerusalem. This period of time beginning with David's reign in Hebron and leading up to his reign in Jerusalem foreshadows the time from Yeshua's death and resurrection to His ultimate triumphant entry into Jerusalem as the conquering king.

David reigns over Judah. (2 Sam. 2:4a)

A. The Road to Jerusalem (Lu. 10:1-2, Lu. 12:1, Lu. 13:22, Lu. 13:32-33, Lu. 14:25, Lu. 17:11, Lu. 18:31-33, Lu. 19:1-3, Lu. 19:11, Mat. 21:1-5, Zec. 9:9, Lu. 19:37-38, Acts 1:6-8)

B. Both David and Yeshua were initially accepted as king by only part of Israel. (2Sam. 2:7-9, 2Sam. 5:2, John 5:36-37, John 10:24-25, John 19:12-15)

Yeshua is still today the king over some of the Jews. The first believers were Jews as are many believers today. (Acts 2:41, Acts 6:7)

C. While David reigned in Hebron, there was conflict between his followers and the followers of Ishbosheth. (1Sam. 26:9-11a, 2Sam. 4:9-12, Rom. 11:27-29)

God's judgment on Assyria and Babylon (Isa. 10:5-7, 12, Jer. 25:11-13)

Blessings and curses (Gen. 12:2-3, Gen. 27:29, Num. 24:9)

D. David and Yeshua are anointed as king over all Israel. (2Sam. 5:3, 1Sam. 28:24-25, Gen. 19:3, 2Sam. 2:10, Gen. 45:6, 1Sam. 28:19, 1Sam. 31:7)

E. Conquering Jerusalem (2Sam. 5:6-7)

> *So when he had feasted them, and treated them kindly, he sent them out to bring all the people to him. (Josephus, <u>The Antiquities of the Jews</u>, Book 7, Chapter 2:54)*

Gathering the people (Jer. 29:14, Eze. 37:21-22, 24-25))

F. The nations come against both David and Yeshua in Jerusalem. (2Sam. 5:17-19, 1Chr. 14:15)

> *"... but let him know that all Syria and Phoenicia, with many other nations also, came to their assistance, and had a share in this war; -- which thing was the only cause why, when they had been so often conquered, and had lost so many ten thousands of their men, they still came upon the Hebrews with greater armies. (Josephus, <u>The Antiquities of the Jews</u>, Book 7, Chapter 3; 74-75)*

Prophecy against the nations that come against Jerusalem (Eze. 39:3-6, Zec. 14:2-4, Ps. 45:6-7)

G. David and Yeshua rejoice in their triumphs. (1Chr. 15:25-28, 2Sam. 6:14)

Prophet, Priest and king! (Isa. 51:11, Isa. 52:7-9)

Discussion Questions for David's Reign and Yeshua's Second Coming

1. We read that Yeshua rode the donkey into Jerusalem from the Mt. of Olives. What are some other events that have happened or will happen on the Mt. of Olives?

2. While in Jericho, Yeshua related a parable to His disciples because they thought the kingdom of God would come immediately. Read the parable in Luke 19:11-17. How does the parable address the issue of the kingdom of God?

3. In the above parable, the man is already a nobleman yet he goes to receive a kingdom and then returns to the first kingdom. What do you think the two kingdoms are?

4. Israel first chose Saul's son Ishbosheth over David as king of Israel. The name Ishbosheth means "man of shame." In 1 Chronicles 8:33 in the listing of the sons of Saul, Ishbosheth is recorded as Ish-Baal which means "man of Baal." Baal is a Canaanite god. Jeremiah 11:3 equates the word "bosheth" or shame to Baal in a Hebrew word play. In what way is Ishbosheth a "man of shame?" Yeshua said that in the days leading up to His return that, if it were possible, false messiahs would fool even the elect (Matt 24:24). How is Ishbosheth like a false Messiah?

5. Read Psalm 83. Which nations will conspire against Israel? How does this compare with the nations Josephus said came against Israel when David became king over all Israel? What does the Psalmist ask God to do to their enemies? How does that compare with what God says He will do as recorded by Ezekiel and Zechariah?

6. Read 1 Kings 1:32-40, the account of the coronation of Solomon, the son of David. Reread Matthew 21:1-5 and Luke 19:37-38 about Yeshua's triumphal entry. Compare these two accounts. How is Yeshua asserting that He is the Son of David?

Sealed For the Day of Redemption

Eph 4:30 *And do not grieve the Holy Spirit of God, by whom you were sealed for the day of redemption.* (NKJV)

What is Paul talking about when he says we are sealed for the day of redemption? What is the seal? In Jewish tradition, everyone's life comes up for review before God on the Feast of Trumpets and judgment is rendered by Yom Kippur, the Day of Atonement, on whether that person will live or die for the coming year. A traditional greeting for the days leading up to Rosh Hashanah is, "May you be written and sealed for the coming year." The wish is that a person's name is written in the book of life and that the book is sealed. There will be no changing after the book is sealed. There are two parts to this greeting—being written in the book of life and having your name sealed in the book.

A. The Book of Life: What does Paul say about the book of life?

> Php 4:3 And I urge you also, true companion, help these women who labored with me in the gospel, with Clement also, and the rest of my fellow workers, whose names are in the Book of Life. (NKJV)

Paul says that his fellow workers in Christ have their names written in the Book of Life.

> Mal 3:16 Then those who feared the LORD spoke to one another, And the LORD listened and heard them; So a book of remembrance was written before Him For those who fear the LORD And who meditate on His name. (NKJV)

Malachi wrote that those who fear the LORD and keep thoughts of God uppermost in their minds will be written in the Book of Remembrance.

> Re 3:5 "He who overcomes shall be clothed in white garments, and I will not blot out his name from the Book of Life; but I will confess his name before My Father and before His angels. (NKJV)

Yeshua, through the prophet John, says that those who overcome will be written in the Book of Life and that He will confess his name before God the Father. Those who are written in the Book of Life belong to Yeshua and through Him to God the Father. In His prayer at the close of His last Passover Seder, Yeshua prays for those God has given Him. He is able to keep and guard those who have received and believed God's words.

> Joh 17:6-9, 12 "I have manifested Your name to the men whom You have given Me out of the world. They were Yours, You gave them to Me, and they have kept Your word. 7 "Now they have known that all things which You have given Me are from You. 8 "For I have given to them the words which You have given Me; and they have received them, and have known surely that I came forth from You; and they have believed that You sent Me. 9 "I pray for them. I do not pray for the world

but for those whom You have given Me, for they are Yours… 12 "While I was with them in the world, I kept them in Your name. Those whom You gave Me I have kept; and none of them is lost except the son of perdition, that the Scripture might be fulfilled. (NKJV)

Only those who are written in the Book of Life will be able to enter the New Jerusalem.

Re 21:27 But there shall by no means enter it anything that defiles, or causes an abomination or a lie, but only those who are written in the Lamb's Book of Life. (NKJV)

B. What is the opposite of being written in the Book of Life? Yeshua, again through the prophet John, says that those who are not written in the book of life belong to the Beast and will be thrown into the lake of fire.

Re 13:8 All inhabitants of the earth will worship the beast-- all whose names have not been written in the book of life belonging to the Lamb that was slain from the creation of the world. (NIV)

Re 17:8 The beast, which you saw, once was, now is not, and will come up out of the Abyss and go to his destruction. The inhabitants of the earth whose names have not been written in the book of life from the creation of the world will be astonished when they see the beast, because he once was, now is not, and yet will come. (NIV)

Re 20:12, 15 And I saw the dead, great and small, standing before the throne, and books were opened. Another book was opened, which is the book of life. The dead were judged according to what they had done as recorded in the books.15 If anyone's name was not found written in the book of life, he was thrown into the lake of fire. (NIV)

David records a Psalm asking God that those who hate him, that do iniquity or moral evil be blotted out of the Book of Life.

Ps 69:27-28 Add iniquity to their iniquity, And let them not come into Your righteousness. 28 Let them be blotted out of the book of the living, And not be written with the righteous. (NKJV)

Those who aren't written in the Book of Life are destined to be thrown into the lake of fire. Being written in the Book of Life means eternal life. We are not only written in the Book, we are sealed into it.

C. What is the seal Paul speaks of in Ephesians, "…by whom you were sealed for the day of redemption?" The seal has its origins in the priesthood described in Exodus.

> Ex 28:36-38 "Make a plate of pure gold and engrave on it as on a seal: HOLY TO THE LORD. 37 Fasten a blue cord to it to attach it to the turban; it is to be on the front of the turban. 38 It will be on Aaron's forehead, and he will bear the guilt involved in the sacred gifts the Israelites consecrate, whatever their gifts may be. It will be on Aaron's forehead continually so that they will be acceptable to the LORD. (NIV))

The word we translate "seal" is from Strong's #2368 חותם chowtham, kho-thawm' or chotham {kho-thawm'}; from 2856; a signature-ring:--seal, signet.

A signet was used to seal correspondence. The document would be rolled up or folded, wax would be dripped onto the opening, then the signet would be pressed into the hot wax to seal the document. The only way to open the document was to break the seal. Also, the signet was used to "notarize" a signature on a document. The wax would be dripped onto the document and the signet would be pressed onto it to attest to the signature. As an alternate, blood would be dripped onto the document and the signet pressed into the blood. This is where we get the phrase "sealed in blood."

The high priest wore the plate with the name "Holy to the LORD." The word holy means to be separate or to be set aside. The high priest was set aside to the LORD. In a sense, he has God's signature on his forehead. Paul paraphrases from Isaiah 52:11 and Ezekiel 20:41 as he tells us that we also are called to be holy, to be set aside for God.

> 2Co 6:17 "Therefore come out from them and be separate, says the Lord. Touch no unclean thing, and I will receive you." (NIV)

The plate was worn on the forehead. Everyone who looked at the high priest saw that he was "Holy to the LORD." God also told the Israelites to wear the word of God on their foreheads as well as their hands.

> De 6:6, 8 These commandments that I give you today are to be upon your hearts…
> 8 Tie them as symbols on your hands and bind them on your foreheads. (NIV)

A tiny scroll with the words from passages with the commandment to bind the commandments on their foreheads and hands is placed in a small leather box and bound on the foreheads and left hand. The left hand is chosen because it is closer to the heart. By doing so, they are reminded that God's commands should be on their minds (forehead) and that they should apply them in their lives (hand). An alternate explanation given by the sages is to tie them on the weaker hand showing that true strength comes from God.

D. Satan is always trying to imitate God. Notice the placement of the mark of the beast.

> Re 13:15-16 He was granted power to give breath to the image of the beast, that the image of the beast should both speak and cause as many as would not worship the image of the beast to be killed. 16 He causes all, both small and great, rich and

poor, free and slave, to receive a mark on their right hand or on their foreheads, (NKJV)

The mark is on the forehead and the right hand. The mark of the beast is a counterfeit seal. The right hand is chosen instead of the left. It is usually the stronger arm so they are relying on their own strength. Further, God's strength is symbolized by "His strong right hand."

Ex 15:6 "Your right hand, O LORD, has become glorious in power; Your right hand, O LORD, has dashed the enemy in pieces. (NKJV)

The beast is trying to put himself in the place of God demanding the worship of his followers. Notice that he is not trying to be Christ, the Messiah. He is not trying to bring about the salvation of mankind nor bring about reconciliation of any type. He is not claiming to be anointed or sent by God; instead he is claiming to be god himself.

Those who worship the beast will receive its mark and be granted power by the beast.

Re 13:17-18 and that no one may buy or sell except one who has the mark or the name of the beast, or the number of his name. 18 Here is wisdom. Let him who has understanding calculate the number of the beast, for it is the number of a man: His number is six hundred and sixty-six. (NKJV)

But the power of the beast is temporary. The beast and the false prophet will be thrown in the lake of fire.

Re 15:2 And I saw something like a sea of glass mingled with fire, and those who have the victory over the beast, over his image and over his mark and over the number of his name, standing on the sea of glass, having harps of God. (NKJV)

Re 19:20 Then the beast was captured, and with him the false prophet who worked signs in his presence, by which he deceived those who received the mark of the beast and those who worshiped his image. These two were cast alive into the lake of fire burning with brimstone. (NKJV)

Here's our take on the number 666. Six is the number of man. Man and the serpent were created on the sixth day. Man was to labor six days. With the addition of God, represented by the number one, we have seven, spiritual completeness. But without God we have only 6, secular completeness or man's attempt at completeness by his own works. The number 6 is repeated three times. Three is the number of divine completeness as represented in the Godhead, Father, Son and Spirit. The simplest geometric figure requires three sides to be complete. The number 6 repeated three times represents man elevating himself to be God. It is the pinnacle of humanism advocating that man by his own efforts can achieve anything; that we are evolving into a more noble being. We believe that the beast will exalt himself specifically and mankind in general. He will speak of the great power and nobility and character of mankind. Those who have the name of the beast on their forehead have their minds on the great achievements of man. Paul says that the beast will set himself up as God.

> 2Th 2:4 He will oppose and will exalt himself over everything that is called God or is worshiped, so that he sets himself up in God's temple, proclaiming himself to be God. (NIV)

Moses declares the greatness of God after the crossing of the Red Sea.

> Ex 15:11 "Who among the gods is like you, O LORD? Who is like you-- majestic in holiness, awesome in glory, working wonders? (NIV)

Those who worship the beast will proclaim the beast to be unsurpassed imitating Moses' song.

> Re 13:4 Men worshiped the dragon because he had given authority to the beast, and they also worshiped the beast and asked, "Who is like the beast? Who can make war against him?" (NIV)

But what do those who have victory over the beast sing? They sing the song of Moses and the Lamb.

> Re 15:3-4 They sing the song of Moses, the servant of God, and the song of the Lamb, saying: "Great and marvelous are Your works, Lord God Almighty! Just and true are Your ways, O King of the saints! 4 Who shall not fear You, O Lord, and glorify Your name? For You alone are holy. For all nations shall come and worship before You, For Your judgments have been manifested." (NKJV)

E. The observance of the Feast of Unleavened Bread was like a sign on the hand or forehead for the purpose of reminding the Israelites that the law of the LORD is to be on their lips. It is to be ingrained in every part of their lives.

> Ex 13:6-9 For seven days eat bread made without yeast and on the seventh day hold a festival to the LORD. 7 Eat unleavened bread during those seven days; nothing with yeast in it is to be seen among you, nor shall any yeast be seen anywhere within your borders. 8 On that day tell your son, 'I do this because of what the LORD did for me when I came out of Egypt.' 9 This observance will be for you like a sign on your hand and a reminder on your forehead that the law of the LORD is to be on your lips. For the LORD brought you out of Egypt with his mighty hand. (NIV)

God brought them out of Egypt to be a nation of priests and holy to the LORD. We also are priests before God.

> Ex 19:6 'And you shall be to Me a kingdom of priests and a holy nation.' These are the words which you shall speak to the children of Israel." (NKJV)

> 1Pe 2:5 you also, as living stones, are being built up a spiritual house, a holy priesthood, to offer up spiritual sacrifices acceptable to God through Jesus Christ. (NKJV)

> 1Pe 2:9 But you are a chosen generation, a royal priesthood, a holy nation, His own special people, that you may proclaim the praises of Him who called you out of darkness into His marvelous light; (NKJV)

Yeshua was crucified on Passover which is the afternoon before the Feast of Unleavened Bread begins. Yeshua was buried and resurrected during the Feast of Unleavened Bread. Since unleavened bread does not decay or become moldy, it symbolizes the fact that Yeshua was not left in the grave to decay.

> Ps 16:8-10 I have set the LORD always before me. Because he is at my right hand, I will not be shaken. 9 Therefore my heart is glad and my tongue rejoices; my body also will rest secure, 10 because you will not abandon me to the grave, nor will you let your Holy One see decay. (NIV)

> Ac 2:24-27 But God raised him from the dead, freeing him from the agony of death, because it was impossible for death to keep its hold on him. 25 David said about him: "'I saw the Lord always before me. Because he is at my right hand, I will not be shaken. 26 Therefore my heart is glad and my tongue rejoices; my body also will live in hope, 27 because you will not abandon me to the grave, nor will you let your Holy One see decay. (NIV)

It is also a promise to us who are "Holy to the LORD" that we will have a new body which is eternal and will not decay.

> 1Co 15:42-44, 54-55 So also is the resurrection of the dead. The body is sown in corruption, it is raised in incorruption. 43 It is sown in dishonor, it is raised in glory. It is sown in weakness, it is raised in power. 44 It is sown a natural body, it is raised a spiritual body. There is a natural body, and there is a spiritual body. 54 So when this corruptible has put on incorruption, and this mortal has put on immortality, then shall be brought to pass the saying that is written: "Death is swallowed up in victory." 55 "O Death, where is your sting? O Hades, where is your victory?" (NKJV)

F. In addition to wearing the commandments on the forehead and hands, the Israelites were to wear tassels on their garments to remind them of all the commands of the LORD.

> Nu 15:38-39 "Speak to the Israelites and say to them: 'Throughout the generations to come you are to make tassels on the corners of your garments, with a blue cord on each tassel. 39 You will have these tassels to look at and so you will remember all the commands of the LORD, that you may obey them and not prostitute yourselves by going after the lusts of your own hearts and eyes. (NIV)

There is an interesting connection between the plate the high priest wears and the tassels all the Israelites wear. The word for the plate the high priest wears is tzitz.

Plate: #6731: ציץ tsiyts, tseets or tsits {tseets}; from 6692; properly, glistening, i.e. a burnished plate; also a flower (as bright-colored); a wing (as gleaming in the air):-- blossom, flower, plate, wing.

The word for tassels is just the feminine form of the word for the plate. Both are for the purpose of setting the wearer apart for God. The plate and the tassels reminded anyone who saw them that the wearer belonged to God and followed His commandments.

Tassels: #6734. ציצת tsiytsith, tsee-tseeth' feminine of 6731; a floral or wing-like projection, i.e. a forelock of hair, a tassel:--fringe, lock.

G. God's name on our foreheads sets us aside for him. At the time of the destruction of the first temple, God held off judgment until those who belonged to Him were marked on their foreheads.

> Eze 9:3-6 Now the glory of the God of Israel had gone up from the cherub, where it had been, to the threshold of the temple. And He called to the man clothed with linen, who had the writer's inkhorn at his side; 4 and the LORD said to him, "Go through the midst of the city, through the midst of Jerusalem, and put a mark on the foreheads of the men who sigh and cry over all the abominations that are done within it." 5 To the others He said in my hearing, "Go after him through the city and kill; do not let your eye spare, nor have any pity. 6 "Utterly slay old and young men, maidens and little children and women; but do not come near anyone on whom is the mark; and begin at My sanctuary." So they began with the elders who were before the temple. (NKJV)

The mark placed on their foreheads was the letter tav,□ ת. The Hebrew word for mark is literally tav spelled in Hebrew using the tav and the vav. Read right to left, it is תו meaning mark or the letter tav. In Ezekiel's day the shape of the ת was like a slanted cross, ✗.

Hebrew word Picture: Hebrew is read right to left.

Mark: תו

Tav: A sign, a cross, to covenant, to seal

Vav: Nail, "and," to secure, to add

Mark: The covenant secured.

We are marked with the cross which is symbolic of the crucifixion of Yeshua. On the day of Pentecost, the Feast of Weeks, when the Holy Spirit fell, Peter instructed the people.

Ac 2:38-39 Then Peter said to them, "Repent, and let every one of you be baptized in the name of Jesus Christ for the remission of sins; and you shall receive the gift of the Holy Spirit. 39 "For the promise is to you and to your children, and to all who are afar off, as many as the Lord our God will call." (NKJV)

Part of the gift of the Holy Spirit is that He seals us as a promise of our eternal redemption.

Eph 1:13-14 In Him you also trusted, after you heard the word of truth, the gospel of your salvation; in whom also, having believed, you were sealed with the Holy Spirit of promise,14 who is the guarantee of our inheritance until the redemption of the purchased possession, to the praise of His glory. (NKJV)

The Tablets of the Ten Commandments were written by the finger of God.

Ex 31:18 And when He had made an end of speaking with him on Mount Sinai, He gave Moses two tablets of the Testimony, tablets of stone, written with the finger of God. (NKJV)

Yeshua compares the "finger of God" with the Holy Spirit. Luke and Matthew both describe Yeshua driving demons out of a man. Luke says Yeshua used the phrase "finger of God" and Matthew said the phrase was "Spirit of God."

Lu 11:20 "But if I cast out demons with the finger of God, surely the kingdom of God has come upon you. (NKJV)

Mat 12:28 "But if I cast out demons by the Spirit of God, surely the kingdom of God has come upon you. (NKJV)

The Holy Spirit is the finger of God who wrote the Ten Commandments on the Tablets of stone. The same Holy Spirit writes those same commandments on our hearts bringing us into the New Covenant and sealing us for the day of redemption.

2Co 3:3 clearly you are an epistle of Christ, ministered by us, written not with ink but by the Spirit of the living God, not on tablets of stone but on tablets of flesh, that is, of the heart. (NKJV)

Eph 4:30 And do not grieve the Holy Spirit of God, by whom you were sealed for the day of redemption. (NKJV)

Student Notes: Sealed For the Day of Redemption

Eph 4:30 *And do not grieve the Holy Spirit of God, by whom you were sealed for the day of redemption.* (NKJV)

What is Paul talking about when he says we are sealed for the day of redemption? What is the seal? In Jewish tradition:

A. The Book of Life: (Php. 4:3, Mal. 3:16, Rev. 3:5, John 17:6-9, 12, Rev. 21:27)

Those who are written in the Book of Life belong to:

He is able to:

B. What is the opposite of being written in the Book of Life? (Rev. 13:8, Rev 17:8, Rev. 20:12, 15, Ps. 69:27-28)

Those who are not written in the book of life belong to:

C. What is the seal Paul speaks of in Ephesians, "…by whom you were sealed for the day of redemption?"

The priesthood: (Ex. 28:36-38)
Seal: Strong's Dictionary #2368 חותם chowtham, kho-thawm' or chotham {kho-thawm'}; from 2856; a signature-ring:--seal, signet.

The people: (2Cor. 6:17, Deu. 6:6, 8)

D. Satan is always trying to imitate God. Notice the placement of the mark of the beast. (Rev. 13:15-16, Ex. 15:6, Rev. 13:17-18, Rev. 15:2, Rev. 19:20)

The number 3 means:

The beast will set himself up as God. (2Thes. 2:4, Ex. 15:11, Rev. 13:4, Rev. 15:3-4)

E. The observance of the Feast of Unleavened Bread was like a sign on the hand or forehead. (Ex. 13:6-9, Ex. 19:6, 1Pet. 2:5, 9)

Yeshua was not left _____ (Ps. 16:8-10, Acts 2:24-27, 1Cor. 15:42-44, 54-55)

F. The tassels worn on the garments are connected to the plate of the high priest. (Nu. 15:38-39)

Plate: #6731. צִיץ tsiyts, tseets or tsits {tseets}; from 6692; properly, glistening, i.e. a burnished plate; also a flower (as bright-colored); a wing (as gleaming in the air):-- blossom, flower, plate, wing.

Tassels: #6734. צִיצִת tsiytsith, tsee-tseeth' feminine of 6731; a floral or wing-like projection, i.e. a forelock of hair, a tassel:--fringe, lock.

G. God's name on our foreheads sets us aside for him. (Eze. 9:3-6, Acts 2:38-39)

Mark: tav תו meaning mark or the letter tav.
In Ezekiel's day the shape was like a slanted cross, ✗ .

> Hebrew word Picture: Hebrew is read right to left.
>
> Mark: תו
>
> Tav: A sign, a cross, to covenant, to seal
>
> Vav: Nail, "and," to secure, to add
>
> Mark: The covenant secured.

The Holy Spirit is the finger of God. (Eph. 1:13-14. Ex. 31:18, Lu. 11:20, Mat. 12:28, 2 Cor. 3:3)

Eph 4:30 *And do not grieve the Holy Spirit of God, by whom you were sealed for the day of redemption.* (NKJV)

Discussion questions for Sealed for the Day of Redemption

1. Read Exodus 32:30-33. In this passage, Moses is interceding with God on behalf of the children of Israel after they built and worshipped the golden calf. Discuss Moses' offer to be blotted out of God's book in the context of intercession.

2. Read Romans 9:1-5. How is Paul's desire similar to Moses' offer in Exodus 32:30-33? How is what Moses and Paul offered to do like what Yeshua did on the cross?

3. God's deliverance of the children of Israel out of Egypt is a picture of our deliverance from sin. Reread Exodus 13:6-9. The observance of the Feast of Unleavened Bread is to be like the sign on the hand and forehead to remind them to speak God's Torah. How does that apply to us as the recipients of deliverance from sin?

4. Continuing with Exodus 13:6-9, not only was Torah to be on the lips of the children of Israel, the Holy Spirit would write it on their hearts (Jer. 31:31-32). Yeshua refers to the New Covenant when He is observing His last Passover Seder. Since we are under the New Covenant, how do these instructions apply to us?

5. Read Leviticus 28:40-43 about a priest's garments. How do we put on the garments of the priesthood?

The Commandment to Read the Torah before the Assembly

De 31:10-13 And Moses commanded them, saying: "At the end of every seven years, at the appointed time in the year of release, at the Feast of Tabernacles, 11 "when all Israel comes to appear before the LORD your God in the place which He chooses, you shall read this law (Torah) before all Israel in their hearing. 12 "Gather the people together, men and women and little ones, and the stranger who is within your gates, that they may hear and that they may learn to fear the LORD your God and carefully observe all the words of this law, 13 "and that their children, who have not known it, may hear and learn to fear the LORD your God as long as you live in the land which you cross the Jordan to possess." (NKJV)

This commandment is a rehearsal of the time Yeshua Himself will read Torah to the nations. The event will occur at a specific time of year, "the appointed time of release at the Feast of Tabernacles." We need some background about the Biblical calendar to understand the significance of the timing of this event. See Appendix B for additional details about the Biblical Calendar. All of the events mentioned here occur in the month of Tishrei. Tishrei corresponds to September/October of the Gregorian calendar. The official New Year when the year number changes is Tishrei 1, but the days from Tishrei 1 to Tishrei 22 are all counted as the end of one year and the beginning of the next. It's like having a three week celebration to end each year and start the next. Because of this, end of year and beginning of year activities overlap. The following chart shows the sequence of events.

Tishrei 1	Tishrei 10	Tishrei 15
Feast of Trumpets	Day of Atonement	Feast of Tabernacles Begins
Official Calendar New Year 100 Trumpets blasts are sounded to signal the beginning of the fall feasts.	Shofar is blown to announce the start of the Year of Jubilee	Reading of the Torah at the end of the year of release

We need to keep this chart in mind while we study this passage phrase by phrase.

A. "At the end of every seven years, at the appointed time in the year of release…"

The year of release is the Sabbath year. Every seventh year was to be observed as a Sabbath year. During this year, the land is to observe a Sabbath rest; it is not to be plowed or tilled. The produce that comes up voluntarily can be used for food but is not to be preserved or sold.

In addition to the rest for the land, debts are forgiven, so the Sabbath year is also called the year of release.

De 15:1-3 "At the end of every seven years you shall grant a **release** of debts. 2 "And this is the form of the release: Every creditor who has lent anything to his neighbor shall **release** it; he shall not require it of his neighbor or his brother, because it is called the LORD'S **release**. 3 "Of a foreigner you may require it; but you shall give up your claim to what is owed by your brother, (NKJV)

It is at the end of this year, after the land has observed its Sabbath and debts are released that the Torah is read before the Assembly. The land and the debtor experience a new beginning. The first act of this new beginning is to remember the LORD by reading His Torah.

Another example of release is that slaves are set free in the seventh year of service. This seventh year may or may not be a Sabbath year, but the cycle is seven years like that of the Sabbath cycle.

De 15:12-15 "If your brother, a Hebrew man, or a Hebrew woman, is sold to you and serves you six years, then in the seventh year you shall let him go free from you. 13 "And when you send him away free from you, you shall not let him go away empty-handed; 14 "you shall supply him liberally from your flock, from your threshing floor, and from your winepress. From what the LORD has blessed you with, you shall give to him. 15 "You shall remember that you were a slave in the land of Egypt, and the LORD your God redeemed you; therefore I command you this thing today. (NKJV)

When the slaves were released, they were to be provided with provisions for a new start.

If a Hebrew is sold to a Gentile, then the term of service is until the Year of Jubilee unless a relative redeems him earlier.

Le 25:47-48 'Now if a sojourner or stranger close to you becomes rich, and one of your brethren who dwells by him becomes poor, and sells himself to the stranger or sojourner close to you, or to a member of the stranger's family, 48 'after he is sold he may be redeemed again. One of his brothers may redeem him; (NKJV)

Le 25:54-55 'And if he is not redeemed in these years, then he shall be **released** in the Year of Jubilee-he and his children with him. 55 'For the children of Israel are servants to Me; they are My servants whom I brought out of the land of Egypt: I am the LORD your God. (NKJV)

The Year of Jubilee is the fiftieth year; it follows the seventh Sabbath year. In fact, the Year of Jubilee begins five days before the end of the seventh Sabbath year! Refer to the chart on the previous page. The Year of Jubilee begins on Tishrei 10 and the year of release ends on Tishrei 15.

Le 25:8-10 'And you shall count seven sabbaths of years for yourself, seven times seven years; and the time of the seven sabbaths of years shall be to you forty-nine years. 9 'Then you shall cause the trumpet of the Jubilee to sound on the **tenth day of the seventh month**; on the Day of Atonement you shall make the trumpet to sound throughout all your land. 10 'And you shall consecrate the fiftieth year, and **proclaim liberty** throughout all the land to all its inhabitants. It shall be a Jubilee for you; and each of you shall return to his possession, and each of you shall return to his family. (NKJV)

In the Sabbath year, debts are released and the land has a rest. Like the Sabbath year, the land rests in the Year of Jubilee. In addition, all slaves go free even those sold to fellow Hebrews who haven't served for six years.

Le 25:39-40 'And if one of your brethren who dwells by you becomes poor, and sells himself to you, you shall not compel him to serve as a slave. 40 'As a hired servant and a sojourner he shall be with you, and shall serve you until the Year of Jubilee. (NKJV)

Everyone goes free in the Year of Jubilee! Also in the Year of Jubilee, the Land reverts to the family that originally owned it, and each person returns to his land and his family. The key phrase for the Year of Jubilee is "proclaim liberty." Whenever we see this phrase, we know we are talking about a Year of Jubilee event.

Isaiah writes about preaching good tidings proclaiming liberty, the release of debts, and freedom from slavery.

Isa 61:1-3 "The Spirit of the Lord GOD is upon Me, Because the LORD has anointed Me To preach good tidings to the poor; He has sent Me to heal the brokenhearted, To **proclaim liberty** to the captives, **And the opening of the prison** to those who are bound; 2 To proclaim the acceptable year of the LORD, And the day of vengeance of our God; To comfort all who mourn, 3 To console those who mourn in Zion, To give them beauty for ashes, The oil of joy for mourning, The garment of praise for the spirit of heaviness; That they may be called trees of righteousness, The planting of the LORD, that He may be glorified." (NKJV)

God says that His Messiah will be the one to fulfill this prophecy.

Isa 42:5-7 Thus says God the LORD, Who created the heavens and stretched them out, Who spread forth the earth and that which comes from it, Who gives breath to the people on it, And spirit to those who walk on it: 6 "I, the LORD, have called You in righteousness, And will hold Your hand; I will keep You and give You as a covenant to the people, As a light to the Gentiles, 7 To open blind eyes, **To bring out prisoners** from the prison, Those who sit in darkness from the prison house. (NKJV)

When Yeshua announced the beginning of His ministry in the synagogue at Nazareth, He quoted the first part of the passage in Isaiah 61:1-3, but He stopped in the middle of verse two. The completion of this prophecy will be at His second return.

Lu 4:18 "The Spirit of the LORD is upon Me, Because He has anointed Me To preach the gospel to the poor; He has sent Me to heal the brokenhearted, To **proclaim liberty** to the captives And recovery of sight to the blind, To set at liberty those who are oppressed; (NKJV)

Yeshua is proclaiming a Year of Jubilee as He begins His public ministry. Yeshua will fulfill the second part of the prophecy in Isaiah 61 at another Year of Jubilee. This could be exactly 2000 years after the Year of Jubilee which began His ministry. When Yeshua came the first time, He set us free from slavery to sin that leads to death. In His second coming He will set us free from physical death, mourning, and the spirit of heaviness while at the same time proclaiming the vengeance of God.

The reading of the Torah in the year of release becomes especially significant at the end of the 49th year because it inaugurates a year of Jubilee. As the trumpet is blown signaling the beginning of the Year of Jubilee, all the slaves are set free and ownership of the land reverts to its original owners. Five days later, the seventh Sabbath Year, during which all debts had been released, ends. All the people gather to hear the reading of the Torah.

B. "… at the appointed time … at the Feast of Tabernacles…"

There are three Pilgrimage feasts each year, the Feast of Unleavened Bread, the Feast of Weeks, and the Feast of Tabernacles. All males were to go to Jerusalem and appear before the LORD with an offering on each of these feasts.

De 16:16 "Three times a year all your males shall appear before the LORD your God in the place which He chooses: at the Feast of Unleavened Bread, at the Feast of Weeks, and at the Feast of Tabernacles; and they shall not appear before the LORD empty-handed. (NKJV)

The Feast of Tabernacles occurs at the end of the harvest year. The command is to rejoice during the Feast of Tabernacles.

De 16:13-15 "You shall observe the Feast of Tabernacles seven days, when you have gathered from your threshing floor and from your winepress. 14 "And you shall rejoice in your feast, you and your son and your daughter, your male servant and your female servant and the Levite, the stranger and the fatherless and the widow, who are within your gates. 15 "Seven days you shall keep a sacred feast to the LORD your God in the place which the LORD chooses, because the LORD your God will bless you in all your produce and in all the work of your hands, so that you surely rejoice. (NKJV)

They rejoice in God's abundant provision both from the land and through the work of the artisans. The time of the final harvest, though, is not joyful for everyone. The judgment of God at the end times is described as the harvest of the earth, mentioning specifically the grape harvest which is the final harvest leading up to the Feast of Tabernacles.

Joel describes the time of judgment in terms of the winepress.

> Joe 3:12-13 "Let the nations be wakened, and come up to the Valley of Jehoshaphat; For there I will sit to judge all the surrounding nations. 13 Put in the sickle, for the harvest is ripe. Come, go down; For the winepress is full, The vats overflow-For their wickedness is great." (NKJV)

Yeshua says the harvest is the end of the age. It will be a time of judgment. Those who belong to Him will shine with His righteousness. Isaiah 42 says God calls Israel in righteousness. In contrast, those who belong to Satan will face eternal punishment. This is the final harvest.

> Mat 13:38-43 The field is the world, and the good seed stands for the sons of the kingdom. The weeds are the sons of the evil one, 39 and the enemy who sows them is the devil. The harvest is the end of the age, and the harvesters are angels. 40 "As the weeds are pulled up and burned in the fire, so it will be at the end of the age. 41 The Son of Man will send out his angels, and they will weed out of his kingdom everything that causes sin and all who do evil. 42 They will throw them into the fiery furnace, where there will be weeping and gnashing of teeth. 43 Then the righteous will shine like the sun in the kingdom of their Father. He who has ears, let him hear. (NIV)

The passage in Joel also mentions that God will liberate the slaves in the end times, specifically those sold into slavery by the "nations." The slaves are set free and God returns the land to Israel. The Day of Judgment occurs in the Year of Jubilee.

> Joe 3:1-3, 6-7 "For behold, in those days and at that time, When I bring back the captives of Judah and Jerusalem, 2 I will also gather all nations, And bring them down to the Valley of Jehoshaphat; And I will enter into judgment with them there On account of My people, My heritage Israel, Whom they have scattered among the nations; They have also divided up My land. 3 They have cast lots for My people, Have given a boy as payment for a harlot, And sold a girl for wine, that they may drink... 6 Also the people of Judah and the people of Jerusalem You have sold to the Greeks, That you may remove them far from their borders. 7 "Behold, I will raise them Out of the place to which you have sold them, And will return your retaliation upon your own head. (NKJV)

Hebrew word picture: Hebrew is read right to left.

Jehoshaphat: יהושפט The LORD's judgment

Yood-hey-vav: יהו Abbreviated form of the name of God, יהוה

Sheen: ש teeth- destroy or consume

Pey: פ mouth- to speak, to open, a word

Tet: ט snake, to twist, to surround

Jehoshaphat: The LORD destroys the mouth of the serpent.

At the end of the harvest, the righteous will shine and there will be great rejoicing. This event will happen after the nations divide the land of Israel. This is happening right now. The United States and the United Nations are pressuring Israel to give up land to the Palestinians to enforce a two state solution in Israel. This is the first time that multiple nations have been involved in dividing up the land.

C. "… when all Israel comes to appear before the LORD your God in the place which He chooses... Gather the people together, men and women and little ones, and the stranger who is within your gates…"

We read in Deuteronomy 16:16 that at a normal pilgrimage feast, only the males were required to appear before the LORD. In the Sabbath year, all Israel including women, children and the strangers who live in Israel were all to appear before the LORD at the Feast of Tabernacles. The gathering was called the Hakhel or the Great Assembly.

The word for gather is "qahal" which can be used as a verb or a noun.

Gather: Strong's #6950 קהל qahal, 'kaw-hal' a primitive root; to convoke:--assemble (selves) (together), gather (selves) (together)

Strong's #06951. קהל qahal, kaw-hawl' from 6950; assemblage (usually concretely):--assembly, company, congregation, multitude.

This special gathering of the people was not an assembly but **The** assembly. The word in Hebrew becomes הקהל or "hakhel." In the Septuagint, this word is translated as ecclesia, In English hakhel is translated as church.

Hebrew word picture: Hebrew is read right to left.

Hakhel: הקהל : The Assembly

Hey: ה window, lattice, "the," to reveal, behold

Quph: ק back of the head, behind, the last, the least, to follow

Hey: ה window, lattice, "the," to reveal, behold

Lamed: ל cattle goad, staff – prod, toward, control, authority

The Assembly: Behold, follow the revealed authority.

The writer of Hebrews tells us not to forsake the assembly especially as we approach the end times.

Heb 10:25 Not forsaking the assembling of ourselves together, as the manner of some is; but exhorting one another: and so much the more, as ye see the day approaching. (KJV)

The Hakhel is an appointed time—a time when God promises to meet with His people. David writes about the Great Assembly in three of his Psalms—Psalm 22, 35 and 40. Psalm 22 begins with the words Yeshua quoted while on the cross.

Psalms 22:1 NKJV 1 <<To the Chief Musician. Set to "The Deer of the Dawn." A Psalm of David.>> My God, My God, why have You forsaken Me? Why are You so far from helping Me, And from the words of My groaning?

David continues prophesying in Psalm 22 that Messiah's bones would be out of joint, His hands and feet would be pierced, and that they would gamble over who would get His garments.

Ps 22:14-18 I am poured out like water, And all My bones are out of joint; My heart is like wax; It has melted within Me. 15 My strength is dried up like a potsherd, And My tongue clings to My jaws; You have brought Me to the dust of death. 16 For dogs have surrounded Me; The congregation of the wicked has enclosed Me. They pierced My hands and My feet; 17 I can count all My bones. They look and stare at Me. 18 They divide My garments among them, And for My clothing they cast lots. (NKJV)

All these verses are about Yeshua's death. But then we come to verse 21.

Ps 22:21 Save me from the mouth of a lion: --And--from the horns of the high places Thou hast answered me! (YLT)

In one sentence, the tone of the Psalm changes; God answered from the horns or the strength of the high places. The Psalm becomes a psalm of praise to God declared in the Great Assembly.

Ps 22:22-28 I will declare Your name to My brethren; In the midst of the **assembly** I will praise You. 23 You who fear the LORD, praise Him! All you descendants of Jacob, glorify Him, And fear Him, all you offspring of Israel! 24 For He has not despised nor abhorred the affliction of the afflicted; Nor has He hidden His face from Him; But when He cried to Him, He heard. 25 My praise shall be of You in the **great assembly**; I will pay My vows before those who fear Him. 26 The poor shall eat and be satisfied; Those who seek Him will praise the LORD. Let your heart live forever! 27 All the ends of the world Shall remember and turn to the LORD, And all the families of the nations Shall worship before You. 28 For the kingdom is the LORD'S, And He rules over the nations. (NKJV)

God has answered His Messiah who was afflicted for us. He hasn't hidden His face from His Messiah. Yeshua will praise the LORD, Yehovah, in the Great Assembly! We see the year of Jubilee reflected in this Psalm because the poor eat and are satisfied. This is a time of praise and rejoicing for those who love Him and seek Him! Messiah is on the throne and all the people come up to Jerusalem to worship before the LORD!

Zechariah confirms that at this first Hakhel at the time of Yeshua's return, all the saints who came with Yeshua in the clouds and all the people left after the battle of Armageddon will come to Jerusalem to worship God.

> Zec 14:16 And it shall come to pass, that every one that is left of all the nations which came against Jerusalem shall even go up from year to year to worship the King, the LORD of hosts, and to keep the feast of tabernacles. (KJV)

The place God has chosen for the Hakhel, the assembly, is Jerusalem. He chose Jerusalem at the time of David and Zechariah confirms that God will again choose Jerusalem as the place for His name.

> 2Ch 6:6 'Yet I have chosen Jerusalem, that My name may be there; and I have chosen David to be over My people Israel.' (NKJV)

> Zec 2:12 The LORD will inherit Judah as his portion in the holy land and will again choose Jerusalem. (NIV)

Further, Zechariah said the observation of the Feast of Tabernacles, and by extension, the Hakhel, will continue throughout the millennium. Every seven years during the millennium, all the peoples of the earth will assemble to hear the reading of the Torah.

D. "… you shall read this law before all Israel in their hearing. Gather the people… "

The word "you" in this passage is singular. One specific person was to read the law before all Israel. Further, that person would gather the people. The priest could and did read the Torah but he couldn't gather the people. Only one person had the authority to do both. That person was the king.

David gathered the people to celebrate bringing the Ark of the Covenant into Jerusalem.

> 1Ch 15:3 And David gathered all Israel together to Jerusalem, to bring up the ark of the LORD unto his place, which he had prepared for it. (KJV)

Solomon gathered all the people for the dedication of the first temple.

> 2Ch 5:2-3 Then Solomon assembled the elders of Israel, and all the heads of the tribes, the chief of the fathers of the children of Israel, unto Jerusalem, to bring up the ark of the covenant of the LORD out of the city of David, which is Zion. 3 Wherefore all the men of Israel assembled themselves unto the king in the feast which was in the seventh month. (KJV)

At the time of Hezekiah, the Books of Moses had been stored away. When Hezekiah became king, he ordered the repair and cleaning of the temple. He first gathered all the priests and Levites and ordered them to put the LORD's house in order.

> 2Ch 29:4 And he brought in the priests and the Levites, and gathered them together into the east street, (KJV)

After the repairs to the temple were complete, he gathered the people to celebrate the Passover. Even though Judah and Israel were two separate kingdoms, Hezekiah included all Israel in his decree.

> 2Ch 30:1 And Hezekiah sent to all Israel and Judah, and wrote letters also to Ephraim and Manasseh, that they should come to the house of the LORD at Jerusalem, to keep the Passover unto the LORD God of Israel. (KJV)

When King Josiah reigned, he also gathered the people. He was the last good king of Judah. Because of Josiah's humble and repentant heart, judgment against Judah was held off until his son's reign. When Josiah became king, the Torah was rediscovered and King Josiah read it in the presence of all the people.

> 2Ch 34:29-31 Then the king sent and **gathered together** all the elders of Judah and Jerusalem. 30 And the king went up into the house of the LORD, and all the men of Judah, and the inhabitants of Jerusalem, and the priests, and the Levites, and all the people, great and small: and **he read** in their ears all the words of the book of the covenant that was found in the house of the LORD. 31 And the king stood in his place, and made a covenant before the LORD, to walk after the LORD, and to keep his commandments, and his testimonies, and his statutes, with all his heart, and with all his soul, to perform the words of the covenant which are written in this book. (KJV)

When Messiah comes, He will read the Torah to the gathered saints in Jerusalem. Throughout the millennium, He will read the Torah to the gathered nations.

> De 33:2-5 And he said: "The LORD came from Sinai, And dawned on them from Seir; He shone forth from Mount Paran, And He came with ten thousands of saints; From His right hand Came a fiery law for them. 3 Yes, He loves the people; All His saints are in Your hand; They sit down at Your feet; Everyone receives Your words. 4 Moses commanded a law (Torah) for us, A heritage of the congregation of Jacob. 5 And He was King in Jeshurun, When the leaders of the people were gathered, All the tribes of Israel together. (NKJV)

Jeshurun: Strong's #03484. ישרון Yeshuruwn, yesh-oo-roon' from 3474; upright; a name for Israel, the upright or righteous one.

While Yeshua was here on earth, he taught in the temple during the Feast of Tabernacles.

Joh 8:2 Now early in the morning He came again into the temple, and all the people came to Him; and He sat down and taught them. (NKJV)

David writes that Messiah will declare the character of the Father.

Psalms 40:7-10 NKJV 7 Then I said, "Behold, I come; In the scroll of the book it is written of me. 8 I delight to do Your will, O my God, And Your law is within my heart." 9 I have proclaimed the good news of righteousness In the great assembly; Indeed, I do not restrain my lips, O LORD, You Yourself know. 10 I have not hidden Your righteousness within my heart; I have declared Your faithfulness and Your salvation; I have not concealed Your lovingkindness and Your truth From the great assembly.

What will Yeshua teach when He returns?

E. "… that they may hear and that they may learn to fear the LORD your God … and that their children, who have not known it, may hear and learn to fear the LORD your God…"

When Yeshua reads the Torah during the millennium, all the people of the earth will learn to fear and obey God. He will be the King in Jeshurun or righteousness.

Ps 33:8-9 Let all the earth fear the LORD; let all the people of the world stand in awe of Him. 9 For He spoke, and it was done; He commanded, and it stood. (MKJV)

Yeshua will teach the way and the truth.

Ps 25:4-5 Show me Your ways, O LORD; Teach me Your paths. 5 Lead me in Your truth and teach me, For You are the God of my salvation; On You I wait all the day. (NKJV)

The name Yeshua or Jesus comes from the same root as this word for salvation.

Salvation: #3468. ישע yesha`, yeh'-shah or yeshai {yay'-shah}; from 3467; liberty, deliverance, prosperity:--safety, salvation, saving.

Jesus: Yeshua: #3442. ישוע Yeshuwa`, yay-shoo'-ah for 3091; he will save
Strong's #3091. יהושוע Yahowshuwa`, yeh-ho-shoo'-ah or Yhowshua {yeh-ho-shoo'-ah}; from 3068 and 3467; Jehovah-saved; Jehoshua (i.e. Joshua), Jehoshua, Jehoshuah, Joshua.

Yehovah is the God of Yeshua. And Yeshua, He who brings salvation, will teach us His ways and lead us in truth.

F. "…as long as you live in the land …"

This command can only be kept while Israel is living in the land and has control of Jerusalem. Although Israel has control of most of Jerusalem, the temple mount is in the hands of the Muslims. The Jews have access to only a small area of the temple mount for a short period of time each day. The year 2008 on the Gregorian calendar, or 5768 on the Jewish calendar was believed to be a Sabbath year. Some Jews wished to honor the commandment to read the Torah at the Feast of Tabernacles. Each day during the feast, they took advantage of the opportunity to go to the area of the temple mount they had access to and read portions of the Torah to the people who were gathered there. Only a small group of people were allowed on the temple mount at a time but to the best of their ability, they carried out the command.

When Yeshua gathers the people for the wedding supper of the Lamb after the final battle, He will fulfill the entire prophecy and truly read the Torah in the presence of all the people. The prophet Isaiah describes this time.

> Is 51:3-6 The LORD will surely comfort Zion and will look with compassion on all her ruins; he will make her deserts **like Eden**, her wastelands like the **garden of the LORD**. Joy and gladness will be found in her, thanksgiving and the sound of singing. 4 **"Listen to me, my people; hear me, my nation: The law (Torah) will go out from me;** my justice will become a light to the nations. 5 My righteousness draws near speedily, my salvation is on the way, and my arm will bring justice to the nations. The islands will look to me and wait in hope for my arm. 6 **Lift up your eyes to the heavens, look at the earth beneath; the heavens will vanish like smoke, the earth will wear out like a garment** and its inhabitants die like flies. But my salvation will last forever, my righteousness will never fail. (NIV)

We recognize this as after the Battle of Armageddon because He restores the land of Israel to be like the Garden of Eden, He rules over the nations, and the Torah is again taught from Jerusalem.

> Is 2:3 Many people shall come and say, "Come, and let us go up to the mountain of the LORD, To the house of the God of Jacob; He will teach us His ways, And we shall walk in His paths." For out of Zion shall go forth the law, And the word of the LORD from Jerusalem. (NKJV)

Student Notes: The Commandment to Read the Torah Before the Assembly

This commandment is a rehearsal of the time Jesus Himself will read Torah to the nations. (Deu. 31:10-13)

The timing of the events surrounding the reading of the Torah is the month of Tishrei.

Tishrei 1	Tishrei 10	Tishrei 15
Feast of Trumpets	Day of Atonement	Feast of Tabernacles Begins
Official Calendar New Year 100 Trumpets blasts are sounded to signal the beginning of the fall feasts.	Shofar is blown to announce the start of the Year of Jubilee	Reading of the Torah at the end of the year of release

A. "At the end of every seven years, at the appointed time in the year of release…" (Deu. 15:1-3, 12-15)

    1. Rest for _____

    2. Debts are _____

    3. Slaves are _____

The Year of Jubilee (Lev. 25:47-48, 54-55, Lev. 25:8-10, Lev. 25:39-40)

Isaiah's good tidings are a proclamation of the Year of Jubilee. (Isa. 61:1-3, Isa. 42:5-7, Lu. 4:18)

B. "… at the appointed time … at the Feast of Tabernacles…" (Deu. 16:16, Deu. 16:13-15)

End time judgment (Joel 3:12-13, Mat. 13:38-43, Joel 3:1-3, 6-7)

Hebrew word picture: Hebrew is read right to left.

Jehoshaphat: יהושפט The LORD's judgment

Yood-hey-vav: יהו Abbreviated form of the name of God, יהוה

Sheen: ש teeth- destroy or consume

Pey: פ mouth- to speak, to open, a word

Tet: ט snake, to twist, to surround

Jehoshaphat: The LORD destroys the mouth of the serpent.

C. "… when all Israel comes to appear before the LORD your God in the place which He chooses... Gather the people together, men and women and little ones, and the stranger who is within your gates…"

Gather: #6950. קהל qahal, 'kaw-hal' a primitive root; to convoke:--assemble (selves) (together), gather (selves) (together)

Assembly: #6951. קהל qahal, kaw-hawl' from 6950; assemblage (usually concretely):--assembly, company, congregation, multitude.

The assembly הקהל or "hakhel"

Hebrew word picture: Hebrew is read right to left.

Hakhel: הקהל : The Assembly

Hey: ה window, lattice, "the," to reveal, behold

Quph: ק back of the head, behind, the last, the least, to follow

Hey: ה window, lattice, "the," to reveal, behold

Lamed: ל cattle goad, staff – prod, toward, control, authority

The Assembly: Behold, follow the revealed authority.

The Great Assembly (Heb. 10:25, Ps. 22:1, Ps. 22:14-18, Ps. 22:21, Ps. 22:22-28, Zech. 14:16, 2 Chr. 6:6, Zec. 2:12)

D. "… you shall read this law before all Israel in their hearing. Gather the people… "

    1. David (1Chr. 15:3)

    2. Solomon (2Chr. 5:2-3)

3. Hezekiah (2Chr. 29:4, 2Chr. 30:1)

4. Josiah (2Chr. 34:29-31)

5. Messiah (Deu. 33:2-5, John. 8:2, Ps. 40:7-10)

Jeshurun: Strong's #3484. ישרון Yeshuruwn, yesh-oo-roon' from 3474; upright; a name for Israel, the upright or righteous one.

E. "… that they may hear and that they may learn to fear the LORD your God … and that their children, who have not known it, may hear and learn to fear the LORD your God…"

When Yeshua reads the Torah (Ps. 33:8-9, Ps. 25:4-5)

Salvation: #3468. ישע yesha`, yeh'-shah or yeshai {yay'-shah}; from 3467; liberty, deliverance, prosperity:--safety, salvation, saving.

Jesus: Yeshua: #3442. ישוע Yeshuwa`, yay-shoo'-ah for 3091; he will save
Strong's #3091. יהושע Yahowshuwa`, yeh-ho-shoo'-ah; from 3068 and 3467; Jehovah-saved; Jehoshua (i.e. Joshua), the Jewish leader:--Jehoshua, Jehoshuah, Joshua.

F. "…as long as you live in the land …" (Isa. 51:3-6, Isa. 2:3)

Discussion questions for the Commandment to read the Torah

1. The Israelites were to read the Torah at the end of every Sabbath year for the Land. How is the Sabbath for the Land like the weekly Sabbath for man?

2. In the year of Jubilee everyone was freed so they could return to his land or possession and his family. What does that mean for the land of Israel today? What does that mean when Yeshua proclaims the year of Jubilee when He returns?

3. In the year of Jubilee, land was restored to the original owner's family (Lev 25:23-28). How does this apply to Yeshua as the son of David? How does this apply to Yeshua as the Son of God?

4. Read Nehemiah 7:73b-8:18 about Ezra reading the Torah before the Assembly for the first time in seventy years. Who all were assembled to hear Ezra? What was their reaction? During which feast did Ezra read the Torah?

5. The reason for reading the Torah is so that "they may hear and learn to fear the LORD your God." Read the following passages about those who fear the LORD, then discuss what it means to fear the LORD. Read Proverbs 9:10, Psalm 111:10, Psalm 1184, Psalm 19:9-11, 1 Samuel 12:23-24, and Psalm 33:8-9.

6. David writes of praising God in the Great Assembly. Read Psalm 22:22-31. How are David's words consistent with the reading of the Torah in the year of release at the Feast of Tabernacles?

The Queen Who Saved Her People

At the time of the Book of Esther, the Jewish people were in captivity in the empire of the Persians. They faced certain destruction—the decree for the genocide of the Jews had been signed and a date for their death was set. They needed a redeemer, a savior. They turned to Esther as one who was in a position to intercede for them. Esther becomes a type of Messiah foreshadowing the ultimate redemption of Israel by Yeshua.

A. Esther was chosen to be the queen after an elaborate procedure designed to pick the most beautiful woman of face and form as well as manner.

> Es 2:2 Then said the king's servants that ministered unto him, Let there be fair young virgins sought for the king: (KJV)

> Es 2:12 Each young woman's turn came to go in to King Ahasuerus after she had completed twelve months' preparation, according to the regulations for the women, for thus were the days of their preparation apportioned: six months with oil of myrrh, and six months with perfumes and preparations for beautifying women. (NKJV)

Esther was noted for her outward as well as inner beauty.

> Es 2:7 And Mordecai had brought up **Hadassah, that is, Esther**, his uncle's daughter, for she had neither father nor mother. The young woman was lovely and beautiful. When her father and mother died, Mordecai took her as his own daughter. (NKJV)

The word translated beautiful also refers to character, literally she was good.

Beautiful #2896 טוב towb, tobe from 2895; good (as an adjective) in the widest sense; (good, a good or good thing, a good man or woman; the good, goods or good things, good men or women)-- beautiful, best, better, bountiful, cheerful, at ease

Yeshua was also highly regarded. During one Passover trip to Jerusalem when He was twelve years old, he was found in discussion with the teachers of the Law. Luke reports that He continued to be highly regarded as He grew up.

> Lu 2:46-47 Now so it was that after three days they found Him in the temple, sitting in the midst of the teachers, both listening to them and asking them questions. 47 And all who heard Him were astonished at His understanding and answers. (NKJV)

> Lu 2:52 And Jesus increased in wisdom and stature, and in favor with God and men. (NKJV)

B. The choice of Esther as queen was made by the king. She and the other candidates for queen were presented before the king one by one. When Esther's turn came, she impressed the king with her beauty and demeanor, and he selected her to be queen.

> Es 2:17 The king loved Esther more than all the other women, and she obtained grace and favor in his sight more than all the virgins; so he set the royal crown upon her head and made her queen instead of Vashti. (NKJV)

Yeshua was selected as our Passover lamb by God Himself but He was also presented before the people as without spot or blemish.

> 1Pe 1:20 He was chosen before the creation of the world, but was revealed in these last times for your sake. (NIV)

When Yeshua entered Jerusalem for that last Passover, many people including Pharisees, Sadducees, Herodians, Pilate, and even Herod questioned and tested Him. The Centurion, for one, testified that "surely this was a righteous man" (Luke 23:47).

C. In her role of queen, Esther did not reveal that she was Jewish. She went by the Persian name of Esther instead of her Hebrew name of Hadassah. She lived among the gentiles of the land and they saw her only as their queen. No one, not even the king knew she was Jewish.

> Es 2:10 Esther had not revealed her people or family, for Mordecai had charged her not to reveal it. (NKJV)

> Es 2:18, 20 Then the king made a great feast, the Feast of Esther, for all his officials and servants; and he proclaimed a holiday in the provinces and gave gifts according to the generosity of a king... 20 Now Esther had not revealed her family and her people, just as Mordecai had charged her, for Esther obeyed the command of Mordecai as when she was brought up by him. (NKJV)

In the second and third century A.D., the believers in Yeshua as Messiah were separated from the greater Jewish faith. Believers were rejected in the synagogues where they had met from the time the Holy Spirit fell at the Feast of Weeks (Pentecost) and Yeshua was first proclaimed as Messiah. In turn, believers rejected their Jewish brothers who did not believe in Messiah and formed their own sect. They eventually rejected all the Jews and their own Jewish heritage. In time, "Christians" forgot that Yeshua was even Jewish! To the Jewish people today, Yeshua does not appear to be Jewish and we present Him as if He did not live a Jewish life. He, like Esther, is hidden among the Gentiles with a Gentile name.

D. When the decree to kill all the Jews was signed and Mordecai learned of it, he urged Esther to intercede for her people. Esther replied that to go before the king without being summoned could mean her death.

> Es 4:10-11 Then Esther spoke to Hathach, and gave him a command for Mordecai: 11 "All the king's servants and the people of the king's provinces know that any man or woman who goes into the inner court to the king, who has not been called, he has but one law: put all to death, except the one to whom the king holds out the golden scepter, that he may live. Yet I myself have not been called to go in to the king these thirty days." (NKJV)

Going before the king was like going into the Holy of Holies. Access to the Holy of Holies was limited to once a year and only by the high priest.

> Le 16:1-2 Now the LORD spoke to Moses after the death of the two sons of Aaron, when they offered profane fire before the LORD, and died; 2 and the LORD said to Moses: "Tell Aaron your brother not to come at just any time into the Holy Place inside the veil, before the mercy seat which is on the ark, lest he die; for I will appear in the cloud above the mercy seat. (NKJV)

Mordecai's reply to Esther was that perhaps she was in the position of queen just to save her people.

> Es 4:14 "For if you remain completely silent at this time, relief and deliverance will arise for the Jews from another place, but you and your father's house will perish. Yet who knows whether you have come to the kingdom for such a time as this?" (NKJV)

Yeshua, our Passover lamb, did indeed come into the world specifically for our salvation.

> Joh 3:17 For God sent not his Son into the world to condemn the world; but that the world through him might be saved. (KJV)

E. Esther instructed the people to fast for her for three days before she attempted going before the king. She was willing to risk her life for her people.

> Es 4:16 "Go, gather all the Jews who are present in Shushan, and fast for me; neither eat nor drink for three days, night or day. My maids and I will fast likewise. And so I will go to the king, which is against the law; and if I perish, I perish!" (NKJV)

The timing of the event is interesting. The decree to kill the Jews was signed on Nisan 13, the day before Passover.

> Es 3:12 Then the king's scribes were called on the thirteenth day of the first month, and a decree was written according to all that Haman commanded-to the king's satraps, to the governors who were over each province, to the officials of all people, to every province according to its script, and to every people in their language. In the name of King Ahasuerus it was written, and sealed with the king's signet ring. (NKJV)

If the communication between Esther and Mordecai occurred the day after the decree was signed, Nisan 14, the three day fast decreed by Esther would coincide with the dates of Yeshua's death, burial and resurrection. Yeshua died and was buried just before sunset at the end of the day of Nisan 14. He was in the grave two days and on the third day, he rose again. Yeshua spoke of His death and resurrection both before and after His crucifixion.

> Lu 18:33 And they shall scourge him, and put him to death: and the third day he shall rise again. (KJV)

> Lu 24:45-46 Then opened he their understanding, that they might understand the scriptures, 46 And said unto them, Thus it is written, and thus it behooved Christ to suffer, and to rise from the dead the third day: (KJV)

F. On the third day of the fast, Esther put on her royal robes and went before the king who was sitting on his throne facing the entrance of the inner court. She entered with trepidation not knowing if she would live or die.

> Es 5:1 Now it happened on the third day that Esther put on her royal robes and stood in the inner court of the king's palace, across from the king's house, while the king sat on his royal throne in the royal house, facing the entrance of the house. (NKJV)

On the third day, the day of His resurrection, Yeshua also presented Himself before the King. This King was God His father.

> Joh 20:17 Jesus saith unto her, Touch me not; for I am not yet ascended to my Father: but go to my brethren, and say unto them, I ascend unto my Father, and your Father; and to my God, and your God. (KJV)

Unlike Esther, Yeshua was confident of the reception that He would receive when He entered into the presence of the King. Yeshua says that He will sit at the right hand of God.

> Lu 22:69 Hereafter shall the Son of man sit on the right hand of the power of God. (KJV)

The day Esther goes before the king is the Feast of Firstfruits. Esther is a type of firstfruits from the dead. When the king saw Esther, he favored her and extended his scepter sparing her life. She counted herself as dead accepting that "if I perish, I perish," but the king granted her life back to her.

> Es 5:2 So it was, when the king saw Queen Esther standing in the court, that she found favor in his sight, and the king held out to Esther the golden scepter that was in his hand. Then Esther went near and touched the top of the scepter. (NKJV)

Yeshua is resurrected on the Feast of Firstfruits, and Paul says He is the offering of Firstfruits to God.

1Co 15:20 But now is Christ risen from the dead, and become the firstfruits of them that slept. (KJV)

G. Esther intercedes with the king on behalf of her people after spending a couple of days showing her regard for the king by preparing a banquet for him. She is counted worthy to receive honor from the king even to half his kingdom. She asks for her life and the life of her people and denounces Haman as their enemy.

Es 7:2-6 And on the second day, at the banquet of wine, the king again said to Esther, "What is your petition, Queen Esther? It shall be granted you. And what is your request, up to half the kingdom? It shall be done!" 3 Then Queen Esther answered and said, "If I have found favor in your sight, O king, and if it pleases the king, let my life be given me at my petition, and my people at my request. 4 "For we have been sold, my people and I, to be destroyed, to be killed, and to be annihilated. Had we been sold as male and female slaves, I would have held my tongue, although the enemy could never compensate for the king's loss." 5 So King Ahasuerus answered and said to Queen Esther, "Who is he, and where is he, who would dare presume in his heart to do such a thing?" 6 And Esther said, "The adversary and enemy is this wicked Haman!" So Haman was terrified before the king and queen. (NKJV)

The king removed the authority he had given to Haman. Haman is then hanged on the very gallows he had erected in anticipation of having Mordecai executed for failing to pay him proper respect.

Yeshua also intercedes for His people and by His intercession we are granted redemption.

Heb 9:24 For Christ has not entered the holy places made with hands, which are copies of the true, but into heaven itself, now to appear in the presence of God for us; (NKJV)

Heb 7:25-26 Therefore He is also able to save to the uttermost those who come to God through Him, since He always lives to make intercession for them. 26 For such a High Priest was fitting for us, who is holy, harmless, undefiled, separate from sinners, and has become higher than the heavens; (NKJV)

Yeshua is also counted as worthy by God to receive honor from God.

Ps 8:5-6 For You have made him a little lower than the angels, And You have crowned him with glory and honor. 6 You have made him to have dominion over the works of Your hands; You have put all things under his feet, (NKJV)

He is even now seated at the right hand of God until the time when He will defeat His enemies.

Ps 110:1-2 A Psalm of David. The LORD said to my Lord, "Sit at My right hand,

Till I make Your enemies Your footstool." 2 The LORD shall send the rod of Your strength out of Zion. Rule in the midst of Your enemies! (NKJV)

H. Although Haman was hanged, the decree to kill all the Jews can't be overturned. Esther again goes before the king and pleads for the lives of her countrymen. In like manner, the sentence of death hangs over all people because of the sin of Adam. The decree cannot be overturned.

Es 8:7-8 King Xerxes replied to Queen Esther and to Mordecai the Jew, "Because Haman attacked the Jews, I have given his estate to Esther, and they have hanged him on the gallows. 8 Now write another decree in the king's name in behalf of the Jews as seems best to you, and seal it with the king's signet ring-- for no document written in the king's name and sealed with his ring can be revoked." (NIV)

Ro 5:14 Nevertheless death reigned from Adam to Moses, even over those who had not sinned according to the likeness of the transgression of Adam, who is a type of Him who was to come. (NKJV)

But a new decree is written! In the decree, the Jews were given the gift of the right to defend themselves.

Es 8:9, 11-12 At once the royal secretaries were summoned-- on the twenty-third day of the third month, the month of Sivan. They wrote out all Mordecai's orders to the Jews, and to the satraps, governors and nobles of the 127 provinces stretching from India to Cush. These orders were written in the script of each province and the language of each people and also to the Jews in their own script and language. 11 The king's edict granted the Jews in every city the right to assemble and protect themselves; to destroy, kill and annihilate any armed force of any nationality or province that might attack them and their women and children; and to plunder the property of their enemies. 12 The day appointed for the Jews to do this in all the provinces of King Xerxes was the thirteenth day of the twelfth month, the month of Adar. (NIV)

This decree went out in all the languages of the people in the month of Sivan just after the Feast of Weeks, also known as Pentecost. During the Feast of Weeks after Yeshua's ascension, the Holy Spirit fell on the disciples, and they spoke in the languages of all the people gathered in Jerusalem for the Feast.

Ac 2:1-6 When the Day of Pentecost had fully come, they were all with one accord in one place. 2 And suddenly there came a sound from heaven, as of a rushing mighty wind, and it filled the whole house where they were sitting. 3 Then there appeared to them divided tongues, as of fire, and one sat upon each of them. 4 And they were all filled with the Holy Spirit and began to speak with other tongues, as the Spirit gave them utterance. 5 And there were dwelling in Jerusalem Jews, devout men, from every nation under heaven. 6 And when this sound occurred, the multitude came together, and were confused, because everyone heard them speak in his own language. (NKJV)

The "decree" that was sent out at this Feast of Weeks was, first, an acclamation of the glory of God and, second, a promise that all who call upon the name of the LORD shall be saved. We are given the gift of salvation through the actions of one man, Yeshua.

> Ac 2:11 " --we hear them speaking in our own tongues the wonderful works of God." (NKJV)

> Ac 2:20 The sun shall be turned into darkness, And the moon into blood, Before the coming of the great and awesome day of the LORD. 21 And it shall come to pass That whoever calls on the name of the LORD Shall be saved.' (NKJV)

> Ro 5:15 But the free gift is not like the offense. For if by the one man's offense many died, much more the grace of God and the gift by the grace of the one Man, Jesus Christ, abounded to many. (NKJV)

When all the nations come against Israel, God says that He will defend them. The power of God will give them the faith and strength of David.

> Zec 12:8 "In that day the LORD will defend the inhabitants of Jerusalem; the one who is feeble among them in that day shall be like David, and the house of David shall be like God, like the Angel of the LORD before them. (NKJV)

I. The day on which the Jewish people can defend themselves is still almost nine months away.

> Es 8:12 …on one day in all the provinces of King Ahasuerus, on the thirteenth day of the twelfth month, which is the month of Adar. (NKJV)

The decree for their redemption has been sealed and delivered but the day is not yet come. Similarly, the redemption of Israel and all mankind has been sealed and delivered but the day has not yet come. In Revelation, Yeshua, the Lamb of God, is the only one counted worthy to open the scrolls containing the last judgments on man.

> Re 5:2 And I saw a strong angel proclaiming with a loud voice, Who is worthy to open the book, and to loose the seals thereof? 3 And no man in heaven, nor in earth, neither under the earth, was able to open the book, neither to look thereon. 4 And I wept much, because no man was found worthy to open and to read the book, neither to look thereon. 5 And one of the elders saith unto me, Weep not: behold, the Lion of the tribe of Juda, the Root of David, hath prevailed to open the book, and to loose the seven seals thereof. (KJV)

J. In the meantime, many people became Jews because the fear of the Jews "fell on them."

> Es 8:17 And in every province and city, wherever the king's command and decree

came, the Jews had joy and gladness, a feast and a holiday. Then many of the people of the land became Jews, because fear of the Jews fell upon them. (NKJV)

At the Feast of Weeks when the Holy Spirit fell and the disciples spoke in all the languages of man, the fear of God overtook those who witnessed the event and the subsequent miracles done by the apostles. Many Jews believed that Yeshua was the Messiah.

Ac 2:43 Then fear came upon every soul, and many wonders and signs were done through the apostles. (NKJV)

Ac 2:47b And the Lord added to the church daily those who were being saved. (NKJV)

When the end times come, many people will join themselves to the Jews because of the fear of the LORD.

Zec 8:23 "Thus says the LORD of hosts: 'In those days ten men from every language of the nations shall grasp the sleeve of a Jewish man, saying, "Let us go with you, for we have heard that God is with you."'" (NKJV)

K. On the appointed day, the enemies of the Jewish people came against them led by the ten sons of Haman. The shadow of Messiah now shifts from Esther to her uncle Mordecai. Esther's role as intercessor fades into the background. Mordecai steps to the forefront as the one who leads the Jewish people to victory.

Es 9:1-5 Now in the twelfth month, that is, the month Adar, on the thirteenth day of the same, when the king's commandment and his decree drew near to be put in execution, in the day that the enemies of the Jews hoped to have power over them, (though it was turned to the contrary, that the Jews had rule over them that hated them;) 2 The Jews gathered themselves together in their cities throughout all the provinces of the king Ahasuerus, to lay hand on such as sought their hurt: and no man could withstand them; for the fear of them fell upon all people. 3 And all the rulers of the provinces, and the lieutenants, and the deputies, and officers of the king, helped the Jews; because the fear of Mordecai fell upon them. 4 For Mordecai was great in the king's house, and his fame went out throughout all the provinces: for this man Mordecai waxed greater and greater. 5 Thus the Jews smote all their enemies with the stroke of the sword, and slaughter, and destruction, and did what they would unto those that hated them. (KJV)

On the appointed day, Yeshua will return and the victory will belong to God. Those who are enemies of God will be judged.

Re 14:14-16 And I looked, and behold a white cloud, and upon the cloud one sat like unto the Son of man, having on his head a golden crown, and in his hand a sharp sickle. 15 And another angel came out of the temple, crying with a loud voice to him that sat on the cloud, Thrust in thy sickle, and reap: for the time is come for thee to reap; for the harvest of the earth is ripe. 16 And he that sat on the cloud thrust in his sickle on the earth; and the earth was reaped. (KJV)

The next day, the ten sons of Haman, although they were already dead, are hung on the same gallows as their father Haman.

> Es 9:12-13 And the king said to Queen Esther, "The Jews have killed and destroyed five hundred men in Shushan the citadel, and the ten sons of Haman. What have they done in the rest of the king's provinces? Now what is your petition? It shall be granted to you. Or what is your further request? It shall be done." 13 Then Esther said, "If it pleases the king, let it be granted to the Jews who are in Shushan to do again tomorrow according to today's decree, and let Haman's ten sons be hanged on the gallows." (NKJV)

During the times approaching Yeshua's return, the book of Revelation reveals that there will arise ten horns and a beast which will be given authority to rule for a short time.

> Re 17:12 "The ten horns which you saw are ten kings who have received no kingdom as yet, but they receive authority for one hour as kings with the beast. (NKJV)

The ten sons of Haman, through Haman, were given authority by the king for a short time. It was during this time when Haman had the authority of the king that he had the decree written to kill all the Jews.

> Es 3:1, 10 After these things King Ahasuerus promoted Haman, the son of Hammedatha the Agagite, and advanced him and set his seat above all the princes who were with him... 10 So the king took his signet ring from his hand and gave it to Haman, the son of Hammedatha the Agagite, the enemy of the Jews. (NKJV)

In the same way, the beast will be given authority to come against the people of God and the ten kings will give their authority over to the beast. Their sole purpose is to destroy God's people.

> Re 13:6-7 Then he opened his mouth in blasphemy against God, to blaspheme His name, His tabernacle, and those who dwell in heaven. 7 It was granted to him to make war with the saints and to overcome them. And authority was given him over every tribe, tongue, and nation. (NKJV)

> Re 17:13-14 These (*the ten horns*) have one mind, and shall give their power and strength unto the beast. 14 These shall make war with the Lamb, and the Lamb shall overcome them: for he is Lord of lords, and King of kings: and they that are with him are called, and chosen, and faithful. (KJV)

The end for the "ten horns" will be same as it was for Haman's ten sons. The Lamb of God shall overcome them.

L. After their victory over Haman and his followers, the Jewish people held a celebration. The people feasted and gave presents to one another. The days that would have been days of mourning, instead became days of gladness.

> Es 9:20-22 And Mordecai wrote these things and sent letters to all the Jews, near and far, who were in all the provinces of King Ahasuerus, 21 to establish among them that they should celebrate yearly the fourteenth and fifteenth days of the month of Adar, 22 as the days on which the Jews had rest from their enemies, as the month which was turned from sorrow to joy for them, and from mourning to a holiday; that they should make them days of feasting and joy, of sending presents to one another and gifts to the poor. (NKJV)

After Yeshua defeats the nations that come against Jerusalem, the days of mourning will be turned to gladness and cheerful feasts. Even the fast days on which the Jewish people currently mourn the various events leading up to the destruction and captivity of Jerusalem and all Judah by the Babylonians will be turned to days of gladness.

> Zec 8:19 "Thus says the LORD of hosts: 'The fast of the fourth month, The fast of the fifth, The fast of the seventh, And the fast of the tenth, Shall be joy and gladness and cheerful feasts For the house of Judah. Therefore love truth and peace.' (NKJV)

Through Mordecai's assistance, the kingdom prospered. He watched over and sought the good of his people. In other words, he did not seek his own gain.

> Es 10:3 For Mordecai the Jew was second to King Ahasuerus, and was great among the Jews and well received by the multitude of his brethren, seeking the good of his people and speaking peace to all his countrymen. (NKJV)

The authority that had been granted to Haman was transferred to Mordecai. Likewise, the authority given to Satan is transferred to Yeshua. We await the day that He will assert that authority and destroy the beast and Satan.

Yeshua, when He reigns, will reign with justice and righteousness under the authority given to Him by God.

> Isa 9:7 Of the increase of His government and peace There will be no end, Upon the throne of David and over His kingdom, To order it and establish it with judgment and justice From that time forward, even forever. The zeal of the LORD of hosts will perform this. (NKJV)

> 1Co 15:27-28 For "He has put all things under His feet." But when He says "all things are put under Him," it is evident that He who put all things under Him is excepted. 28 Now when all things are made subject to Him, then the Son Himself will also be subject to Him who put all things under Him, that God may be all in all. (NKJV)

Student Notes: The Queen Who Saved Her People

At the time of the Book of Esther, the Jewish people were in captivity in the empire of the Persians. They faced certain destruction—the decree for the genocide of the Jews had been signed and a date for their death was set. They needed a redeemer, a savior. They turned to Esther as one who was in a position to intercede for them. Esther becomes a type of Messiah foreshadowing the ultimate redemption of Israel by Yeshua.

A. The procedure for selection (Est. 2:2, Est. 2:12, Est. 2:7, Lu. 2:46-47, Lu. 2:52)

Beautiful: #2896 טוֹב towb, tobe from 2895; good (as an adjective) in the widest sense; (good, a good or good thing, a good man or woman; the good, goods or good things),-- beautiful, best, better, bountiful, cheerful, at ease

B. The King makes the choice. (Est. 2:17, 1Pet. 1:20)

C. A hidden identity. (Est. 2:10, 18, 20)

D. To intercede means death. (Est. 4:10-11, Lev. 16:1-2, Est. 4:14, John 3:17)

E. The three day fast (Est. 4:16, Est. 3:12, Lu. 18:33, Lu. 24:45-46)

F. On the third day….. (Est. 5:1, John 20:17, Lu. 22:69)

.

Feast of Firstfruits (Est. 5:2, 1Cor. 15:20)

G. The intercessor is deemed worthy. (Est. 7:2-6, Heb. 9:24, Heb. 7:25-26, Ps. 8:5-6, Ps. 110:1-2)

H. The first decree cannot be overturned so a new decree is written. (Est. 8:7-8, Rom. 5:14, Est. 8:9, 11-12, Acts 2:1-6, Acts 2:11, Acts 2:20, Rom. 5:15, Zec. 12:8)

I. The day has not yet come. (Est. 8:12, Rev. 5:2-5)

J. Many people became Jews. (Est. 8:17, Acts 2:43, Acts 2:47b, Zec. 8:23)

K. On the appointed day, the victory belonged to the Jewish people. (Est. 9:1-5, Rev. 14:14-16, Est. 9:12-13, Rev. 17:12, Est. 3:1, 10, Rev. 13:6-7, Rev. 17:13-14)

L. Mourning turns to gladness. (Est. 9:20-22, Zec. 8:19, Est. 10:3, Isa. 9:7, 1Cor. 15:27-28)

Discussion questions for the Queen Who Saved Her People

1. Haman relied on chance to choose the day to destroy the Jewish people (Est. 3:7). How does this differ from the appointed days of the LORD (Lev. 23 1-3)? Discuss the underlying philosophies of each position.

2. Esther goes into the king on Nisan 17 and invites him to a banquet that day. That night, King Ahasuerus couldn't sleep. What honor is bestowed upon Mordecai the next day (Est. 6:6-11)? How does this show the beginning of the shift of the Messianic role from Esther to Mordecai? How does this apply to Yeshua after His resurrection on Nisan 17?

3. Mordecai eventually rules second to King Ahasuerus (Est. 10:3). What do we know about the reign of Yeshua (1 Cor. 15:25-28)?

4. Read Mordecai's words to Esther in Esther 4:13-14. Discuss how this can apply to any believer.

5. The days of Adar which would have been days of sorrow were turned into days of joy (Est. 9:20-22). Read Zechariah 8:19. The fast days written about here all involve the destruction of Jerusalem and the temple by the Babylonians. Discuss the connection between the days of Adar becoming days of joy and the fasts becoming days of joy.

6. The Book of Esther is the only book in the Bible that doesn't mention God even once. He is a hidden player in the events of the book of Esther. Within the book itself, Esther is a hidden player behind the scenes to stop Haman who doesn't know that she is Jewish. How can we apply this idea to today and God, the Father, as well as Yeshua, the Son, acting behind the scenes?

The Promise: Melchizedek meets Abram

A. Melchizedek and Abram are both types of Messiah. In Genesis 14, Melchizedek who is already established as the king of Salem and is a type of Messiah, meets Abram and recognizes his role in bringing the promise of a Redeemer closer. In Abram, we see the beginning of the plan of redemption. In Melchizedek, we see the end and the reign of the eternal king of righteousness. In essence, the beginning meets the end with Satan trying to come between the two.

The background of this meeting is in God's promise to Abram. God revealed His promises to Abram in parts. When Abram first enters the land, God promised to give him the land (Gen.12:6). After Abram and his nephew Lot separated, God reiterated the promise to Abram saying that He would give Abram all the land he could see. He then commanded Abram to walk the land taking the promise one step further. It is at this point that Abram begins to take possession of the land. In a sense Abram is laying claim to the land by walking it. Similarly, we have prayer walks, where believers will pray as they walk around a block, neighborhood, or city laying claim to it in the name of Yeshua, the Son of God. We can see Abram doing the same thing here. He is acting in belief that God would give him the land.

> Ge 13:17 "Arise, walk in the land through its length and its width, for I give it to you." (NKJV)

1. After this promise, an alliance of four Kings from the Babylonian region attacked five kings of the plains near where the Dead Sea would be. They plundered Sodom and Gomorrah taking Abram's nephew Lot captive.

> Ge 14:14 Now when Abram heard that his brother was taken captive, he armed his three hundred and eighteen trained servants who were born in his own house, and went in pursuit as far as Dan. (NKJV)

Abram, with his 318 men, and the men from his allies the Amorites from the Hebron region win a miraculous victory. He recovered all the goods as well as all the people who were taken captive including Lot. Abram delivers not just his nephew Lot but the entire land by ridding them of the Babylonian confederacy. He is acting as the protector of the land and the kinsman redeemer of Lot.

2. The three-way meeting between the king of Sodom, Melchizedek and Abram after this battle is replete with symbolic meaning. Melchizedek is a type of Messiah "like unto the Son of God" representing Messiah as reigning king. But the time of the fulfillment of Messiah the Son of God is not yet come. So Melchizedek passes the mantle back to Abram through whom the promised Seed will come. The king of Sodom is present as a representative of the serpent and the worldly system. What he offers is in contrast to what God offers. We read of this meeting in Genesis 14.

Ge 14:17-24 Then after his return from the defeat of Chedorlaomer and the kings who were with him, the king of Sodom went out to meet him at the valley of Shaveh (that is, the King's Valley). 18 And Melchizedek king of Salem brought out bread and wine; now he was a priest of God Most High. 19 And he blessed him and said, "Blessed be Abram of God Most High, Possessor of heaven and earth; 20 And blessed be God Most High, Who has delivered your enemies into your hand." And he gave him a tenth of all. 21 And the king of Sodom said to Abram, "Give the people to me and take the goods for yourself." 22 And Abram said to the king of Sodom, "I have sworn to the LORD God Most High, possessor of heaven and earth, 23 that I will not take a thread or a sandal thong or anything that is yours, lest you should say, 'I have made Abram rich.' 24 "I will take nothing except what the young men have eaten, and the share of the men who went with me, Aner, Eshcol, and Mamre; let them take their share." (NASB)

B. Melchizedek's name and city proclaim him as a type of Messiah.

1. The name Melchizedek means king of righteousness.
Melchizedek: #4442. מלכי צדק Malkiy-Tsedeq, mal-kee-tseh'-dek is from #4428 מלך malek meaning king and #6664 צדק tsedeq, tseh'-dek meaning the right or righteous; king of righteousness.

2. Yeshua is our king of righteousness and He will rule in righteousness. One of His names is The LORD Our Righteousness. This name for the King from the branch of David incorporates the very name of God, יהוה, sometimes pronounced Jah-weh or Yahovah, which is not even spoken among the Jewish people lest it accidentally be profaned.

Jer 23:5-6 "Behold, the days are coming," says the LORD, "That I will raise to David a Branch of righteousness; A King shall reign and prosper, And execute judgment and righteousness in the earth. 6 In His days Judah will be saved, And Israel will dwell safely; Now this is His name by which He will be called: THE LORD יהוה OUR RIGHTEOUSNESS. (NKJV)

Ps 45:6-7 Your throne, O God, is forever and ever; A scepter of righteousness is the scepter of Your kingdom. 7 You love righteousness and hate wickedness; Therefore God, Your God, has anointed You With the oil of gladness more than Your companions. (NKJV)

3. Melchizedek is the king of Salem. Salem means peace, so the King of Righteousness is the king or prince of peace.

Salem: #8004. שלם Shalem, shaw-lame' the same as 8003; peaceful; Shalem, an early name of Jerusalem:--Salem. 08003. שלם shalem, shaw-lame' from #7999; complete (literally or figuratively); especially friendly:--full, just, made ready, peaceable, perfect(-ed), quiet, whole.

4. Yeshua is our Prince of Peace. He shall have a government of peace.

Is 9:6-7 For a child will be born to us, a son will be given to us; And the government will rest on His shoulders; And His name will be called Wonderful Counselor, Mighty God, Eternal Father, Prince of Peace. 7 There will be no end to the increase of His government or of peace, On the throne of David and over his kingdom, To establish it and to uphold it with justice and righteousness From then on and forevermore. The zeal of the LORD of hosts will accomplish this. (NASB)

5. The name Salem suggests not only peace but perfection and completeness. Salem has the same root word as the Hebrew greeting shalom meaning peace. Isaiah describes the time of Messiah as a time of righteousness and of the peace that comes from trusting in God.

Is 26:1-3 In that day this song will be sung in the land of Judah: "We have a strong city; God will appoint salvation (Yashuwah) for walls and bulwarks. 2 Open the gates, That the righteous nation which keeps the truth may enter in. 3 You will keep him in perfect peace, Whose mind is stayed on You, Because he trusts in You. (NKJV)

Hebrew Word Picture: Hebrew is read right to left.

Peace: Shalom: שלם

ש Shin: Teeth, destroy, consume

ל Lamed: The staff, authority

ם Mem: Water, chaos

Peace is to destroy the authority of chaos.

---

6. This idea of peace, perfection and completion is emphasized by Melchizedek's offering of bread and wine to Abram. Each week, the Sabbath begins with the lighting of the Sabbath candles and then the blessings over the bread and the wine. In English, these blessings are "Blessed are You, Lord our God, creator and king of the universe who brings forth bread from the earth." The blessing over the wine is similar, "Blessed are You, Lord our God, creator and king of the universe who creates the fruit of the vine." The Sabbath is a day to remember God's completed work of creation.

Ex 20:8, 11 "Remember the Sabbath day, to keep it holy…11 For in six days the LORD made the heavens and the earth, the sea, and all that is in them, and rested the seventh day. Therefore the LORD blessed the Sabbath day and hallowed it. (NKJV)

7. The city of Salem is now known as Jerusalem. We can trace the name changes through the scriptures. Psalm 76 equates Salem with Zion.

Ps 76:2 In Salem also is His tabernacle And His dwelling place in Zion. (NKJV)

Zion is then equated with Jerusalem, the city David conquers and where he establishes his reign. Zion is specifically the fortress or stronghold on the southern hill of Jebus which would be renamed Jerusalem. When the fortress was taken, the whole city fell to David and his army.

1Ch 11:4-5 And David and all Israel went to Jerusalem, which is Jebus, where the Jebusites were, the inhabitants of the land. 5 Then the inhabitants of Jebus said to David, "You shall not come in here!" Nevertheless David took the stronghold of Zion (that is, the City of David). (NKJV)

8. The name Jerusalem comes from two Hebrew words and means "established peaceful or instruction in peace."

Jerusalem: #3389. ירושלם Yeruwshalaim, yer-oo-shaw-lah'-im probably from (the passive participle of) #3384 and #7999; founded peaceful; the capital city of Israel:-- Jerusalem.

We saw that the second part of the name Jerusalem, Salem, comes from the root word shalam meaning safe, complete or peaceful.

#7999. שלם shalam, shaw-lam' a primitive root; to be safe (in mind, body or estate); figuratively, to be (causatively, make) completed; by implication, to be friendly; by extension, to reciprocate (in various applications):--make amends, (make an) end, finish, full, give again, make good, (re-)pay (again), (make) (to) (be at) peace(-able), that is perfect, perform, (make) prosper(-ous), recompense, render, requite, make restitution, restore, reward.

The first part of the name Jerusalem comes from the same root as the root for Torah.

#3384. ירה yarah, yaw-raw' a primitive root; properly, to flow as water (i.e. to rain); transitively, to lay or throw (especially an arrow, i.e. to shoot); figuratively, to point out (as if by aiming the finger), to teach:--(+) inform, instruct, lay, shew, shoot, teach(-er,- ing)

The word Torah comes from this same root word and means "teaching or instruction." As we look at the broader meaning of the root words for Jerusalem, we see Jerusalem as the place where we receive instruction in peace. Isaiah says that during Messiah's reign, the Torah will be taught from Jerusalem. Further, those who love the Torah will have peace.

Is 2:3 Many people shall come and say, "Come, and let us go up to the mountain of the LORD, To the house of the God of Jacob; He will teach (yarah #3384) us His ways, And we shall walk in His paths." For out of Zion shall go forth the law (Torah #8451), And the word of the LORD from Jerusalem. (NKJV)

Ps 119:165 Great peace have those who love Your law (Torah), And nothing causes them to stumble. (NKJV)

Melchizedek was the king of righteousness who reigned in the city of peace, perfection or completeness. Yeshua will be our righteous king reigning as the Prince of Peace from the city from which instruction in peace will flow. Indeed, Yeshua Himself will teach our children.

Is 54:13 All your children shall be taught by the LORD, And great shall be the peace of your children. (NKJV)

Hebrew Word Picture: Hebrew is read right to left.

Jerusalem: Yeruwshalaim: ירושלם

י Yod: Hand, actions, deeds

ר Resh: head, the highest, a person

ו Vav: nail, "and," to secure

ש Shin: Teeth, destroy, consume

ל Lamed: The staff, authority

ם Mem: Water, chaos

Jerusalem: The hand of the highest secures the destruction of the authority of chaos.

C. Melchizedek is a priest of God Most High and Yeshua will be a priest of the same order.

1. The writer of Hebrews specifically says that this order is different from the Aaronic priesthood. The priests according to Aaron are called first by lineage. They must be of the family of Aaron.

Ex 28:1 "Now take Aaron your brother, and his sons with him, from among the children of Israel, that he may minister to Me as priest, Aaron and Aaron's sons: Nadab, Abihu, Eleazar, and Ithamar. (NKJV)

Being merely men, they are weak and subject to sin.

Heb 7:23 Also there were many priests, because they were prevented by death from continuing.

Heb 7:28a For the law appoints as high priests men who have weakness,

They were anointed to serve in the earthly temple which is a pattern of the heavenly temple.

Ex 25:8-9 "And let them make Me a sanctuary, that I may dwell among them. 9 "According to all that I show you, that is, the pattern of the tabernacle and the pattern of all its furnishings, just so you shall make it. (NKJV)

2. The priest called according to Melchizedek is perfect and everlasting. The writer of Hebrews says that since no lineage is given and no death is recorded for Melchizedek, it is as if he came directly from God.

Heb 7:1-3 For this Melchizedek, king of Salem, priest of the Most High God, who met Abraham returning from the slaughter of the kings and blessed him, 2 to whom also Abraham gave a tenth part of all, first being translated "king of righteousness," and then also king of Salem, meaning "king of peace," 3 without father, without mother, without genealogy, having neither beginning of days nor end of life, but made like the Son of God, remains a priest continually. (NKJV)

Melchizedek is not mentioned again in the history of the Promised Land. It is as if he exists just for this moment at the beginning of the possession of the Promised Land as a glimpse forward to the ultimate possession of the land when Yeshua will reign as king and priest forever.

Ps 110:4 The LORD has sworn and will not change his mind: "You are a priest forever, in the order of Melchizedek." (NIV)

3. Melchizedek is also said to be "made like the Son of God." The only other place this phrase is used is when Nebuchadnezzar threw Shadrach, Meshach and Abednego into the fiery furnace. In the midst of the furnace was a fourth man described as being "like the Son of God."

Da 3:24-25, 28 Then King Nebuchadnezzar was astonished; and he rose in haste and spoke, saying to his counselors, "Did we not cast three men bound into the midst of the fire?" They answered and said to the king, "True, O king." 25 "Look!" he answered, "I see four men loose, walking in the midst of the fire; and they are not hurt, and the form of the fourth is like the Son of God." 28 Nebuchadnezzar spoke, saying, "Blessed be the God of Shadrach, Meshach, and Abed-Nego, who sent His Angel and delivered His servants who trusted in Him, and they have frustrated the king's word, and yielded their bodies, that they should not serve nor worship any god except their own God! (NKJV)

The fourth being is described by Nebuchadnezzar as an Angel. The Aramaic word used is malak translated by Young's Literal Translation as messenger. (Much of the Book of Daniel is written in Aramaic.)

Angel #4398. מלאך mal'ak (Aramaic), mal-ak' (Aramaic) corresponding to 4397; an angel:--angel.

#4397. מלאך mal'ak, mal-awk' from an unused root meaning to despatch as a deputy; a messenger; specifically, of God, i.e. an angel (also a prophet, priest or teacher):--ambassador, angel, king, messenger.

This Angel, being like the Son of God brings deliverance to Shadrach, Meshach and Abednego. Yeshua is not like the Son of God; He is the Son of God. The writer of Hebrews says that the Son of God is the King of righteousness.

> Heb 1:8 But to the Son He says: "Your throne, O God, is forever and ever; A scepter of righteousness is the scepter of Your Kingdom. (NKJV)

4. The Jewish sages speculate that Melchizedek could have been Noah's son Shem who was still alive at this time. Noah passed on the blessing of a future redemption to Shem.

> Ge 9:26 And he said: "Blessed be the LORD, The God of Shem, And may Canaan be his servant. (NKJV)

Shem serves the LORD. He would have inherited the priesthood from his father Noah. It would be fitting that Shem would rule over a city in the midst of the Canaanites. If Melchizedek were Shem, it would still be as if he had no lineage and had no beginning of life because he passed through the flood gaining his life back as it were from the dead.

5. What Aaron's priesthood couldn't fulfill, Yeshua could.

> Heb 7:11 Therefore, if perfection were through the Levitical priesthood (for under it the people received the law (Torah)), what further need was there that another priest should rise according to the order of Melchizedek, and not be called according to the order of Aaron? (NKJV)

> Heb 9:11-12 But Christ came as High Priest of the good things to come, with the greater and more perfect tabernacle not made with hands, that is, not of this creation. 12 Not with the blood of goats and calves, but with His own blood He entered the Most Holy Place once for all, having obtained eternal redemption. (NKJV)

Aaron's priesthood, being a shadow of the heavenly priesthood, couldn't attain salvation. Only faith in God's mercy and the promise of God's redemption that was realized through the death and resurrection of Messiah brings eternal redemption.

D. Melchizedek, in his role as priest and king of Salem, brings out bread and wine and blesses Abram. It is as if the future meets the present. Melchizedek testifies to Abram's standing with God. Abram is of "God Most High."

Ge 14:19 And he blessed him and said, "Blessed be Abram of God Most High, Possessor of heaven and earth;

He testifies that it is God who worked and will continue to work through Abram to deliver the land.

Ge 14:20 And blessed be God Most High, Who has delivered your enemies into your hand." (NKJV)

Seen from the future, God has already accomplished the deliverance of all Abram's enemies into his hand. The Babylonian kings Abram defeated in this incident had not come against Abram. They had come against the kings of the land but they are described as Abram's enemies and being delivered into Abram's hand. Yeshua, our priest like Melchizedek, sits at God's right hand and God will deliver His enemies into His hand.

Ps 110:1 A Psalm of David. The LORD said to my Lord, "Sit at My right hand, Till I make Your enemies Your footstool." (NKJV)

Melchizedek looks back from the fulfillment of the promise to the beginning of the promise. Abram looks forward from the beginning to the fulfillment. This is like a time travel movie in which Yeshua, King of Israel, travels back in time to stand with Abram when Abram faces a crucial choice. Yeshua blesses Abram as the one from whom the promise seed will come, and Abram recognizes Yeshua as the king to come.

E. Abram gave a tithe to Melchizedek.

1. In Moses' instructions to the Israelites before they entered the land, he told them to tithe of the produce of the land and fields in the place God would choose. This was to be shared with God through His priests.

De 14:22-23 "You shall truly tithe all the increase of your grain that the field produces year by year. 23 "And you shall eat before the LORD your God, in the place where He chooses to make His name abide, the tithe of your grain and your new wine and your oil, of the firstborn of your herds and your flocks, that you may learn to fear the LORD your God always. (NKJV)

We know that God would ultimately choose Jerusalem as the place where He would place His name. He chose Jerusalem at the time of David, and Zechariah says that God will again choose Jerusalem for His dwelling place.

Zec 2:11-12 "Many nations shall be joined to the LORD in that day, and they shall become My people. And I will dwell in your midst. Then you will know that the LORD of hosts has sent Me to you. 12 "And the LORD will take possession of Judah as His inheritance in the Holy Land, and will again choose Jerusalem. (NKJV)

2. A tithe or a tenth was also considered the king's share. Samuel describes the portion due a king when the Israelites demand that he appoint a king over them.

> 1Sa 8:15-17 And he will take the tenth of your seed, and of your vineyards, and give to his officers, and to his servants. 16 And he will take your menservants, and your maidservants, and your goodliest young men, and your asses, and put them to his work. 17 He will take the tenth of your sheep: and ye shall be his servants. (KJV)

3. Whether Melchizedek received the tithe as a priest of God Most High or as the King of Righteousness or both, he typifies the reigning Messiah. Abram recognizes Melchizedek as one who deserves tribute by his voluntary offer of a tithe. He gives his allegiance to God through his acknowledgment of Melchizedek the priest of God Most High and king of Salem. When Yeshua is king, everyone will acknowledge that He is king over all the earth. All the nations will pay tribute to the ruler of Jerusalem, the Prince of Peace.

> Php 2:9-11 Therefore God also has highly exalted Him and given Him the name which is above every name, 10 that at the name of Jesus every knee should bow, of those in heaven, and of those on earth, and of those under the earth, 11 and that every tongue should confess that Jesus Christ is Lord, to the glory of God the Father. (NKJV)

Isaiah writes that all the Gentiles will serve the king of Jerusalem.

> Is 60:11-12 Therefore your gates shall be open continually; They shall not be shut day or night, That men may bring to you the wealth of the Gentiles, And their kings in procession. 12 For the nation and kingdom which will not serve you shall perish, And those nations shall be utterly ruined. (NKJV)

F. In the meantime, the king of Sodom, who was also present at this meeting, makes his presence known. He is the representative of the worldly system controlled by Satan and is the king of a city that was known to be wicked.

> Ge 13:13 But the men of Sodom were exceedingly wicked and sinful against the LORD. (NKJV)

He tacitly lays claim to all the spoils with a proposal to divide them between himself and Abram. He acts as if the spoils are his to award.

> Ge 14:21 Now the king of Sodom said to Abram, "Give me the persons, and take the goods for yourself." (NKJV)

1. But Abram has the promise from God that the land belongs to him not the king of Sodom. The king of Sodom offers Abram the wealth of this world asking only for the

"people." But the word "people" doesn't convey the depth of meaning in this passage. The Hebrew word translated as people is "nephesh."

#5315. נפש nephesh, neh'-fesh from 5314; properly, a breathing creature, i.e. animal of (abstractly) vitality; used very widely in a literal, accommodated or figurative sense (bodily or mental):--any, appetite, beast, body, breath, creature, soul

The emphasis of the word is on the life that is contained within the man or creature. It is the word used when God breathed life into Adam.

> Ge 2:7 And the LORD God formed man of the dust of the ground, and breathed into his nostrils the breath of life; and man became a living soul (nephesh). (KJV)

The king of Sodom was after the living beings, the life that was in the people. He wanted their souls. In the same way, Satan offers worldly riches to Yeshua in exchange for His life when He tempted Him in the wilderness.

> Mat 4:8-10 Again, the devil took Him up on an exceedingly high mountain, and showed Him all the kingdoms of the world and their glory. 9 And he said to Him, "All these things I will give You if You will fall down and worship me." 10 Then Jesus said to him, "Away with you, Satan! For it is written, 'You shall worship the LORD your God, and Him only you shall serve.'" (NKJV)

But the entire world already belongs to Yeshua through God's promise just like the land belonged to Abram and all the earth was originally under the dominion of Adam. If Yeshua had chosen the kingdoms of the world as offered by Satan, then all the souls of everyone ever born would have belonged to Satan. Yeshua refused to give us up!

2. Like Yeshua, Abram refused most emphatically the lure of the world and the temptation of Satan. He refused any share of the spoils other than that owed to the Amorites who went with him.

> Ge 14:22-24 But Abram said to the king of Sodom, "I have raised my hand to the LORD, God Most High, the Possessor of heaven and earth, 23 "that I will take nothing, from a thread to a sandal strap, and that I will not take anything that is yours, lest you should say, 'I have made Abram rich' - 24 "except only what the young men have eaten, and the portion of the men who went with me: Aner, Eshcol, and Mamre; let them take their portion." (NKJV)

Abram wants all the credit for his prosperity to go to God. He doesn't want any man to be able to take credit for God's blessings.

When Abram refused the king of Sodom's offer of wealth, he makes an oath to God. In his oath, Abram invokes the words of Melchizedek's blessing over him that God is the Possessor of heaven and earth adding the name LORD, יהוה. The name LORD, יהוה, indicates God's grace and mercy to man. This name is used only in God's dealings with man. This takes us back to the name of the King, The LORD OUR RIGHTEOUSNESS (Jer. 23:5).

3. Further, in the second part of the blessing to Abram, Melchizedek blesses God with these words, "And blessed be God Most High, Who has delivered your enemies into your hand." The word delivered can also mean "to shield," reminding Abram that God is His shield.

Delivered: #4042. מָגֵן magan, maw-gan' a denominative from #4043; properly, to shield; encompass with; figuratively, to rescue, to hand safely over (i.e. surrender):-- deliver.

Abram's shield or deliverance and reward was not in the worldly wealth offered by the king of Sodom but was in the covenant that God would make with him and his descendants.

> Ge 15:1 After these things the word of the LORD came to Abram in a vision, saying, "Do not be afraid, Abram. I am your shield, your exceedingly great reward." (NKJV)

Yeshua confirms the covenant that He is the promised deliverer with bread and wine shared with His disciples before His death.

> Lu 22:19-20 And he took bread, gave thanks and broke it, and gave it to them, saying, "This is my body given for you; do this in remembrance of me." 20 In the same way, after the supper he took the cup, saying, "This cup is the new covenant in my blood, which is poured out for you. (NIV)

Abram refused the reward offered to him by man embracing the promise from God. Let us also reject the reward of the world and Satan, and embrace the reward promised to us when Yeshua comes and takes possession of the world which is His through the promise of God.

> Heb 10:35-37 Therefore do not cast away your confidence, which has great reward. 36 For you have need of endurance, so that after you have done the will of God, you may receive the promise: 37 "For yet a little while, And He who is coming will come and will not tarry. (NKJV)

He is our exceeding great reward.

Student Notes: The Promise: Melchizedek meets Abram

A. Melchizedek and Abram are both types of Messiah. In Genesis 14, Melchizedek who is already established as the king of Salem and is a type of Messiah, meets Abram and recognizes his role in bringing the promise of a Redeemer closer.

Background: God's covenant with Abram was delivered to him in parts. When Abram first enters the land, God promised to give it to him. After Abram and his nephew Lot separated, God reiterated the promise to Abram saying that He would give Abram all the land he could see. He then commanded Abram to walk the land taking the promise one step further. It is at this point that Abram begins to take possession of the land. In a sense Abram is laying claim to the land by walking it. Similarly, we have prayer walks, where believers will pray as they walk around a block, neighborhood or city laying claim to it in the name of Yeshua, the Son of God. We can see Abram doing the same thing here. He is acting in belief that God would give him the land. (Gen. 13:17)

    1. Abram goes to the rescue: (Gen. 14:14)

    2. The three way meeting: (Gen. 14:17-24)

Melchizedek represents:

Abram represents:

The king of Sodom represents:

B. Melchizedek's name and city proclaim him as a type of Messiah.

    1. The name means:

Melchizedek: #4442. מלכי צדק Malkiy-Tsedeq, mal-kee-tseh'-dek is from #4428 מלך malek meaning king and #6664 צדק tsedeq, tseh'-dek meaning the right or righteous; king of righteousness.

2. Yeshua is our King of righteousness and He will rule in righteousness. (Jer. 23:5-6, Ps. 45:6-7)

3. The name Salem means:

Salem: #8004. שלם Shalem, shaw-lame' the same as 8003; peaceful; Shalem, an early name of Jerusalem:--Salem. 08003. שלם shalem, shaw-lame' from #7999; complete (literally or figuratively); especially friendly:--full, just, made ready, peaceable, perfect(-ed), quiet, whole.

4. Yeshua is our Prince of Peace. (Isa. 9:6-7)

5. The name Salem suggests perfection and completeness. (Isa. 26:1-3)

Hebrew Word Picture: Hebrew is read right to left.
Peace: Shalom: שלם
ש Shin: Teeth, destroy, consume
ל Lamed: The staff, authority
ם Mem: Water, chaos
Peace is to destroy the authority of chaos.

---

6. This idea of peace, perfection and completion is emphasized by Melchizedek's offering of bread and wine to Abram. (Ex. 20:8, 11)

7. The city of Salem is now known as Jerusalem. (Ps. 76:2, 1Chr. 11:4-5)

8. Jerusalem and the Torah. (Isa.2:3, Ps. 119:165, Isa. 54:13)

Jerusalem: #3389. ירושלם Yeruwshalaim, yer-oo-shaw-lah'-im probably from (the passive participle of) #3384 and #7999; founded peaceful; the capital city of Israel:-- Jerusalem.

#7999. שלם shalam, shaw-lam' a primitive root; to be safe (in mind, body or estate); figuratively, to be (causatively, make) completed; by implication, to be friendly; by extension, to reciprocate (in various applications):--make amends, (make an) end, finish, full, give again, make good, (re-)pay (again), (make) (to) (be at) peace(-able), that is perfect, perform, (make) prosper(-ous), recompense, render, requite, make restitution, restore, reward.

#3384. ירה yarah, yaw-raw' a primitive root; properly, to flow as water (i.e. to rain); transitively, to lay or throw (especially an arrow, i.e. to shoot); figuratively, to point out (as if by aiming the finger), to teach:--(+) archer, cast, direct, inform, instruct, lay, shew, shoot, teach(-er,-ing), through

---

Hebrew Word Picture: Hebrew is read right to left.

Jerusalem: Yeruwshalaim: ירושלם

י Yod: Hand, actions, deeds

ר Resh: head, the highest, a person

ו Vav: nail, "and," to secure

ש Shin: Teeth, destroy, consume

ל Lamed: The staff, authority

מ Mem: Water, chaos

Jerusalem: The hand of the highest secures the destruction of the authority of chaos.

C. Melchizedek is a priest of God Most High and Yeshua will be a priest of the same order.

1. The order of Aaron: (Ex. 28:1, Heb. 7:23, Heb. 7:28a, Ex. 25:8-9)

2. The order of Melchizedek: (Heb. 7:1-3, Ps. 110:4)

3. "Like the Son of God": (Dan. 3:24-25, 28, Heb. 1:8))

Angel #4398. מלאך mal'ak (Aramaic), mal-ak' (Aramaic) corresponding to 4397; an angel:--angel.

#4397. מלאך mal'ak, mal-awk' from an unused root meaning to despatch as a deputy; a messenger; specifically, of God, i.e. an angel (also a prophet, priest or teacher):--ambassador, angel, king, messenger.

4. The Jewish sages speculate that Melchizedek could have been Noah's son Shem who was still alive at this time. (Gen. 9:26)

5. What Aaron's priesthood couldn't fulfill, Yeshua could. (Heb. 7:11, Heb. 9:11-12)

D. The future meets the present. (Gen. 14:19, Gen. 14:20, Ps. 110:1)

E. The tithe:

    1. God's share: (Deu. 14:22-23, Zec. 2:11-12)

    2. The king's share (1Sam. 8:15-17)

    3. Priest and King: (Php. 2:9-11, Isa. 60:11-12)

F. The king of Sodom is the representative of the worldly system (Gen. 13:13, Gen. 14:21)

    1. The offer of wealth: (Gen. 2:7, Mat. 4:8-10)

#5315. נפש nephesh, neh'-fesh from 5314; properly, a breathing creature, i.e. animal of (abstractly) vitality; used very widely in a literal, accommodated or figurative sense (bodily or mental):--any, appetite, beast, body, breath, creature, soul

    2. The oath of refusal: (Gen. 14:22-24)

    Adds His Name: LORD: יהוה   Yah-weh

    3. Deliverer and reward: (Gen. 15:1, Lu. 22:19-20, Heb. 10:35-37)

Delivered: #4042. מען magan, maw-gan' a denominative from #4043; properly, to shield; encompass with; figuratively, to rescue, to hand safely over (i.e. surrender):-- deliver.

Discussion questions for the Promise: Melchizedek Meets Abram

1. Abram's meeting with Melchizedek and the king of Sodom took place in the King's Valley (Gen. 14:17). Read 2 Samuel 18:18. How is Absalom like the king of Sodom?

2. Abram refuses to give up the people in exchange for the wealth offered to him by the king of Sodom. Read Genesis 15:1-5. What did God promise Abram? Compare the promise of God with the promise of the king of Sodom.

3. The king of Sodom tries to place Abram under obligation to him; he wants Abram to acknowledge his right to decide the disposition of the rescued people and plunder. Instead Abram acknowledges God as the one who bestows riches on him. Read Genesis 15:18. What property had God bestowed on Abram and his descendants?

4. After God promises the Land to Abram, He says that Abram's descendants wouldn't receive it until the sins of the Amorites is full. But, the sins of Sodom and Gomorrah, two of the cities that Abram rescued, are already almost full. Just a few years after their rescue by Abram, God destroyed them. Read Joshua 10:4-14. Who are the Amorite kings and how many are there? Compare them with Abram's allies when he rescues Lot. How did God act for the Israelites in the battle against the Amorites?

5. Compare the worldly wealth of Sodom with the worldly wealth of Babylon as described in Revelation 18.

6. Melchizedek is at Abram's side when Abram refuses the "offer" from the king of Sodom. How is this like having Yeshua at our side when we face temptation?

I Am the LORD Who Brought You Out...

In Genesis 15, God makes a formal Covenant with Abram. In a formal Covenant, the two parties need to be identified. Who is it that is making the covenant? God identifies Himself to Abram as the LORD who brought him out of Ur of the Chaldees.

> Ge 15:7 7 And he said unto him, I am the LORD that brought thee out of Ur of the Chaldees, to give thee this land to inherit it. (KJV)

A. Who is the LORD?

The word we translate LORD with all capital letters is composed of four Hebrew letters, יהוה, read right to left, the yood-hey-vav-hey. We translate it LORD in our Bibles with all the letters capitalized. Among Orthodox Jews this Hebrew word is never spoken. But is referred to as the Tetragrammaton, literally "the four letters." The pronunciation of this name is said to have been either lost or held as a closely guarded secret. The sages say it will once again be spoken when Messiah comes. The Jewish translation of this verse in The Chumash translates יהוה as HaShem meaning "The Name." Strong's Dictionary defines יהוה as the self-existent or Eternal and is pronounced Yehovah.

LORD: #3068. יהוה Yehovah, yeh-ho-vaw' (the) self-Existent or Eternal; probably from #1961 ha-yah היה the verb to be or become. I was who I was, I am who I am, and I will be who I will be.

Others say the name should be pronounced Yahweh. What makes this name so important and its pronunciation a matter of debate? What makes the name יהוה unique among the names of God? We can begin to answer these questions by looking at what the LORD Himself says about His name. To start with, all during creation, God referred to Himself as Elohim, the Creator.

> Ge 1:1 In the beginning God (Elohim) created the heaven and the earth. (KJV)

Elohim: #430. אלהים 'elohiym, el-o-heem' plural of #433; gods in the ordinary sense; but specifically used (in the plural thus, especially with the article) of the supreme God;

When it came to the creation of man, the scriptures describe God as the LORD יהוה God.

> Ge 2:7 And the LORD God formed man of the dust of the ground, and breathed into his nostrils the breath of life; and man became a living soul. (KJV)

God identifies Himself as יהוה in this intimate interaction between God and man. The LORD Himself handled the dust of the ground to form man. Then He breathed life into Adam's nostrils. He spoke creation into existence but He was personally involved in Adam's creation. The original Hebrew text reinforces this concept of God's personal involvement. The Hebrew word translated as "formed" is yatzar, יצר, which begins with the letter yood, י. The letter yood is a hand symbolizing actions or deeds. In this verse, yatzar is written וייצר, with two yoods. God used both of His hands to form Adam!

B. The LORD reveals more about the uniqueness of His name to Moses. At the burning bush, God identifies Himself as the God of his fathers.

> Ex 3:6 Moreover he said, I am the God of thy father, the God of Abraham, the God of Isaac, and the God of Jacob. And Moses hid his face; for he was afraid to look upon God. (KJV)

Moses isn't sure about who God is. He inquires further. God's response is that He is the LORD, יהוה.

> Ex 3:13-15 Then Moses said to God, "Indeed, when I come to the children of Israel and say to them, 'The God (Elohim) of your fathers has sent me to you,' and they say to me, 'What is His name?' what shall I say to them?" 14 And God said to Moses, "I AM (hayah)WHO I AM (hayah)." And He said, "Thus you shall say to the children of Israel, 'I AM (hayah) has sent me to you.'"15 Moreover God said to Moses, "Thus you shall say to the children of Israel: 'The LORD (Yah-weh) God of your fathers, the God of Abraham, the God of Isaac, and the God of Jacob, has sent me to you. This is My name forever, and this is My memorial to all generations.' (NKJV)

His title is God, but His name is יהוה. It is His name and memorial forever. This is how we are to remember God.

We get further understanding of this name after the Exodus from Egypt when Israel sins by making and worshipping the golden calf. Moses interceded for the Israelites and pleads for the LORD's presence to go with them to the Promised Land. This must have pleased the LORD because He tells Moses that He knows his name and then promises to reveal to Moses His own Name.

> Ex 33:17-19 So the LORD said to Moses, "I will also do this thing that you have spoken; for you have found grace in My sight, and I know you by name." 18 And he said, "Please, show me Your glory." 19 Then He said, "I will make all My goodness pass before you, and **I will proclaim the name of the LORD** before you. I will be gracious to whom I will be gracious, and I will have compassion on whom I will have compassion." (NKJV)

As Moses goes up Mt. Sinai with the new tablets on which God would once again write the Ten Commandments, God places Moses in a cleft of rock and proclaims His Name starting with repeating His name, יהוה, twice.

Ex 34:5-7 And the LORD descended in the cloud, and stood with him there, and proclaimed the name of the LORD. 6 And the LORD passed by before him, and proclaimed, The LORD, The LORD God, merciful and gracious, longsuffering, and abundant in goodness and truth, 7 Keeping mercy for thousands, forgiving iniquity and transgression and sin, and that will by no means clear the guilty; visiting the iniquity of the fathers upon the children, and upon the children's children, unto the third and to the fourth generation. (KJV)

The Jewish people call these the thirteen attributes of HaShem. These describe the character of the LORD. The qualities associated with mercy and kindness dominate the list. It is only when repentance is missing that judgment comes. **(See handout: The Thirteen Attributes of God.)**

Elohim is the God of creation; He fixed all the laws of the universe. There is no breaking these laws. If someone falls from a window, the law of gravity ensures that he will fall. There are no do-overs. In contrast, with יהוה there is mercy, grace, and forgiveness.

This is the LORD who brought Abram out of Ur of the Chaldees and established His covenant with him. Each time God uses this phrase, "I am the LORD who brought you out," it is in connection with deliverance or redemption.

C. The LORD brought Abram out of Ur of the Chaldees. The word Ur literally means fire.

Ur: #218 from #217 flame, the East as being the region of light, fire, light.

The Jewish sages tell the story that Abram's family made idols for Nimrod the ruler of the Babylonian region. One day, Abram smashed all the idols except one in his father Terah's shop. When Terah questioned Abram, Abram replied that the one remaining idol must have destroyed the others. Terah said that it was impossible for the idol to have done so. Abram confronted his father with the words, "Why then do you worship these powerless idols?"

When Terah had no idols to deliver to Nimrod, Nimrod had Abram thrown into a fiery furnace. Like Shadrach, Meshach and Abednego, the fire did not harm Abram. Nimrod then asked Abram's brother Haran whose God he served. When Haran saw that Abram was not burned, he said that he stood with Abram. But because he chose to stand with Abram only after Abram was thrown in the fire, Haran perished when he was thrown into the fire with Abram. Thus, "Haran died in Ur (the fire) of the Chaldees." (Gen. 11:28)

Shortly after Abram went to the Promised Land, there was a famine and Abram proceeded to Egypt. God arranged to have him kicked out of Egypt, in a sense delivering him a second time, this time from Egypt.

Ge 12:19-20 "Why did you say, 'She is my sister'? I might have taken her as my wife. Now therefore, here is your wife; take her and go your way." 20 So Pharaoh commanded his men concerning him; and they sent him away, with his wife and all that he had. (NKJV)

So, the LORD called Abram out of Ur of the Chaldees and delivered him from Nimrod, as well as a very mad Pharaoh. He delivered Abram "to give you this land to inherit it." (Gen. 15:7) Genesis 15:13-16 gives the details of how the covenant will be fulfilled which we will examine in "Cycles of Prophetic Fulfillment." Genesis 15 concludes with a repeat of the promise "Unto thy seed have I given this land."

D. The next time God identifies Himself with the phrase, "I am the LORD who…" is at the time of the Exodus when God delivers the Israelites from slavery in Egypt.

> Ex 6:6-7 "Therefore say to the children of Israel: 'I am the LORD; I will bring you out from under the burdens of the Egyptians, I will rescue you from their bondage, and I will redeem you with an outstretched arm and with great judgments. 7 'I will take you as My people, and I will be your God. Then you shall know that **I am the LORD your God who brings you out** from under the burdens of the Egyptians. (NKJV)

After the Exodus, when the Israelites are at Mt. Sinai, God again identifies Himself in preparation for making the covenant with the nation of Israel.

> Ex 20:1-2 And God spoke all these words, saying: 2 **"I am the LORD your God, who brought you out** of the land of Egypt, out of the house of bondage. (NKJV)

God follows this statement with the rest of the Ten Commandments or Ten Words, the basis of God's covenant with the nation of Israel.

E. A variation of the phrase "I am the LORD who…" is used in the life of Yeshua. Matthew tells us that "Out of Egypt I called my son." This variation of the phrase is used to show that Yeshua fulfills the prophecies about the Messiah. Matthew quotes Hosea 11:1.

> Mt 2:13-15 Now when they had departed, behold, an angel of the Lord appeared to Joseph in a dream, saying, "Arise, take the young Child and His mother, flee to Egypt, and stay there until I bring you word; for Herod will seek the young Child to destroy Him."14 When he arose, he took the young Child and His mother by night and departed for Egypt, 15 and was there until the death of Herod, that it might be fulfilled which was spoken by the Lord through the prophet, saying, "Out of Egypt I called My Son." (NKJV)

> Ho 11:1 "When Israel was a child, I loved him, And out of Egypt I called My son. (NKJV)

The history of Israel is recapitulated in the life of Yeshua. He came to fulfill the Torah and the covenants included in the Torah.

Mat 5:17 "Do not think that I came to destroy the Law (Torah) or the Prophets (Navi-im). I did not come to destroy but to fulfill. (NKJV)

The Jewish scriptures are made of three parts, the Law or Torah, the Prophets or Nevi-im and the Writings or Ketuvim. Yeshua refers to two parts of the Jewish Scriptures in this verse we just read. Yeshua institutes the New Covenant written about by Jeremiah the Prophet.

Jer 31:31-34 "Behold, the days are coming, says the LORD, when I will make a new covenant with the house of Israel and with the house of Judah- 32 "not according to the covenant that I made with their fathers in the day that I took them by the hand to lead them out of the land of Egypt, My covenant which they broke, though I was a husband to them, says the LORD. 33 "But this is the covenant that I will make with the house of Israel after those days, says the LORD: I will put My law (Torah) in their minds, and write it on their hearts; and I will be their God, and they shall be My people. 34 "No more shall every man teach his neighbor, and every man his brother, saying, 'Know the LORD,' for they all shall know Me, from the least of them to the greatest of them, says the LORD. For I will forgive their iniquity, and their sin I will remember no more." (NKJV)

This New Covenant is between the LORD and the houses of Israel and Judah. Part of the agreement or promise of the covenant is that their sins will be forgiven. The same LORD who wrote the Ten Commandments on tablets of stone writes them in their minds and on their hearts.

F. We partake in this same New Covenant because we have been grafted into Israel.

Ro 11:17-18 And if some of the branches were broken off, and you, being a wild olive tree, were grafted in among them, and with them became a partaker of the root and fatness of the olive tree, 18 do not boast against the branches. But if you do boast, remember that you do not support the root, but the root supports you. (NKJV)

Peter tells us that we also are "called out" and that the promise of the covenant is to all whom God will call. We are heirs together with Messiah.

Ac 2:38-39 Then Peter said to them, "Repent, and let every one of you be baptized in the name of Jesus Christ for the remission of sins; and you shall receive the gift of the Holy Spirit. 39 "For the promise is to you and to your children, and to all who are afar off, as many as the Lord our God will call." (NKJV)

Ro 8:16-17 The Spirit Himself bears witness with our spirit that we are children of God, 17 and if children, then heirs--heirs of God and joint heirs with Christ, if indeed we suffer with Him, that we may also be glorified together. (NKJV)

G. God will again identify Himself as "the LORD who…" during the Latter times when He gathers the Jewish people from all the nations and brings them back to Israel.

> Jer 23:7-8 "Therefore, behold, the days are coming," says the LORD, "that they shall no longer say, 'As the LORD lives who brought up the children of Israel from the land of Egypt,' 8 "but, 'As **the LORD lives who brought up** and led the descendants of the house of Israel from the north country and from all the countries where I had driven them.' And they shall dwell in their own land." (NKJV)

The pattern is that a covenant or the reminder of a covenant or promise will follow the statement "I am the LORD who…" This time, it is the fulfillment of all the covenants that will follow. They will take possession of the Promised Land fulfilling the Covenant with Abram for his seed to possess the land. This will occur when Yeshua, the Branch of David, comes again to reign from David's throne in Jerusalem.

> Zec 2:12 "And the LORD will take possession of Judah as His inheritance in the Holy Land, and will again choose Jerusalem. (NKJV)

> Jer 33:14-15 'Behold, the days are coming,' says the LORD, 'that I will perform that good thing which I have promised to the house of Israel and to the house of Judah: 15 'In those days and at that time I will cause to grow up to David A Branch of righteousness; He shall execute judgment and righteousness in the earth. (NKJV)

The final fulfillment will be when the new heaven and earth are created.

> Re 21:3 And I heard a loud voice from heaven saying, "Behold, the tabernacle of God is with men, and He will dwell with them, and they shall be His people. God Himself will be with them and be their God. (NKJV)

H. How can we be sure that, in this day of broken contracts, covenants, and marriages, the LORD God will keep His covenant? Let's look at what a covenant meant in the time of Abraham, Moses, and Yeshua. God formalizes the covenant with Abram in the traditional format of covenant agreements.

> Ge 15:9-12, 17 So He said to him, "Bring Me a three-year-old heifer, a three-year-old female goat, a three-year-old ram, a turtledove, and a young pigeon." 10 Then he brought all these to Him and cut them in two, down the middle, and placed each piece opposite the other; but he did not cut the birds in two. 11 And when the vultures came down on the carcasses, Abram drove them away. 12 Now when the sun was going down, a deep sleep fell upon Abram; and behold, horror and great darkness fell upon him.17 And it came to pass, when the sun went down and it was dark, that behold, there appeared a smoking oven and a burning torch that passed between those pieces. (NKJV)

This is an irrevocable covenant. When the parties to a covenant bring a sacrifice, cut the parts and walk between the parts they are saying, "May it be to me like the sacrificed animals if I do not keep my oath and pledge." There is no backing out of this type of covenant. Although Abram prepared the parts of the sacrifice animals, he did not walk between the parts, only God walked between the parts. This covenant is not dependent on any further action by Abram. God alone will bring it to fruition. God will keep His promises to Abram.

I. The covenant between God and the nation of Israel after the Exodus was also formalized by a covenant sacrifice. Instead of walking through the parts, Moses sprinkled the altar of God and the people with the blood of the sacrifice.

> Ex 24:4-8 And Moses wrote all the words of the LORD. And he rose early in the morning, and built an altar at the foot of the mountain, and twelve pillars according to the twelve tribes of Israel. 5 Then he sent young men of the children of Israel, who offered burnt offerings and sacrificed peace offerings of oxen to the LORD. 6 And Moses took half the blood and put it in basins, and half the blood he sprinkled on the altar. 7 Then he took the Book of the Covenant and read in the hearing of the people. And they said, "All that the LORD has said we will do, and be obedient." 8 And Moses took the blood, sprinkled it on the people, and said, "This is the blood of the covenant which the LORD has made with you according to all these words." (NKJV)

The LORD is fulfilling the promise to Abram to give his descendants, the Israelites, the Promised Land. In order to keep the Land, they need to agree to obey the commandments of God, to be holy and separate from the nations around them. In accepting the covenant, they are accepting the proviso of "may it be to me like these sacrificed animals." When they are not able to do so, they broke the covenant and invoked the penalty. They needed the New Covenant written about by Jeremiah. Since the nation of Israel was the priest to the nations, everyone, not just Israel, needed the New Covenant!

J. The writer of Hebrews writes of the establishment and continuing fulfillment of the New Covenant prophesied by Jeremiah. It is detailed in Hebrews 9:15-18. This passage may not have made sense to you before. That is because a couple of words have been mistranslated. First, let's read them in the New King James Version. Other versions may vary significantly.

> Heb 9:15-18 And for this reason He is the Mediator of the new covenant, by means of death, for the redemption of the transgressions under the first covenant, that those who are called may receive the promise of the eternal inheritance.16 For where there is a **testament**, there must also of necessity be the death of the **testator**.17 For a **testament** is in force **after men are dead**, since it has no power at all while the **testator** lives.18 Therefore not even the first covenant was dedicated without blood. (NKJV)

Verse 15 of Hebrews 9 is about a covenant although it mentions an inheritance. We looked at our inheritance earlier and know that the promised inheritance is part of the agreement of the New Covenant—the forgiveness of sins (Jer. 31:34). Paul said that we are heirs together with Yeshua, not heirs of Yeshua! Our inheritance is not a result of Yeshua dying and passing on His possessions to us. Our inheritance is a gift of God.

> Ro 6:22-23 But now having been set free from sin, and having become slaves of God, you have your fruit to holiness, and the end, everlasting life. 23 For the wages of sin is death, but the gift of God is eternal life in Christ Jesus our Lord. (NKJV)

Notice that Hebrews 9:15 talks about a transgression of the covenant. Remember, the transgression of a covenant requires the death of the party who broke the covenant. Also, a new covenant requires a new covenant sacrifice. A covenant is an agreement between two people. It goes into effect when the covenant sacrifice dies not when one party to the agreement dies.

To make sense of this, we need to look at some Hebrew, Greek, Latin and English back in Jeremiah 31:31-32. The King James Version reads:

> Jer 31:31-32a Behold, the days come, saith the LORD, that I will make a new **covenant** with the house of Israel, and with the house of Judah: 32 Not according to the **covenant** that I made with their fathers… (KJV)

Hebrews 8:8-9a quotes this Jeremiah passage:

> Hebrews 8:8-9 For finding fault with them, he saith, Behold, the days come, saith the Lord, when I will make a new **covenant** with the house of Israel and with the house of Judah: 9 Not according to the **covenant** that I made with their fathers… (KJV)

As we look at the Greek and Latin translations of Jeremiah 31:31-32 and Hebrews 8:8-9, we see a difference in the Latin Vulgate.

Verse	KJV English	Hebrew	Greek	Vulgate Latin: KJV
Jer. 31:31	Covenant	Brit	Diatheke	Foedus-Alliance
Jer. 31:32	Covenant	Brit	Diatheke	Pactum: Covenant
Heb. 8:8	Covenant	Brit	Diatheke	Testamentum: Testament
Heb. 8:9	Covenant	Brit	Diatheke	Testamentum: Testament

In Jeremiah 31:31-32 the Latin words foedus and pactum are similar; both are agreements between two parties. But in Hebrews 8:8-9 the same Greek word, diatheke, was translated as testamentum or testament in the Latin Vulgate.

In the Pocket Webster School and Office Dictionary these words are defined as follows:

Covenant: A solemn agreement or compact. Promises made by God to man as set forth in scriptures.

Testament: A solemn authentic instrument in writing disposing of the estate of a person deceased. i.e. a will.

What are some characteristics of a covenant?

It is an agreement between two or more parties.

Sometimes a mediator will act to bring the parties to agreement.

If one party dies, the covenant is no longer in force unless arrangements are made to continue it.

In ancient times, it was ratified over the body of an animal.

The parties would walk between the parts and/or be sprinkled with the blood.

What are some characteristics of a testament?

One person writes it.

It is a transfer of property after the original owner dies.

The person writing it must die before it goes into effect.

The person receiving property may know nothing until the testator dies.

It does not require the agreement of the person receiving property (although the bequest can be rejected).

As we look at the Greek and Latin of Hebrews 9:15-18, we see the Latin mistranslation following into the English. By the way, it is from this passage in Hebrews that we get the idea that there is an Old Testament and a New Testament. The other words in the passage that are also mistranslated from the Latin are "testator" and "after men are dead." The table shows the original Greek words, the literal translation of those Greek words, and the New King James translation.

Verse	Greek	Young's Literal Translation	NKJV
16-17	diatheke	covenant	Testament
16-17	diatithemai	covenant-victim	Testator
17	epi-nekrois	over dead victims/bodies	After men are dead

We see the Greek **diatheke** ignored in favor of the Latin testamentum showing up as testament in the New King James Version. The next Greek word is the word **diatithemai** from the same root as **diatheke** which we saw means a **covenant**. The New King James Version again ignores the Greek in favor of the Latin translating the word as **testator** while Young's Literal Translation translates it as **covenant-victim.**

Finally the Greek phrase **"epi nekrois"** is translated "after men are dead." It literally means **"over dead bodies."** We know that covenants are formalized over the covenant sacrifice so "over dead bodies" makes sense in the context of a covenant. Young's Literal Translation uses the phrase "over dead victims" referring to the covenant-victim.

Young's Literal Translation reads as follows:

Heb 9:15 And because of this, of a new covenant he is mediator, that, death having come, for redemption of the transgressions under the first covenant, those called may receive the promise of the age-during inheritance, 16 for where a **covenant** is, the death of the **covenant-victim** to come in is necessary, 17 for a **covenant over dead victims** is stedfast, since it is no force at all when the **covenant-victim** liveth,

The grammatical structure is a little hard to understand in the Young's Literal Translation so, let's read the New King James passage with the correct translation from the Greek. Replace the word testament with covenant, the word testator with covenant-victim, and the phrase "after men are dead" with the phrase "over dead bodies." It all of sudden makes sense! The changes are marked in bold type with the original English in parentheses.

> Heb 9:15-18 And for this reason He is the Mediator of the new covenant, by means of death, for the redemption of the transgressions under the first covenant, that those who are called may receive the promise of the eternal inheritance.16 For where there is a **covenant** (testament), there must also of necessity be the death of the **covenant victim** (testator).17 For a **covenant** (testament) is in force **over dead bodies** (after men are dead), since it has no power at all while the **covenant victim** (testator) lives.18 Therefore not even the first covenant was dedicated without blood.

God put in place and formalized the New Covenant over the covenant victim of His one and only Son. Yeshua gave His life both for the transgression of the first covenant as representative of the Israelites who broke the covenant and as the covenant sacrifice for the New Covenant. This is what the writer of Hebrews is referring to in Hebrews 10:8-9.

> Hebrews 10:8-9 Previously saying, "Sacrifice and offering, burnt offerings, and offerings for sin You did not desire, nor had pleasure in them" (which are offered according to the law), 9 then He said, "Behold, I have come to do Your will, O God." He takes away the first that He may establish the second. (NKJV)

The breaking of the covenant required the death of the children of Israel who broke the covenant. Sacrifices and offerings could not achieve payment for breaking the covenant. Only the death of Yeshua as an Israelite could pay that price. He takes away the penalty of the first and establishes the second. Remember, we participate in that redemption as we are grafted into Israel. We are now under the New Covenant with the Torah written in our minds and on our hearts.

Since the redemption price of the Old Covenant and the establishment of the New Covenant cost God the life of His Son, we can be sure He will keep His covenant!

Remember, a covenant is an agreement between two parties. We need to agree to the covenant by being sprinkled with the blood of the covenant-victim, Yeshua, the Son of God.

> 1Co 11:23-25 For I received from the Lord that which I also delivered to you: that the Lord Jesus on the same night in which He was betrayed took bread; 24 and when He had given thanks, He broke it and said, "Take, eat; this is My body which is broken for you; do this in remembrance of Me." 25 In the same manner He also

took the cup after supper, saying, "This cup is the new covenant in My blood. This do, as often as you drink it, in remembrance of Me." (NKJV)

Joh 3:16-17 "For God so loved the world that He gave His only begotten Son, that whoever believes in Him should not perish but have everlasting life. 17 "For God did not send His Son into the world to condemn the world, but that the world through Him might be saved. (NKJV)

Who is the LORD? He is the LORD who interacted intimately with Adam as He created Adam and desires an intimate relationship with us. He is the LORD who brought us out of slavery to sin and death redeeming us and sealing us into the New Covenant by the death of His son Yeshua both for the transgression of the first covenant and the sacrifice for the New. He will keep His Covenant!

Student Notes For I Am the LORD Who Brought You Out

In Genesis 15, God makes a formal Covenant with Abram. In a formal Covenant, the two parties need to be identified. Who is it that is making the covenant? (Gen. 15:7)

A. Who is the LORD?

The word we translate LORD with all capital letters is composed of four Hebrew letters, יהוה, read right to left, the yood-hey-vav-hey.

LORD: #3068 יהוה : יהוה   יהוה   Yehovah, yeh-ho-vaw' from 1961; (the) self-Existent or Eternal. Sometimes pronounced Yah-weh probably from #1961 ha-yah היה the verb to be or become, I was who I was, I am who I am, I will be who I will be.

Elohim: #430. אלהים 'elohiym, el-o-heem' plural of #433; gods in the ordinary sense; but specifically used (in the plural thus, especially with the article) of the supreme God;

The first action of the LORD God (Gen. 2:7): _____

Formed: ייצר: yatzar with two yoods. God used both of His hands to form Adam!

B. The LORD reveals more about the uniqueness of His name to Moses. (Ex. 3:6, Ex. 3:13-15, Ex. 33:17-19, Ex. 34:5-7))

C. The LORD brought Abram out of Ur of the Chaldees.

Ur: #218 from #217 flame, the East as being the region of light, fire, light.

The Jewish sages tell the story that Abram's family made idols for Nimrod the ruler of the Babylonian region. One day, Abram smashed all the idols except one in his father Terah's shop. When Terah questioned Abram, Abram replied that the one remaining idol must have destroyed the others. Terah said that it was impossible for the idol to have done so. Abram confronted his father with the words, "Why then do you worship these powerless idols?"

When Terah had no idols to deliver to Nimrod, Nimrod had Abram thrown into a fiery furnace. Like Daniel, the fire did not harm Abram. Nimrod then asked Abram's brother Haran whose God he served. When he saw that Abram was not burned, he said that he stood with Abram. But because he chose to stand with Abram only after Abram was thrown in the fire, Haran, when he was thrown into the fire with Abram, perished. Thus, "Haran died in Ur (the fire) of the Chaldees." (Gen. 11:28)

At the time Abram went to the Promised Land, there was a famine and Abram proceeded to Egypt. God arranged to have him kicked out of Egypt, in a sense delivering him a second time, this time from Egypt. (Gen. 12:19-20)

D. The LORD delivers the Israelites from slavery in Egypt. (Ex. 6:6-7, Ex. 20:1-2)

E. Matthew tells us that "Out of Egypt I called my son." (Mat. 2:13-15, Hos. 11:1, Mat. 5:17)

Torah:

Nevi-im:

Ketuvim:

Yeshua establishes the New Covenant: (Jer. 31:31-34)

Who are the parties to the New Covenant?

F. We partake in this same New Covenant.
Grafted in: (Rom. 11:17-18)

Called out: (Acts 2:38-39)

Heirs: (Rom. 8:16-17)

G. God will again identify Himself as "the LORD who…" during the Latter times (Jer. 23:7-8, Zec. 2:12, Jer. 33:14-15, Rev. 21:3)

H. How sure can we be that the LORD God will keep His covenant? (Gen. 15:9-12, 17) God formalizes the covenant with Abram by:

I. The covenant between the LORD and the nation of Israel (Ex. 24:4-8)

Formalized by:

J. The writer of Hebrews writes of the establishment and continuing fulfillment of the New Covenant prophesied by Jeremiah

> Heb 9:15-18 And for this reason He is the Mediator of the new covenant, by means of death, for the redemption of the transgressions under the first covenant, that those who are called may receive the promise of the eternal inheritance.16 For where there is a **testament**, there must also of necessity be the death of the **testator.**17 For a **testament** is in force **after men are dead**, since it has no power at all while the **testator** lives.18 Therefore not even the first covenant was dedicated without blood. (NKJV)

The inheritance mentioned is a provision of the covenant not a will: (Rom. 6:22-23)

To make sense of this, we need to look at some English, Hebrew, Greek and Latin in Jeremiah 31 and Hebrews 8. We can see that Heb. 8:8-9 is a quotation of Jer. 31:31-32.

Verse	KJV English	Hebrew	Greek	Vulgate Latin
Jer. 31:31	Covenant	Brit	Diatheke	Foedus-Alliance
Jer. 31:32	Covenant	Brit	Diatheke	Pactum: Covenant
Heb. 8:8	Covenant	Brit	Diatheke	Testamentum: Testament
Heb. 8:9	Covenant	Brit	Diatheke	Testamentum: Testament

In the Pocket Webster School and Office Dictionary covenant and testament are defined as follows:

Covenant: A solemn agreement or compact. Promises made by God to man as set forth in scriptures.

Testament: A solemn authentic instrument in writing disposing of the estate of a person deceased. i.e. a will.

What are some characteristics of a covenant?	What are some characteristics of a testament?

The other words in the passage of Hebrews 9:15-18 were "testator" and "after men are dead."

Verse	NKJV	Greek	Young's Literal Translation
16-17	testament	diatheke	covenant
16-17	testator	diatithemai	covenant-victim
17	after men are dead	epi-nekrois	over dead victims/bodies

Young's Literal Translation:
Heb 9:15-18 And because of this, of a new covenant he is mediator, that, death having come, for redemption of the transgressions under the first covenant, those called may receive the promise of the age-during inheritance,16 for where a **covenant** is, the death of the **covenant-victim** to come in is necessary,17 for a **covenant over dead victims** is stedfast, since it is no force at all when the **covenant-victim** liveth…

Now the New King James version with the words relating to covenants:
Heb 9:15-18 And for this reason He is the Mediator of the new covenant, by means of death, for the redemption of the transgressions under the first covenant, that those who are called may receive the promise of the eternal inheritance.16 For where there is a **covenant** (testament), there must also of necessity be the death of the **covenant victim** (testator).17 For a **covenant** (testament) is in force **over dead bodies** (after men are dead), since it has no power at all while the **covenant victim** (testator) lives.18 Therefore not even the first covenant was dedicated without blood.

God has formalized the New Covenant spoken of by Jeremiah over the body of His one and only Son. (Heb. 10:8-9, 1 Cor. 11:23-25)

Joh 3:16-17 "For God so loved the world that He gave His only begotten Son, that whoever believes in Him should not perish but have everlasting life. 17 "For God did not send His Son into the world to condemn the world, but that the world through Him might be saved. (NKJV)

Discussion questions for I am the LORD Who Brought You Out

1. God calls Abram to leave "Ur of the Chaldees" in the kingdom of Babylon. The word "ur," Strong's Dictionary #217, means fire. The word "chaldees," Strong's Dictionary #3778, means astrologers. So, God calls Abram to leave the fire of the astrologers in Babylon. Read Revelation 18:4-9. How are these situations similar?

2. The word "Hebrew" comes from "eber" which means to cross over. The literal translation of Genesis 12:6 says Abram crossed over into the land. The children of Israel crossed over both the Red Sea and the Jordan River (Jos. 4:23). How do we also "cross over?"

3. Read the handout of the thirteen attributes of God. Then read John 3:16-18, 2 Peter 3:8-10 and Ezekiel 33:11. Discuss God's desire to have mercy on all people. Contrast that with the ultimate judgment coming to those who don't believe and obey.

4. David knew the LORD. Read Psalm 103. Discuss how the psalm fits in with this lesson. Include the concepts of mercy, righteousness, covenant and commandments.

5. Compare the description of the covenant ceremony between God and Abram in Genesis 15:9-17 with the description of Yeshua as the covenant victim in the Young's Literal Translation of Hebrews 9:15-17.

6. Read Jeremiah 31:31-34 again as well as Romans 2:12-16 and Romans 3:27-31. Describe the fulfillment of the New Covenant. Does the New Covenant as outlined in this passage destroy the law (Torah) or establish it?

Cycles of Prophetic Fulfillment of the Promises to Abram
Genesis 15

A. God promises Abram three different times that the land inhabited by the Canaanites would be his and that his descendant or descendants would inherit that land. (Genesis 12:7, Genesis 13:15, Genesis 15:4-7). In Genesis 15, God expands on the promise telling Abram the sequence of events that would occur as his descendants came to possess the land.

The Jewish concept of time is that it is cyclical. Times of the year, the Feasts, even events in prophecy repeat. For example, the Feasts are proclaimed by God to be His Feasts which are to be observed as holy convocations. The Hebrew word for Feasts is mo'edim meaning appointed times. The Hebrew word for convocation is miqra meaning convocation, assembly, or dress rehearsal. So God's Feasts are His appointed times where we are to meet and rehearse the fulfillment of the Feasts. Year after year, the events repeat. God uses cycles of fulfillment in the same way. They are rehearsals of the ultimate fulfillment of all promises, the restoration of all things when God will again dwell with man.

The promise to Abram starts with a seed, a son, to inherit.

> Ge 15:4 And behold, the word of the LORD came to him, saying, "This one shall not be your heir, but one who will come from your own body shall be your heir." (NKJV)

But before the seed can inherit, certain events will occur. God spoke to Abram in a vision.

> Ge 15:13-16, 18 Then He said to Abram: "Know certainly that your descendants will be strangers in a land that is not theirs, and will serve them, and they will afflict them four hundred years. 14 "And also the nation whom they serve I will judge; afterward they shall come out with great possessions. 15 "Now as for you, you shall go to your fathers in peace; you shall be buried at a good old age. 16 "But in the fourth generation they shall return here, for the iniquity of the Amorites is not yet complete." 18 On the same day the LORD made a covenant with Abram, saying: "To your descendants I have given this land, from the river of Egypt to the great river, the River Euphrates- (NKJV)

The seven parts of the promise progress as follows:

- A seed of your own loins will be your heir.
- Your seed will be strangers in a land not theirs.
- Your seed will be afflicted.
- The nations they serve will be judged.
- They shall come out with great wealth.
- It shall occur at the appointed time.
- Your seed will take possession of the land.

We will look briefly at five cycles of the fulfillment of these events ending with the ultimate fulfillment as Yeshua, the Seed of Abraham, takes possession of the Promised Land and reigns over all the earth.

B. The first cycle of fulfillment is in the establishment of the nation of Israel. This fulfillment is on a grand scale with three descendants of Abram singled out as the seed who would inherit the Promised Land. Although Isaac is the promised son of Abram, we start this cycle of fulfillment with Isaac's son Jacob who would be renamed Israel.

1. Jacob's birth was a miracle because Isaac was married for twenty years before Rebekah was able to conceive.

> Ge 25:20-21, 26 Isaac was forty years old when he took Rebekah as wife, the daughter of Bethuel the Syrian of Padan Aram, the sister of Laban the Syrian. 21 Now Isaac pleaded with the LORD for his wife, because she was barren; and the LORD granted his plea, and Rebekah his wife conceived. 26b Isaac was sixty years old when she bore them. (NKJV)

2. Jacob-Israel and all his descendants went into Egypt where they were eventually afflicted.

> Ex 1:11-14 Therefore they set taskmasters over them to afflict them with their burdens. And they built for Pharaoh supply cities, Pithom and Raamses. 12 But the more they afflicted them, the more they multiplied and grew. And they were in dread of the children of Israel. 13 So the Egyptians made the children of Israel serve with rigor. 14 And they made their lives bitter with hard bondage-in mortar, in brick, and in all manner of service in the field. All their service in which they made them serve was with rigor. (NKJV)

3. Judgment was inflicted upon Pharaoh through the hand of Moses who is another seed of Abraham. Moses' birth, like Jacob's, was a miracle. He was born at a time when all the Hebrew baby boys were being killed at birth.

> Heb 11:23 By faith Moses' parents hid him for three months after he was born, because they saw he was no ordinary child, and they were not afraid of the king's edict. (NIV)

God used Moses to bring plagues against Egypt. Then Moses brought the Israelites out of Egypt with great wealth.

> Ex 3:20-22 "So I will stretch out My hand and strike Egypt with all My wonders which I will do in its midst; and after that he will let you go. 21 "And I will give this people favor in the sight of the Egyptians; and it shall be, when you go, that you shall not go empty-handed. 22 "But every woman shall ask of her neighbor, namely, of her who dwells near her house, articles of silver, articles of gold, and

clothing; and you shall put them on your sons and on your daughters. So you shall plunder the Egyptians." (NKJV)

4. God brought them out at the appointed time. The promise to Abram was that they would live as strangers in a land not theirs for 400 years.

Ge 15:13 Then He said to Abram: "Know certainly that your descendants will be strangers in a land that is not theirs, and will serve them, and they will afflict them four hundred years.(NKJV)

Ex 12:40 Now the sojourning of the children of Israel, who dwelt in Egypt, was four hundred and thirty years. (KJV)

5. After a delay of forty years of wandering in the wilderness, God used Joshua, another seed of Abraham, to bring the Israelites into the Promised Land. Joshua and his aide Caleb were the only adults who came out of Egypt and were numbered among the armies of Israel to actually go into the Promised Land. The others died in the wilderness because of their disobedience and lack of faith.

Nu 14:30 'Except for Caleb the son of Jephunneh and Joshua the son of Nun, you shall by no means enter the land which I swore I would make you dwell in. (NKJV)

After Joshua takes the Promised Land, God gives him and Israel rest. Taking possession of the land is equated with entering God's rest. We will see this symbolism of rest in later cycles of these events.

Jos 23:1 Now it came to pass, a long time after the LORD had given rest to Israel from all their enemies round about, that Joshua was old, advanced in age. (NKJV)

C. The next cycle begins just before the exile of Judah to Babylon

1. The seed of Abram is Josiah. About 40 years before the exile, Josiah became king of Judah. Josiah was unlike any king since David. He not only did what was right in the eyes of the LORD, he removed all the altars to the foreign gods from the temple, Jerusalem, Judah, and all Israel, even into the northern kingdom of fallen Israel! (2 Kings 23) What followed was a huge revival unlike any that had occurred before. Josiah is described as following in the ways of his father David. Like Abraham, Jacob, Moses and Joshua before him, he listened and obeyed God.

2Ch 34:33 Thus Josiah removed all the abominations from all the country that belonged to the children of Israel, and made all who were present in Israel diligently serve the LORD their God. All his days they did not depart from following the LORD God of their fathers. (NKJV)

2Ch 35:18 There had been no Passover kept in Israel like that since the days of Samuel the prophet; and none of the kings of Israel had kept such a Passover as

Josiah kept, with the priests and the Levites, all Judah and Israel who were present, and the inhabitants of Jerusalem. (NKJV)

2. The nation of Judah and the remnant of Israel that had fled to Judah when Israel fell all went into exile to Babylon. The affliction is a bit different however. God sent the exiles away from Judah to preserve their lives. Those who remained in Judah resisting the rule of Babylon were afflicted.

Jer 27:12-13 I also spoke to Zedekiah king of Judah according to all these words, saying, "Bring your necks under the yoke of the king of Babylon, and serve him and his people, and live! 13 "Why will you die, you and your people, by the sword, by the famine, and by the pestilence, as the LORD has spoken against the nation that will not serve the king of Babylon? (NKJV)

Jer 25:8-10 "Therefore thus says the LORD of hosts: 'Because you have not heard My words, 9 'behold, I will send and take all the families of the north,' says the LORD, 'and Nebuchadnezzar the king of Babylon, My servant, and will bring them against this land, against its inhabitants, and against these nations all around, and will utterly destroy them, and make them an astonishment, a hissing, and perpetual desolations. 10 'Moreover I will take from them the voice of mirth and the voice of gladness, the voice of the bridegroom and the voice of the bride, the sound of the millstones and the light of the lamp. (NKJV)

So, the people who would not serve the King of Babylon were afflicted; their cities destroyed, their people enslaved.

3. God brought judgment against the nation they served—the Babylonians as prophesied by Jeremiah the prophet.

Jer 25:11-12 'And this whole land shall be a desolation and an astonishment, and these nations shall serve the king of Babylon seventy years. 12 'Then it will come to pass, when seventy years are completed, that I will punish the king of Babylon and that nation, the land of the Chaldeans, for their iniquity,' says the LORD; 'and I will make it a perpetual desolation. (NKJV)

The book of Daniel records the fall of the Babylonian empire. King Belshazzar desecrated the goblets from the temple and that very night, Darius the Mede took over the kingdom bringing in the rule of the Medeo-Persians.

Da 5:26-28, 30-31 "This is the interpretation of each word. MENE: God has numbered your kingdom, and finished it; 27 "TEKEL: You have been weighed in the balances, and found wanting; 28 "PERES: Your kingdom has been divided, and given to the Medes and Persians." 30 That very night Belshazzar, king of the Chaldeans, was slain. 31 And Darius the Mede received the kingdom, being about sixty-two years old. (NKJV)

4. God brought Abraham's descendents out at the appointed time. We saw from the passage in Jeremiah that Israel would serve the nation of Babylon for 70 years. After the death of Belshazzar, they continued to serve the Medeo-Persians in Babylon until the 70 years were complete. We would expect another event like the Exodus but that didn't happen. We would expect that the Israelites would come out with great wealth, but that didn't happen. They came out with some wealth; Cyrus returned the articles belonging to the temple that were taken by Nebuchadnezzar.

> Ezr 1:7-11 King Cyrus also brought out the articles of the house of the LORD, which Nebuchadnezzar had taken from Jerusalem and put in the temple of his gods; 8 and Cyrus king of Persia brought them out by the hand of Mithredath the treasurer, and counted them out to Sheshbazzar the prince of Judah. 9 This is the number of them: thirty gold platters, one thousand silver platters, twenty-nine knives, 10 thirty gold basins, four hundred and ten silver basins of a similar kind, and one thousand other articles. 11 All the articles of gold and silver were five thousand four hundred. All these Sheshbazzar took with the captives who were brought from Babylon to Jerusalem. (NKJV)

This is a pittance compared to the wealth taken out of Egypt. The number of people who came out of Babylon was a mere 42,360, less than a tenth of the number who came out of Egypt.

> Ezr 2:64-67 The whole assembly together was forty-two thousand three hundred and sixty, 65 besides their male and female servants, of whom there were seven thousand three hundred and thirty-seven; and they had two hundred men and women singers. 66 Their horses were seven hundred and thirty-six, their mules two hundred and forty-five, 67 their camels four hundred and thirty-five, and their donkeys six thousand seven hundred and twenty. (NKJV)

Again, this number compares badly with the 675,000 men who came out of Egypt together with a "mixed multitude" plus women and children. In fact, Babylon remained the center of Jewish learning and authority well into the 19th century.

5. The temple was rebuilt symbolizing the retaking of the land but through all this, the Israelites were still the subjects of the Medeo-Persian kings.

> Ezr 6:13-15 Then Tattenai, governor of the region beyond the River, Shethar-Boznai, and their companions diligently did according to what King Darius had sent. 14 So the elders of the Jews built, and they prospered through the prophesying of Haggai the prophet and Zechariah the son of Iddo. And they built and finished it, according to the commandment of the God of Israel, and according to the command of Cyrus, Darius, and Artaxerxes king of Persia. 15 Now the temple was finished on the third day of the month of Adar, which was in the sixth year of the reign of King Darius. (NKJV)

Could this possibly be the return spoken of by Jeremiah when God said He would bring His people Israel back from captivity and restore their land (Jer. 30:3)? God said he would break the yoke from off their necks and they wouldn't serve foreigners anymore, that he would restore their fortunes and that they would have rest in their land. Most importantly that their ruler would be one of their own, totally devoted to God; he would be David their king.

> Jer 30:8-10 'For it shall come to pass in that day,' Says the LORD of hosts, 'That I will break his yoke from your neck, And will burst your bonds; Foreigners shall no more enslave them. 9 But they shall serve the LORD their God, And David their king, Whom I will raise up for them. 10 'Therefore do not fear, O My servant Jacob,' says the LORD, 'Nor be dismayed, O Israel; For behold, I will save you from afar, And your seed from the land of their captivity. Jacob shall return, have rest and be quiet, And no one shall make him afraid. (NKJV)

None of this has really happened yet. Israel went from being the possession of the Persians, to the Greeks to the Romans and then exile. They had a brief period of autonomy under the Hasmonean kings during the transition from the Greek to Roman Empire. During that time, the kings of Israel were from the priestly family not the tribe of Judah. Judah Maccabees led the revolt against Antiochus Epiphanes IV, the ruler of the portion of the divided Greek Empire that contained Israel. There was never real peace during that time. The sons and grandsons of Judah Maccabees were fighting amongst themselves for control of Israel. Finally, one of the grandsons enlisted the aid of the Roman Empire on his own behalf resulting in the subjugation of Israel under the Roman Empire.

This cycle remains incomplete. There was only a partial fulfillment of the deliverance and restoration of the seed of Abram. Even today there are nearly as many Jews living outside Israel as there are in Israel. The real return is yet to come.

D. The next cycle begins during the partial restoration of Israel with another miraculous birth. Instead of following the nation of Israel, we follow the life of one Seed of Abram, Yeshua. In this cycle, Yeshua is cast as the suffering servant, the one who would save His people from their sins.

1. Yeshua's birth was miraculous.

> Mat 1:20-21 But while he thought on these things, behold, the angel of the Lord appeared unto him in a dream, saying, Joseph, thou son of David, fear not to take unto thee Mary thy wife: for that which is conceived in her is of the Holy Ghost. 21 And she shall bring forth a son, and thou shalt call his name JESUS: for he shall save his people from their sins.

This occurred at the appointed time as prophesied by Daniel when he was seeking God about the restoration of Israel after the 70 years prophesied by Jeremiah.

Da 9:24-26 "Seventy weeks are determined For your people and for your holy city, To finish the transgression, To make an end of sins, To make reconciliation for iniquity, To bring in everlasting righteousness, To seal up vision and prophecy, And to anoint the Most Holy. 25 Know therefore and understand, That from the going forth of the command To restore and build Jerusalem Until Messiah the Prince, There shall be seven weeks and sixty-two weeks; The street shall be built again, and the wall, Even in troublesome times. 26 "And after the sixty-two weeks Messiah shall be cut off, but not for Himself; And the people of the prince who is to come Shall destroy the city and the sanctuary. The end of it shall be with a flood, And till the end of the war desolations are determined. (NKJV)

The word translated as weeks is the Hebrew word "shavuah" which literally means "seven." Shavuah is sometimes translated as a week because a week is seven days long. In this passage, it is better translated as "seven." So the time until Messiah the Prince is a total of 69 "sevens" or 69 times 7 years which is 483 years. Yeshua was crucified 483 years after the decree was issued to rebuild the temple.

2. Yeshua was a stranger in His own land. His people did not recognize Him.

Joh 1:10-11 He was in the world, and the world was made by him, and the world knew him not. 11 He came unto his own, and his own received him not. (KJV)

He was also exiled from the side of God.

Php 2:6-7 who, being in the form of God, did not consider it robbery to be equal with God, 7 but made Himself of no reputation, taking the form of a bondservant, and coming in the likeness of men. (NKJV)

3. The leaders of the Jewish people mistreated and rejected Yeshua. Yeshua submitted Himself to captivity by the High Priest and Council, and, ultimately, to the sentence of death under Roman rule.

Is 53:3-5 He is despised and rejected by men, A Man of sorrows and acquainted with grief. And we hid, as it were, our faces from Him; He was despised, and we did not esteem Him. 4 Surely He has borne our griefs And carried our sorrows; Yet we esteemed Him stricken, Smitten by God, and afflicted. 5 But He was wounded for our transgressions, He was bruised for our iniquities; The chastisement for our peace was upon Him, And by His stripes we are healed. (NKJV)

4. Yeshua "served" Israel and was mistreated by the leaders of Israel. Yeshua pronounced judgment on Israel.

Mat 23:34-35 "Therefore, indeed, I send you prophets, wise men, and scribes: some of them you will kill and crucify, and some of them you will scourge in your synagogues and persecute from city to city, 35 "that on you may come all the righteous blood shed on the earth, from the blood of righteous Abel to the blood of

Zechariah, son of Berechiah, whom you murdered between the temple and the altar. (NKJV)

5. At the appointed time, Yeshua was delivered from the grave emerging victorious with the keys to death, hell, and the grave.

Mat 16:21 From that time Jesus began to show to His disciples that He must go to Jerusalem, and suffer many things from the elders and chief priests and scribes, and be killed, and be raised the third day. (NKJV)

Re 1:18 "I am He who lives, and was dead, and behold, I am alive forevermore. Amen. And I have the keys of Hades and of Death. (NKJV)

6. When Yeshua completed His task of making atonement for us as High priest, He was restored to the Father's side where He is "resting" until His enemies are brought beneath His feet.

Heb 10:12-14 But this Man, after He had offered one sacrifice for sins forever, sat down at the right hand of God, 13 from that time waiting till His enemies are made His footstool. 14 For by one offering He has perfected forever those who are being sanctified. (NKJV)

E. The fourth cycle of fulfillment is a spiritual fulfillment made possible by the death and resurrection of Yeshua.

1. Each person who believes that Yeshua was the Son of God and died for the sins of all mankind, including himself, is miraculously reborn.

1Pe 1:20-23 He indeed was foreordained before the foundation of the world, but was manifest in these last times for you 21 who through Him believe in God, who raised Him from the dead and gave Him glory, so that your faith and hope are in God. 22 Since you have purified your souls in obeying the truth through the Spirit in sincere love of the brethren, love one another fervently with a pure heart, 23 having been born again, not of corruptible seed but incorruptible, through the word of God which lives and abides forever, (NKJV)

2. Spiritually, we are living as strangers in the world.

1Pe 2:11 Beloved, I beg you as sojourners and pilgrims, abstain from fleshly lusts which war against the soul, (NKJV)

The writer of Hebrews says that all those who live by faith, live as strangers in the world, looking forward to the heavenly country yet to come.

Heb 11:13-16 All these people were still living by faith when they died. They did not receive the things promised; they only saw them and welcomed them from a distance. And they admitted that they were aliens and strangers on earth. 14 People who say such things show that they are looking for a country of their own. 15 If they had been thinking of the country they had left, they would have had opportunity to return. 16 Instead, they were longing for a better country-- a heavenly one. Therefore God is not ashamed to be called their God, for he has prepared a city for them. (NIV)

3. We can expect persecution and mistreatment. Here in the United States, we do not suffer much persecution but in other parts of the world, believers in Yeshua die every day for their faith. Paul tells us that all followers of Yeshua will suffer persecution.

2Tim 3:12 Yes, and all who desire to live godly in Christ Jesus will suffer persecution. (NKJV)

4. Individuals will be judged on how they treat Gods' people.

Mat 16:26-27 "For what profit is it to a man if he gains the whole world, and loses his own soul? Or what will a man give in exchange for his soul? 27 "For the Son of Man will come in the glory of His Father with His angels, and then He will reward each according to his works. (NKJV)

Paul tells us in Romans that God's judgment is based on truth and He will judge all men.

Ro 2:16 This will take place on the day when God will judge men's secrets through Jesus Christ, as my gospel declares. (NIV)

Judgment will come on those who kill the saints.

Re 6:10 They called out in a loud voice, "How long, Sovereign Lord, holy and true, until you judge the inhabitants of the earth and avenge our blood?" (NIV)

5. We receive the riches of God's grace, eternal life, and receive the promised rest in Him.

Eph 1:7-8 In him we have redemption through his blood, the forgiveness of sins, in accordance with the riches of God's grace 8 that he lavished on us with all wisdom and understanding. (NIV)

Heb 4:8-10 For if Joshua had given them rest, God would not have spoken later about another day. 9 There remains, then, a Sabbath-rest for the people of God; 10 for anyone who enters God's rest also rests from his own work, just as God did from his. (NIV)

But this is only the down payment. Like Yeshua and the nation of Israel, we await the completion of the final cycle.

1Joh 3:2 NKJV 2 Beloved, now we are children of God; and it has not yet been revealed what we shall be, but we know that when He is revealed, we shall be like Him, for we shall see Him as He is.

F. This final cycle also began when Yeshua was born. Not only was He born to be the Suffering Servant, He was born the King of the Jews through whom all cycles of prophecy are brought to completion.

1. When the Magi came seeking Yeshua, they asked for the one who was born "king of the Jews." They found Him in Bethlehem where Micah prophesied that he would be born.

Mat 2:2 saying, "Where is He who has been born King of the Jews? For we have seen His star in the East and have come to worship Him." (NKJV)

Mic 5:2 "But you, Bethlehem Ephrathah, Though you are little among the thousands of Judah, Yet out of you shall come forth to Me The One to be Ruler in Israel, Whose goings forth are from of old, From everlasting." (NKJV)

Like in the time of Josiah, there was a revival. Many people believed in Yeshua, followed Him in His lifetime and believed on Him after His resurrection. The apostles and elders in Jerusalem praise God for all the Jews who believe.

Ac 21:20 And when they heard it, they glorified the Lord. And they said to him, "You see, brother, how many myriads of Jews there are who have believed, and they are all zealous for the law; (NKJV)

The word "myriad" means a ten-thousand. There were tens of thousands of Jews who believed Yeshua was the Messiah. Even today, there are many Jewish believers.

2. After Yeshua's resurrection, the Jewish people, including believers, were exiled from Jerusalem in two waves. At the time of the first Jewish revolt in 65 A.D. which led up to the destruction of the temple, many Jews fled Jerusalem or were taken as slaves. The Jewish people revolted again in 135 A.D. This revolt led to the total exile of all the Jewish people from Jerusalem. Emperor Hadrian salted the very land of Jerusalem and made practicing Judaism illegal.

3. Believers in Yeshua, both Jew and Gentile, have been persecuted. At the time of Hadrian, the Gentile believers were also persecuted right along with the Jews because they also followed the tenets of the Jewish faith in imitation of Yeshua their Messiah. The Jewish people have been persecuted throughout the centuries frequently at the hand of the Gentile Christian Church. True believers in Yeshua have been persecuted; this persecution frequently came from a corrupt church hierarchy.

4. The nations of the earth who persecute God's people, either the Jewish people or those who believe in Yeshua, will be judged. The book of Revelation reveals that all

nations that participate in the harlotry of Babylon will suffer plagues. The plagues described in Revelation are reminiscent of the plagues God brought on Egypt.

> Re 18:3-5 "For all the nations have drunk of the wine of the wrath of her fornication, the kings of the earth have committed fornication with her, and the merchants of the earth have become rich through the abundance of her luxury." 4 And I heard another voice from heaven saying, "Come out of her, my people, lest you share in her sins, and lest you receive of her plagues. 5 "For her sins have reached to heaven, and God has remembered her iniquities. (NKJV)

5. This will occur at the appointed time. One of the signs of the appointed time is that the sins of the nations will come before God. The timing for the Exodus from Egypt coincided with the sins of the Amorites reaching full measure. God told Abram that he would not yet receive the land of the Canaanites "... for the sin of the Amorites has not yet reached its full measure." (Gen 15:16b) In Revelation, we see that God takes us out when the sins of Babylon and the nations who copy her rise to heaven.

The Amorites were in the Promised Land at the time of Abraham. Their sin was not yet onerous enough for God to drive them out. But when God led the Israelites into the Land under Joshua, the Amorites along with the rest of the Canaanites were to be completely destroyed otherwise they would lead Israel into idolatry. Unfortunately, the Israelites did not totally drive them out, and they did lead Israel into idolatry.

When Josiah was King of Judah, he tore down all the altars and places where other gods were worshipped. In the time of Messiah, the land will be thoroughly cleaned from all idolatry and there will be no more idol worshippers in the Promised Land.

> Is 52:1 Awake, awake! Put on your strength, O Zion; Put on your beautiful garments, O Jerusalem, the holy city! For the uncircumcised and the unclean Shall no longer come to you. (NKJV)

> Zec 14:20-21 In that day "HOLINESS TO THE LORD" shall be engraved on the bells of the horses. The pots in the LORD'S house shall be like the bowls before the altar. 21 Yes, every pot in Jerusalem and Judah shall be holiness to the LORD of hosts. Everyone who sacrifices shall come and take them and cook in them. In that day there shall no longer be a Canaanite in the house of the LORD of hosts. (NKJV)

(Some versions translate the word for Canaanite as merchant. There are only two places in the Tenakh where this word is translated as merchant, Job 41:6 and Proverbs 31:24. Perhaps here it is best translated in both ways. After all, Yeshua drove the merchants out of the temple. (John 2:16))

6. God will deliver all the Israelites from the nations where they are scattered. When God calls His people out at this time, they will not have a choice to go or stay like they did after the Babylonian exile. He will bring them all out from the nations, but,

like in the original Exodus, God will not allow those who are rebellious to go into the Promised Land.

Jer 16:15-16 "...but, 'The LORD lives who brought up the children of Israel from the land of the north and from all the lands where He had driven them.' For I will bring them back into their land which I gave to their fathers. 16 "Behold, I will send for many fishermen," says the LORD, "and they shall fish them; and afterward I will send for many hunters, and they shall hunt them from every mountain and every hill, and out of the holes of the rocks. (NKJV)

Eze 20:34-38 "I will bring you out from the peoples and gather you out of the countries where you are scattered, with a mighty hand, with an outstretched arm, and with fury poured out. 35 "And I will bring you into the wilderness of the peoples, and there I will plead My case with you face to face. 36 "Just as I pleaded My case with your fathers in the wilderness of the land of Egypt, so I will plead My case with you," says the Lord GOD. 37 "I will make you pass under the rod, and I will bring you into the bond of the covenant; 38 "I will purge the rebels from among you, and those who transgress against Me; I will bring them out of the country where they dwell, but they shall not enter the land of Israel. Then you will know that I am the LORD. (NKJV)

The land is to remain holy to the LORD. The rebels and the disobedient will not enter the land! The believing Gentiles who are grafted into Israel will come out from the nations too! How do we know that both Jews and Gentiles will be brought out of the nations? Because when God brought the people out of Egypt, He brought both the Israelites and the mixed multitude.

Ex 12:37-38 Then the children of Israel journeyed from Rameses to Succoth, about six hundred thousand men on foot, besides children. 38 A mixed multitude went up with them also, and flocks and herds-a great deal of livestock. (NKJV)

Zechariah says that the people of the nations will grab the hem of the garment of a Jewish man and demand to go with him!

Zec 8:23 "Thus says the LORD of hosts: 'In those days ten men from every language of the nations shall grasp the sleeve of a Jewish man, saying, "Let us go with you, for we have heard that God is with you."'" (NKJV)

We, also, will be judged before going into the Promised Land. The passage in Hebrews chapter 4 about the Sabbath rest yet to come for followers of Yeshua continues with a warning. He refers to the generation that came out of Egypt as rebellious and cautions us not to allow the same disobedience in our lives.

Heb 4:11-12 Let us therefore be diligent to enter that rest, lest anyone fall according to the same example of disobedience. 12 For the word of God is living and powerful, and sharper than any two-edged sword, piercing even to the division of soul and spirit, and of joints and marrow, and is a discerner of the thoughts and intents of the heart. (NKJV)

7. Jews and Gentiles will take possession of the Promised Land. When the final trump sounds, we will meet Yeshua in the air.

1Th 4:16-17 For the Lord Himself will descend from heaven with a shout, with the voice of an archangel, and with the trumpet of God. And the dead in Christ will rise first. 17 Then we who are alive and remain shall be caught up together with them in the clouds to meet the Lord in the air. And thus we shall always be with the Lord. (NKJV)

Where is He going when we meet Him in the air? Jerusalem, of course!

Zec 14:4-5 And in that day His feet will stand on the Mount of Olives, Which faces Jerusalem on the east. And the Mount of Olives shall be split in two, From east to west, Making a very large valley; Half of the mountain shall move toward the north And half of it toward the south. 5 Then you shall flee through My mountain valley, For the mountain valley shall reach to Azal. Yes, you shall flee As you fled from the earthquake In the days of Uzziah king of Judah. Thus the LORD my God will come, **And all the saints with You.** (NKJV)

Thus, all the unfulfilled cycles come to completion with the return of Yeshua. The children of the houses of Judah and Israel return to the Promised Land, Yeshua returns with all the saints, and we receive our incorruptible bodies! May He come quickly!

Student Notes for Cycles of Prophetic Fulfillment of the Promises to Abram
Genesis 15

A. God promised Abram three different times that the land inhabited by the Canaanites would be his and that his descendant or descendants would inherit that land. (Genesis 12:7, Genesis 13:15, Genesis 15:4-7). In Genesis 15, God expands on the promise telling Abram the sequence of events that would occur as his descendants came to possess the land.

The Jewish concept of time is that it is cyclical.

The promise starts with a seed, a son, to inherit. (Gen. 15:4)

But before the seed can inherit, certain events will occur. God spoke to Abram in a vision. (Gen. 15:13-16, 18)

The progression of events is:

- A seed of your own loins will be your heir.
- Your seed will be strangers in a land not theirs.
- Your seed will be afflicted.
- The nations they serve will be judged.
- They shall come out with great wealth.
- It shall occur at the appointed time.
- Your seed will take possession of the land.

We will look briefly at five cycles of the fulfillment of these events ending with the ultimate fulfillment as Yeshua, the Seed of Abraham, takes possession of the Promised Land and reigns over all the earth.

B. The establishment of the nation of Israel.
　　1. The seed of Abram
　　　　　Jacob: (Gen. 25:20-21, 26)

2. Into Egypt where they were eventually afflicted. (Ex.1:11-14)

3. Judgment

A second seed: Moses (Heb. 11:23)

Plagues against Egypt and deliverance with great wealth (Ex. 3:20-22)

4. The appointed time (Gen. 15:13, Ex. 12:40)

5. Possession of the Promised Land

Another seed: Joshua (Num. 14:30)

God given rest: (Jos. 23:1)

C. The next cycle begins just before the exile of Judah to Babylon.
1. The seed: Josiah (2 Chr. 34:33, 2 Chr. 35:18)

2. Exile to Babylon
Affliction is a bit different however (Jer. 27:12-13, Jer. 25:8-10)

3. Judgment against Babylon (Jer. 25:11-12, Dan. 5:26-28, 30-31)

4. The appointed time (Ezr. 1:7-11, Ezr. 2:64-67)

Great wealth?

5. Retaking the Promised Land (Ezr. 6:13-15)

Retaking the Land? (Jer. 30:8-10)

D. The Promised Seed
1. Yeshua's birth: (Mat. 1:20-21, Dan. 9:24-26)

2. Yeshua was a stranger in His own land. (John 1:10-11, Php. 2:6-7)

3. Yeshua was mistreated and rejected. (Isa. 53:3-5)

4. Judgment on Israel (Mat. 23:34-35)

5. Delivered from the grave (Mat. 16:21, Rev. 1:18)

6. Restored to the Father's side (Heb. 10:12-14)

E. Spiritual fulfillment

1. The Seed: Rebirth (1Pet. 1:20-23)

2. Strangers in the world (1Pet. 2:11, Heb. 11:13-16)

3. Persecution and mistreatment (2Tim. 3:12)

4. Individuals will be judged. (Mat. 16:26-27, Rom. 2:16, Rev. 6:10)

5. The wealth of God's grace (Eph. 1:7-8, Heb. 4:8-10, 1John 3:2)

F. The promised King

1. Yeshua's birth: (Mat. 2:2, Mic. 5:2, Acts. 21:20)

2. Exiled from Jerusalem

3. Persecution of God's people

4. Judgment (Rev. 18:3-5)

5. This will occur at the appointed time.

Cleansing the Promised Land (Isa. 52:1, Zec. 14:20-21)

6. Delivered from the nations with a catch (Jer. 16:15-16, Eze. 20:34-38)

The Gentiles too? (Ex. 12:37-38, Zec. 8:23, Heb. 4:11-12)

7. We will take possession of the Promised Land. (1The. 4:16-17, Zec. 14:4-5)

Use this chart to summarize the five cycles of prophetic fulfillment in the promise to Abram. How do all cycles finish together when Yeshua returns?

Prophecy	In Egypt--	To Babylon	Yeshua	Spiritual rebirth	Yeshua again
A seed of Your own loins					
A stranger in a foreign land					
Afflicted					
The nations they serve will be judged					
They will come out with great wealth					
At the appointed time					
Take possession of the land					

Discussion questions for Cycles of Prophetic Fulfillment

1. Abram himself experienced a "mini" fulfillment of this same progression of events with himself as the promised seed. Read Genesis 12:10-13:4. Describe the fulfillment of the seven parts of the promise.

2. When the sins of Sodom came to God's attention, what happened (Gen. 19)? How is this like the final judgment of God?

3. Zechariah 14:21 says there will no longer be a Canaanite or merchant in Jerusalem. Who is the chief mourner when Babylon falls (Rev. 18:11-20)? Who did Yeshua drive out of the temple twice at Passover (John 2:13-16, Mark 11:15-17)?

4. Once vessels were used for a holy purpose, they themselves became holy to the LORD and had special rules about how they could then be used. A bronze pot could be washed and then used again for common purposes but an earthen pot had to be broken (Lev 11:33). Zechariah 14:20-21 says that every pot in Jerusalem shall be "holiness to the LORD." Discuss what this means about the city of Jerusalem in the millennial reign.

5. Those who are rebellious against God will not be allowed into the Promised Land (Eze. 20:34-38). Read Hebrews 3:7-4:13. What does the writer of Hebrews say about those who rebel?

6. Today, the nations of the world have joined to afflict Israel. Read Joel 3. What will God do to the nations that afflict Israel?

The End Is Declared From the Beginning

Isaiah writes that God declares His entire plan from the beginning of creation. Not only that it is there but that He actually declares it.

> Is 46:10 Declaring the end from the beginning, And from ancient times things that are not yet done, Saying, 'My counsel shall stand, And I will do all My pleasure,' (NKJV)

The apostle John records that everything was created through Messiah and for the sake of Messiah.

> Joh 1:1-3 In the beginning was the Word, and the Word was with God, and the Word was God. 2 He was in the beginning with God. 3 All things were made through Him, and without Him nothing was made that was made. (NKJV)

Messiah and the entire redemption plan, then, must be in the very first verse in the Bible. As we examine the verse as a whole and each word individually, we see a powerful revelation of God's plan.

> Ge 1:1 In the beginning God created the heavens and the earth.

There are seven words in Genesis 1:1 in the original Hebrew which is read right to left. Seven is the number of spiritual completion. The act of creation took six days and on the seventh day God rested. So, these seven words together show how God will bring about spiritual completion.

The First Word

7	6	5	4	3	2	1
הארץ	ואת	השמים	את	אלהים	ברא	בראשית
the earth	and	the heavens	?	God	created	**in the beginning**

As we examine the first word, we notice that the first letter of the word, in fact the first letter in the whole Bible, the ב (beyt) is enlarged. This is one of those "jots and tittles" of the Bible that Yeshua said would not pass away until the new heavens and earth are created.

> Mat 5:18 "For assuredly, I say to you, till heaven and earth pass away, one jot or one tittle will by no means pass from the law (Torah) till all is fulfilled. (NKJV)

A jot or tittle is an unusual spelling, a break in the text, markings under, above or within a letter or letters, or letters written in unusual ways. Each of these jots and tittles tells us more about the passage in which it occurs. What does the enlarged ב tell us about creation?

In the original Hebrew, each letter was a pictograph. The ב was a house or tent; it represented a house, household or family. As a concept, it represents the idea of "into" or "inclusion." God started His entire body of scripture with this enlarged letter ב. He is showing us that His house and family are the reason for creation. He wants to include us in His family. If we continue to the second letter, we get בר (bar) which is one of the words for son. God wants to build a house or family for His son. He wants a relationship with us and He cares about the relationships we have with each other. Yeshua told us that the two greatest commandments are about the relationships we have with God and with each other.

> Mat 22:37-39 37 Jesus said to him," 'You shall love the LORD your God with all your heart, with all your soul, and with all your mind.' 38 "This is the first and great commandment. 39 "And the second is like it: 'You shall love your neighbor as yourself.' (NKJV)

So, this first verse in Genesis tells us how God is going to bring us into His house and His family! The End is declared from the beginning and we haven't even gotten to the whole first word.

The first word is pronounced "Bre'sheet" in Hebrew. It is from the word ראשית (re'shiyth) with an added ב (beyt) at the beginning of the word. This letter adds the meaning "in" or "**through**," "because of," "**with thought of**." The rest of the word is ראשית (re'shiyth Strong's #7225) which means: the first, in place, time, order or rank, (specifically a firstfruit): beginning, chief(-est), **first fruits, foremost**. Thus, the word is translated "In the beginning." But, the word can also be translated two other ways. In Hebrew thought, each of these translations adds depth of meaning to the word.

So we can translate Gen 1:1 as "In the beginning, with thought of the Firstfruits, through the Foremost, God created the heavens and the earth." This teaches us that God created the heavens and the earth with "Re'sheet" or with the purpose of "Re'sheet."

So who is the Re'sheet or First Fruits of creation? He is Messiah as it says in 1 Corinthians:

> 1Co 15:20 But now Christ is risen from the dead, and has become the firstfruits of those who have fallen asleep. (NKJV)

When we add in the first letter bet, ב, which means the house, to re'sheet, the entire first word can be seen as the "house of the Firstfruits." So God's creation is the "house" of Messiah, His ultimate dwelling place and through Him it was made.

> Heb 1:1 God, who at various times and in various ways spoke in time past to the fathers by the prophets, 2 has in these last days spoken to us by His Son, whom He has appointed heir of all things, through whom also He made the worlds; (NKJV)

He is heir of all created things, thus creation is the house of Firstfruits, which was created through him, the Foremost.

The Second Word

7	6	5	4	3	2	1
הארץ	ואת	השמים	את	אלהים	ברא	בראשית
the earth	and	the heavens	?	God	**created**	in the beginning

The second word in Genesis 1:1 is pronounced "bara" in Hebrew. It implies a direct hand, to physically do.

Create: #1254. ברא bara', baw-raw' a primitive root; meaning to create. To cut down, as in a tree, to feed, create (creator), dispatch, do, make (fat).

There are two word pictures in bara. The first one reinforces that everything was created through Yeshua. The second one introduces the "strong man."

Hebrew word Picture: Hebrew is read right to left.

Created: ברא

Bet reysch: בר "Bar" means "son."

Aleph: א First letter in many of the words for God including Elohim, the name of God in the creation.

Create: The Son of God is in creation.

Hebrew word Picture: Hebrew is read right to left.

Created: ברא

Bet: ב House

Resh: ב Head, highest, person

Aleph: א Strength, first, leader

Create: The strong man of the house is in creation.

Proverbs tell us who this strong man from within the house is.

> Pr 30:4 Who has gone up to Heaven and has come down? Who has gathered the wind in His fists? Who has bound the waters in His garments? Who has established all the ends of the earth? What is His name, and what is His Son's name? Surely you know. (MKJV)

Bara, the second word of Genesis 1:1, is a picture of Messiah as the "Son of God, the strong man within the house" who is the hand of God who "gathers the wind in His fists" and binds the "waters in His garments."

The Third Word

7	6	5	4	3	2	1
האָרץ	ואת	השמים	את	אלהים	ברא	בראשית
the earth	and	the heavens	?	**God**	created	in the beginning

The third word in Genesis 1:1 is one of the names of God used throughout the Torah, Elohim.

#430. אלהים 'elohiym, el-o-heem' plural of 433; gods in the ordinary sense; but specifically used of the supreme God; occasionally applied by way of deference to magistrates; and sometimes as a superlative:--angels, X exceeding, God (gods)(-dess, -ly), X (very) great, judges, X mighty.

According to the Sages, Elohim denotes God in His Attribute of Justice, as Ruler, Lawgiver, and Judge of the world. This name is used exclusively in the creation account until the sixth day. God as Jah-weh is first seen in the Bible when He creates man.

The ancient Hebrew gives a fascinating word picture of the name Elohim.

Elohim: אלהים

Aleph: א - 𐤀   Strength, Leader, First, Ox, Bull

Lamed: ל - 𐤋   Control, Authority, Goad

Hey: ה - 𐤄   To Reveal, Behold

Yood: י - 𐤉   To make, a deed, Hand

Mem: ם - 𐤌   Liquid, Massive, Chaos, Water

Elohim: The First Authority: Behold His Hand is on the Water

The creation begins with the spirit of God moving on the waters.

> Ge 1:2 And the earth was without form and empty. And darkness was on the face of the deep. And the Spirit of God moved on the face of the waters. (MKJV)

In Jerusalem, the pool of Bethesda which means house of kindness or mercy, provided healing when the waters were stirred.

> Joh 5:2-4 Now there is in Jerusalem by the Sheep Gate a pool, which is called in Hebrew, Bethesda, having five porches. 3 In these lay a great multitude of sick people, blind, lame, paralyzed, waiting for the moving of the water. 4 For an angel went down at a certain time into the pool and stirred up the water; then whoever stepped in first, after the stirring of the water, was made well of whatever disease he had. (NKJV)

Yeshua showed Himself the master of the waters when He calmed the storm and the waves of the Sea of Galilee.

> Lu 8:22-25 Now it happened, on a certain day, that He got into a boat with His disciples. And He said to them, "Let us cross over to the other side of the lake." And they launched out. 23 But as they sailed He fell asleep. And a windstorm came down on the lake, and they were filling with water, and were in jeopardy. 24 And they came to Him and awoke Him, saying, "Master, Master, we are perishing!" Then He arose and rebuked the wind and the raging of the water. And they ceased, and there was a calm. 25 But He said to them, "Where is your faith?" And they were afraid, and marveled, saying to one another, "Who can this be? For He commands even the winds and water, and they obey Him!" (NKJV)

We see that Yeshua's hand calmed the water. He has authority over creation. Again, we see that through Him and with the thought of Him God created the heavens and the earth.

Yeshua was with his disciples after his resurrection. He testified that He was given all authority in Heaven and in earth.

> Mt 28:16-19 And the eleven disciples went into Galilee, to the mountain where Jesus had appointed them. 17 And when they saw Him, they worshiped Him. But some doubted. 18 And Jesus came and spoke to them, saying, All authority is given to Me in Heaven and in earth. 19 Therefore go and teach all nations, baptizing them in the name of the Father and of the Son and of the Holy Spirit. (MKJV)

God gave Yeshua authority and His hand is on the water.

The Fourth Word

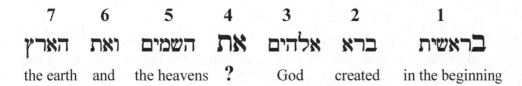

7	6	5	4	3	2	1
הארץ	ואת	השמים	את	אלהים	ברא	בראשית
the earth	and	the heavens	?	God	created	in the beginning

Notice that the fourth word is not translated into English. In fact, it is rarely ever translated because there is no real equivalent in English. Strong's Dictionary and Concordance defines it as follows:

853. אֵת 'eth. In the demonstrative sense of entity; properly, self (but generally used to point out more definitely the object of a verb or preposition, even or namely):--(as such unrepresented in English).

It is a word that emphasizes the object of the verb. In this case, the verb is "created" and the object is the heavens and the earth. The composition of the word, אֵת, 'eth, consists of the first and last letters of the Hebrew alphabet the א Aleph and the ת Tav and is generally taken to represent all the letters of the Hebrew alphabet. As such, אֵת represents all the words God spoke as He created the heavens and the earth. According to the Jewish Sages, the use of the word אֵת in this verse emphasizes that the entire creation was created at this time by the hand of God. We see again the emphasis on the heavens and the earth, the objects of the verb "created."

As we return to the Gospel of John chapter 1 verses 1-3, we see this point emphasized especially in the Modern King James Version.

> Joh 1:1 In the beginning was the Word, and the Word was with God, and the Word was God. 2 He was in the beginning with God. 3 All things came into being through Him, and **without Him not even one thing came into being that has come into being.** (MKJV)

Again we are talking about the entirety of creation. Yeshua identifies Himself with the אֵת in the Revelation to John.

> Re 1:8 "I am the Alpha and the Omega, the Beginning and the End," says the Lord, "who is and who was and who is to come, the Almighty." (NKJV)

The Alpha and Omega are the first and last letters of the Greek alphabet. They are equivalent to the Aleph and Tav. So אֵת is the Messiah, the Living Word, who was there from the beginning and through Him all things were made!

Remember, there are seven Hebrew words in Genesis 1:1. The placement of אֵת as the fourth word places Messiah as the "centerpiece" of creation, the Aleph and the Tav, the beginning and the end! The seven words of Genesis 1:1 are reflected in the seven lamps of the Menorah that lit the Tabernacle of God. The middle lamp of the Menorah was always kept lit.

> Le 24:1-3 Then the LORD spoke to Moses, saying: 2 "Command the children of Israel that they bring to you pure oil of pressed olives for the light, to make the lamps burn continually. 3 "Outside the veil of the Testimony, in the tabernacle of meeting, Aaron shall be in charge of it from evening until morning before the LORD continually; it shall be a statute forever in your generations. (NKJV)

The Jewish Encyclopedia calls this lamp the western Lamp because it was next to the branches on the east side. It was refilled in the evening and was used to light the other lamps. In 1 Samuel it is referred to as the "lamp of God." In Samuel's conversation with Eli, the time is pinpointed by referring to the lamp of God.

> 1Sa 3:2-3 And it came to pass at that time, while Eli was lying down in his place, and when his eyes had begun to grow so dim that he could not see, 3 and before the lamp of God went out in the tabernacle of the LORD where the ark of God was, and while Samuel was lying down, (NKJV)

It is the lamp of God in the Tabernacle of God. Morning had not yet come; the lamp was still lit.

The sun was created on the fourth day to bring light to the world and to separate light from the darkness.

> Ge 1:16-19 Then God made two great lights: the greater light to rule the day, and the lesser light to rule the night. He made the stars also. 17 God set them in the firmament of the heavens to give light on the earth, 18 and to rule over the day and over the night, and to divide the light from the darkness. And God saw that it was good. 19 So the evening and the morning were the fourth day. (NKJV)

Yeshua is the light of the world shining into the darkness. When the New heavens and the new earth are created, there will be no need for the sun because Yeshua is the light.

> Joh 1:4-9 In Him was life, and the life was the light of men. 5 And the light shines in the darkness, and the darkness did not comprehend it. 6 There was a man sent from God, whose name was John. 7 This man came for a witness, to bear witness of the Light, that all through him might believe. 8 He was not that Light, but was sent to bear witness of that Light. 9 That was the true Light which gives light to every man coming into the world. (NKJV)

Again, we have that fourth lamp, the lamp of God which is Yeshua. And he is the aleph-tav, את, the fourth word.

> Re 21:23 The city had no need of the sun or of the moon to shine in it, for the glory of God illuminated it. The Lamb is its light. (NKJV)

In the new creation, the light from Yeshua is so bright that the light of the sun and moon are not needed.

The Fifth Word

7	6	5	4	3	2	1
האָרץ	ואת	השמים	את	אלהים	ברא	בראשית
the earth	and	**the heavens**	?	God	created	in the beginning

The fifth word in Genesis 1:1 is ha'shamayim השמים and means the heavens. The word is composed of the letter hey ה meaning "the" and shamayim שמים meaning "heavens."

Heavens: #8064. שמים shamayim, shaw-mah'-yim. Dual of an unused singular shameh {shaw-meh'}; from an unused root meaning to be lofty; the sky (as aloft; the dual perhaps alluding to the visible arch in which the clouds move, as well as to the higher ether where the celestial bodies revolve):--air, X astrologer, **heaven(-s).**

The word picture of ha'shamayim illustrates the deeper Hebrew meaning of the word which is an illustration of creation.

Hebrew word picture:

The Heavens: השמים

Hey: ה 𐤄 to reveal, behold, "the" (as a prefix), window or lattice.

Sheen: ש ய Teeth, to consume or destroy. An abv. For Almighty God, El Shaddai.

Mem: מ = ∿ Water, massive, chaos

Yood: י = ﹀ Hand, to deed or to make

Mem: ם = ∿ Water, massive, chaos

The Heavens: "Behold, the Almighty God whose hand divides the waters."

This is almost identical to the word picture for Elohim, **The First Authority: Behold His Hand is on the water.** Not only is His hand on the water, it divides the water. The space between the waters is called the heavens.

> Ge 1:6-8 And God said, Let there be a firmament in the midst of the waters, and let it divide the waters from the waters. 7 And God made the firmament, and divided the waters which were under the firmament from the waters which were above the firmament: and it was so. 8 And God called the firmament **Heaven (השמים shamayim).** And the evening and the morning were the second day. (KJV)

Here we see that the hand of God divides the waters above and below the firmament as well as creating the firmament which is called Heaven, **shamayim.** The Hebrew word for firmament is רקיע raqiya.

Firmament: #7549. רקיע raqiya`, raw-kee'-ah. From #7554; properly, **an expanse, i.e. the firmament** or (apparently) visible arch of the sky:--firmament.

According to the sages, this expanse or raqiya includes the entire created universe.

> Ps. 33:6, "By the word of the LORD the heavens were made, And all the host of them by the breath of His mouth." (NKJV)

This 5th word, shamayim, connects us to the first word, בראשית Bre'sheet, which means "In the beginning, for the sake of the Firstfruits, through the Foremost" through the idea of the entire created universe. According to Paul, all of creation was created for Him and by Him.

> Col 1:16-17 For by Him all things were created that are in heaven and that are on earth, visible and invisible, whether thrones or dominions or principalities or powers. All things were created through Him and for Him. 17 And He is before all things, and in Him all things consist. (NKJV)

The word Shamiyim shows a picture of Messiah, the Hand that divided the waters and created the heavens.

The Sixth Word

7	6	5	4	3	2	1
האָרץ	וֵאת	השמים	אֵת	אלהים	ברא	בראשית
the earth	**and**	the heavens	?	God	created	in the beginning

This 6th word is the Hebrew word 'eth (ayth). It is normally translated as "and" but sometimes as "also." It really is not a single word at all but a compound word. In Hebrew, the word "and" is almost always indicated by adding a vav to the beginning of a word. It is like a prefix in English. We see this a lot in the Hebrew language. We saw it in the first word bre'sheet with the Bet ב added in front of re'sheet to form the prefix "in." So "and" is rarely written as a separate word. In this 6th word of Genesis 1:1, we have the ו (vav) connected to the את (aleph tav) connecting us to the fourth word, את, the Messiah which we saw is the "beginning and the end."

So what happens with the sixth word by adding a vav to the את aleph tav? The letter vav is the 6th letter in the Hebrew alphabet and means "to secure." In the ancient picture language, it was depicted as a nail or wooden peg. With the vav meaning to secure or connect, we see that Messiah, the את, is in the midst of creation, in the middle of Heaven *and* Earth. Messiah is the connecting force between man (earth) and God (heaven). He literally is the connection between man and God. To emphasize this further, this is the first appearance of the letter vav in the Torah; it is the 22nd letter of the first verse. Since there are 22 letters in the Hebrew alphabet, this points to all the letters of the alphabet and, thus, by implication connecting all of creation.

He is also the connection between the physical and the spiritual.

> Joh 1:14 And the Word became flesh and dwelt among us, and we beheld His glory, the glory as of the only begotten of the Father, full of grace and truth. (NKJV)

So, He became flesh; He was spiritual and He became physical for us. When the new heavens and the new earth are created, the New Jerusalem connects the heaven and earth.

> Re 21:10-11 And he carried me away in the Spirit to a great and high mountain, and showed me the great city, the holy Jerusalem, descending out of heaven from God, 11 having the glory of God. Her light was like a most precious stone, like a jasper stone, clear as crystal. (NKJV)

The holy Jerusalem comes down out of heaven to earth.

The Seventh Word

7	6	5	4	3	2	1
הארץ	ואת	השמים	את	אלהים	ברא	בראשית
the earth	and	the heavens	?	God	created	in the beginning

The seventh word ties it all together. The seventh word in Genesis is הארץ ha'eretz, which is translated as "the Earth." The root word is ארץ 'erets, or just "earth."

Earth: #776. ארץ 'erets, eh'-rets. From an unused root probably meaning **to be firm; the earth** (at large, or partitively a land):--X common, country, earth, field, ground, land, way, + wilderness, world.

The waters are collected in one place and the dry land which appears is called earth.

> Genesis 1:9-10 And God said, Let the waters under the heavens be gathered together to one place, and let the dry land appear; and it was so. 10 And God called the dry land, Earth. And He called the gathering together of the waters, Seas. And God saw that it was good. (MKJV)

The dry land appears on the third day of creation. It produces the first fruits of creation.

> Ge 1:11-13 Then God said, "Let the earth bring forth grass, the herb that yields seed, and the fruit tree that yields fruit according to its kind, whose seed is in itself,

on the earth"; and it was so. 12 And the earth brought forth grass, the herb that yields seed according to its kind, and the tree that yields fruit, whose seed is in itself according to its kind. And God saw that it was good. 13 So the evening and the morning were the third day. (NKJV)

Yeshua rose from the dead on the third day and is the firstfruits of creation taking us back to the first word, the House of firstfruits and 1 Corinthians 15:20, "But now Christ is risen from the dead, and has become the firstfruits of those who have fallen asleep."

The Garden of Eden was planted on the earth. Man dwelt in the garden with God.

Ge 3:8 And they heard the sound of the LORD God walking in the garden in the cool of the day, and Adam and his wife hid themselves from the presence of the LORD God among the trees of the garden. (NKJV)

God will again dwell with man on the New Earth. The earth will continually produce fruit taking us back to the House of firstfruits once again.

Re 21:3 And I heard a loud voice from heaven saying, "Behold, the tabernacle of God is with men, and He will dwell with them, and they shall be His people. God Himself will be with them and be their God. (NKJV)

The Tabernacle of God will be here on the new earth with man.

Re 22:2-3 In the middle of its street, and on either side of the river, was the tree of life, which bore twelve fruits, each tree yielding its fruit every month. The leaves of the tree were for the healing of the nations. 3 And there shall be no more curse, but the throne of God and of the Lamb shall be in it, and His servants shall serve Him. (NKJV)

The fruit will be produced every month.

God collected the waters in one place and dry land appeared; this calls to mind the fifth word ha'shamayim. God created the heavens by separating the waters and calling the expanse between the waters the heavens, ha'shamayim. As we look at places where God separated water and dry ground appeared, we see two incidents, one in which God separated the water and one in which God gathered the water. We will see in these instances two allegories of Messiah's coming.

The first instance is when God separated the waters of the Red Sea and dry land appeared.

Exodus 14:21-22 Then Moses stretched out his hand over the sea; and the LORD caused the sea to go back by a strong east wind all that night, and made the sea into dry land, and the waters were divided. 22 So the children of Israel went into the midst of the sea on the dry ground, and the waters were a wall to them on their right hand and on their left. (NKJV)

Moses, who is a type of Messiah, stretches his hand over the water and the LORD divides the waters. The dry land appears and the Israelites cross on dry ground out of the slavery of Egypt redeemed by the blood of the Passover lamb. They are the first of the redeemed of the LORD. We also pass through the sea from slavery to sin into freedom in Yeshua.

The generation who came out of Egypt did not believe God could bring them into the Promised Land and thus He allowed them to die in the wilderness instead of entering His Land, His rest. Only two people numbered among the fighting men of that generation entered into the Promised Land.

> Nu 14:30 'Except for Caleb the son of Jephunneh and Joshua the son of Nun, you shall by no means enter the land which I swore I would make you dwell in. (NKJV)

> Heb 3:10-11 Therefore I was angry with that generation, And said, 'They always go astray in their heart, And they have not known My ways.' 11 So I swore in My wrath, 'They shall not enter My rest.'" (NKJV)

The Israelites also crossed the Jordan River on dry ground as they entered the Promised Land. The water was "gathered together in one place" allowing the Israelites to cross on dry land.

> Jos 3:13 "And it shall come to pass, as soon as the soles of the feet of the priests who bear the ark of the LORD, the Lord of all the earth, shall rest in the waters of the Jordan, that the waters of the Jordan shall be cut off, the waters that come down from upstream, and they shall stand as a heap." (NKJV)

The Promised Land is symbolic of entering God's rest; the ultimate redemption of man and the restoration of the Garden of Eden. Ha'eretz is the seventh word in Genesis 1:1 and God rested on the seventh day.

One of the meanings of eretz is to be firm. As the Israelites crossed into the Promised Land, the Ark of God carried by the priests stood firm, eretz, in the middle of the river.

> Jos 3:17 Then the priests who bore the ark of the covenant of the LORD **stood firm on dry ground** in the midst of the Jordan; and all Israel crossed over on dry ground, until all the people had crossed completely over the Jordan. (NKJV)

Hebrews chapter 4 talks about entering God's rest exhorting believers not to fall to unbelief and disobedience as did the generation of the Exodus.

> Heb 4:11 Let us therefore be diligent to enter that rest, lest anyone fall according to the same example of disobedience. (NKJV)

Instead we are encouraged to trust in our High Priest who has passed through the heavens, ha'shamayim, ahead of us. This takes us back again to that fifth word!

Heb 4:14 Seeing then that we have a great High Priest who has passed through the heavens, Jesus the Son of God, let us hold fast our confession. (NKJV)

That Yeshua passed through the heavens takes us back to the fifth word, ha'shamayim, the heavens or the firmament between the waters. The priests stood firm on the dry ground between the waters until everyone had passed through the waters. Yeshua is there on dry ground as we pass through the waters.

Isa 43:2 When you pass through the waters, I will be with you; And through the rivers, they shall not overflow you. When you walk through the fire, you shall not be burned, Nor shall the flame scorch you. (NKJV)

This once again shows that Yeshua links heaven and earth, and spiritual to physical just as the New Jerusalem comes down out of heaven to the earth linking the New Heaven and the New Earth. John relates that when the new earth is created, there will be no more sea. All will be firm earth, eretz.

Re 21:1-2 Now I saw a new heaven and a new earth, for the first heaven and the first earth had passed away. Also there was no more sea. 2 Then I, John, saw the holy city, New Jerusalem, coming down out of heaven from God, prepared as a bride adorned for her husband. (NKJV)

Finally, the word picture of ha'eretz, הארץ, shows that the end is declared from the beginning. We started looking at "the earth," ha'eretz, as the firstfruits of creation. The word picture shows ha'eretz as the final harvest.

> Hebrew word picture
> The earth: הארץ
> Hey: ה = ▥ = behold, window, "the" (as a prefix), lattice
> Aleph: א = 𐤀 = ox, bull, strength, leader
> Resh: ר = 𐤓 = a head, person, highest
> Tsadik: ץ = 𐤑 = fish hook, harvest, need
>
> The earth: Behold the strong man's harvest.

The strong man is the one within the house, the one who creates the heavens and the earth. This goes back to the word picture of the second word create: the strong man of the house is in creation, and He is the one who harvests the earth. Yeshua says the harvest is the end of the age.

Mat 13:36-43 Then he left the crowd and went into the house. His disciples came to him and said, "Explain to us the parable of the weeds in the field." 37 He answered, "The one who sowed the good seed is the Son of Man. 38 The field is the world, and the good seed stands for the sons of the kingdom. The weeds are the sons of the evil one, 39 and the enemy who sows them is the devil. The harvest is the end of the age, and the harvesters are angels. 40 "As the weeds are pulled up and burned in the fire, so it will be at the end of the age. 41 The Son of Man will send out his angels, and they will weed out of his kingdom everything that causes sin and all who do evil. 42 They will throw them into the fiery furnace, where there will be weeping and gnashing of teeth. 43 Then the righteous will shine like the sun in the kingdom of their Father. He who has ears, let him hear. (NIV)

Re 14:14-16 Then I looked, and behold, a white cloud, and on the cloud sat One like the Son of Man, having on His head a golden crown, and in His hand a sharp sickle. 15 And another angel came out of the temple, crying with a loud voice to Him who sat on the cloud, "Thrust in Your sickle and reap, for the time has come for You to reap, for the harvest of the earth is ripe." 16 So He who sat on the cloud thrust in His sickle on the earth, and the earth was reaped. (NKJV)

Yeshua, who was central to creation, is now the one who reaps the earth. This takes us back once again to the first word bre'sheet, the House of Firstfruits.

1 Co 15:22-23 For as in Adam all die, even so in Christ all shall be made alive. 23 But each one in his own order: Christ the firstfruits, afterward those who are Christ's at His coming. (NKJV)

And in the Book of Revelation, Yeshua spoke to John.

Re 21:6-7 And He said to me, "It is done! I am the Alpha and the Omega, the Beginning and the End. I will give of the fountain of the water of life freely to him who thirsts. 7 "He who overcomes shall inherit all things, and I will be his God and he shall be My son. (NKJV)

So you see, the end is declared from the beginning. We become the children of God included in His family taking us back to the beginning with the enlarged ב. The entire redemption story is contained in just the seven words of Genesis 1:1, "In the beginning God created the heavens and the earth."

The cycle is complete with God resting on the seventh day. But cycles in the Bible are always repeating. For instance eight is the number of new beginnings; it begins a new cycle. What is the eighth word in Genesis 1? V'ha'eretz והארץ which means "and the earth." And so we continue with a New Earth.

Isa 65:17-18 "For behold, I create new heavens and a new earth; And the former shall not be remembered or come to mind. 18 But be glad and rejoice forever in what I create; For behold, I create Jerusalem as a rejoicing, And her people a joy. (NKJV)

Student Notes: The End Is Declared From the Beginning

Isa 46:10 Declaring the end from the beginning, And from ancient times things that are not yet done, Saying, 'My counsel shall stand, And I will do all My pleasure,' (NKJV)

Everything was created through Messiah and for the sake of Messiah, as it is written in the Gospel of John:

Joh 1:1-3 In the beginning was the Word, and the Word was with God, and the Word was God. 2 He was in the beginning with God. 3 All things were made through Him, and without Him nothing was made that was made. (NKJV)

Messiah is in each word of the very first verse in the Bible.

Ge 1:1 In the beginning God created the heavens and the earth.

There are seven words in Genesis 1:1 in the original Hebrew which is read right to left. Seven is the number of spiritual completion. The act of creation took six days and on the seventh day God rested.

The First Word

7	6	5	4	3	2	1
האָרץ	ואת	הַשמים	אֵת	אֱלהִים	בּרא	בּראשית
the earth	and	the heavens	?	God	created	**in the beginning**

The first letter ב, bet: house, family, household, into. (Mat. 5:18, Mat. 22:37-39)

The first word is pronounced in Hebrew "Bre'sheet." It is from the word ראשית (re'shiyth) with an added ב (beyt) at the beginning of the word.

Beginning: #7225 ראשית (re'shiyth) means: the first, in place, time, order or rank, (specifically a firstfruit): beginning, chief(-est), first fruits, foremost.

So who is the Re'sheet or First Fruits of creation? (1Cor. 15:20, Heb. 1:1-2)

The Second Word

7	6	5	4	3	2	1
האָרץ	ואת	השמים	את	אלהים	ברא	בראשית
the earth	and	the heavens	?	God	**created**	in the beginning

Create: #1254. ברא bara', baw-raw' a primitive root; meaning to create. To cut down, as in a tree, to feed, create (creator), dispatch, do, make (fat). It implies a direct hand, to physically do.

Hebrew word Picture: Hebrew is read right to left.

Created: ברא

Bet reysch: בר "Bar" means "son."

Aleph: א First letter in one of the words for God, Elohim.

Create: The Son of God is in creation.

Hebrew word Picture: Hebrew is read right to left.

Created: ברא

Bet: ב ◫ House

Resh: ב ঀ Head, highest, person

Aleph: א 𐤀 Strength, first, leader

Created: the strong man of the house is in creation.

Who is this strong man from within the house? (Pro. 30:4)

The Third Word

7	6	5	4	3	2	1
הארץ	ואת	השמים	את	אלהים ברא		בראשית
the earth	and	the heavens	?	**God** created		in the beginning

God: #430. אלהים 'elohiym, el-o-heem' plural of 433; gods in the ordinary sense; but specifically used of the supreme God; occasionally applied by way of deference to magistrates; and sometimes as a superlative:--angels, X exceeding, God (gods)(-dess, -ly), X (very) great, judges, X mighty.

#433. אליה 'elowahh, el-o'-ah, a deity or the Deity:--God, god. See 430.

Elohim: אלהים

Aleph: א - 𐤀   Strength, Leader, First, Ox, Bull
Lamed: ל - 𐤋   Control, Authority, Goad
Hey: ה - 𐤄   To Reveal, Behold
Yood: י - 𐤉   To Add, To Secure, Hand
Mem: ם - 𐤌   Liquid, Massive, Chaos, Water

Elohim: The First Authority: Behold His Hand is on the Water

Creation begins: (Gen. 1:2)

Stirring the waters: (John 5:2-4)

Calming the waters: (Lu. 8:22-25)

Authority: (Mat. 28:16-19)

The Fourth Word

7	6	5	4	3	2	1
האָרץ	ואת	השמים	את	אלהים	ברא	בראשית
the earth	and	the heavens	?	God	created	in the beginning

853. את 'eth. In the demonstrative sense of entity; properly, self (but generally used to point out more definitely the object of a verb or preposition, even or namely):--(as such unrepresented in English).

The verb: _____

The object: _____

The Gospel of John in chapter 1 verse 1-3 also emphasizes this point.

> Joh 1:1 In the beginning was the Word, and the Word was with God, and the Word was God. 2 He was in the beginning with God. 3 All things came into being through Him, and **without Him not even one thing came into being that has come into being.** (MKJV)

The את (Rev. 1:8)

The Menorah (Lev. 24:1-3)

The western Lamp (1Sam. 3:2-3)

The Light: (Gen. 1:16-19, John 1:4-9, Rev. 21:23)

The Fifth Word

7	6	5	4	3	2	1
הארץ	ואת	**השמים**	את	אלהים	ברא	בראשית
the earth	and	**the heavens**	?	God	created	in the beginning

#8064. שמים shamayim, shaw-mah'-yim. Dual of an unused singular shameh {shaw-meh'}; from an unused root meaning to be lofty; the sky (as aloft; the dual perhaps alluding to the visible arch in which the clouds move, as well as to the higher ether where the celestial bodies revolve):--air, X astrologer, **heaven(-s).**

> Hebrew word picture:
> The Heavens: השמים
> Hey: ה to reveal, behold, "the" (as a prefix), window or lattice.
> Sheen: ש Teeth, to consume or destroy. An abv. For Almighty God, El Shaddai.
> Mem: מ = Water, massive, chaos
> Yood: י = Hand, a deed or to make
> Mem: ם = Water, massive, chaos
>
> The Heavens: "Behold, the Almighty God whose hand divides the waters."

The heavens (Gen. 1:6-8, Ps. 33:6, Col. 1:16-17)

Firmament: #7549. רקיע raqiya`, raw-kee'-ah. From #7554; properly, **an expanse, i.e. the firmament** or (apparently) visible arch of the sky:--firmament.

The Sixth Word

7	6	5	4	3	2	1
האָרץ	וְאֵת	הַשָּׁמַיִם אֵת		אֱלֹהִים בָּרָא		בְּרֵאשִׁית
the earth	**and**	the heavens ?		God created		in the beginning

And : 'eth (ayth) and, also
ו (vav): And

את (aleph tav):

He is also the connection between the physical and the spiritual. (John 1:14)

The new heavens and the new earth (Rev. 21:10-11)

The Seventh Word

7	6	5	4	3	2	1
האָרץ	וְאֵת	הַשָּׁמַיִם אֵת		אֱלֹהִים בָּרָא		בְּרֵאשִׁית
the earth	and	the heavens ?		God created		in the beginning

Earth: #776. ארץ 'erets, eh'-rets. From an unused root probably meaning to be firm; the earth (at large, or partitively a land):--X common, country, earth, field, ground, land, way, + wilderness, world.

The waters are collected in one place. (Gen. 1:9-10)

The third day of creation (Gen. 1:11-13)

The Garden of Eden (Gen. 3:8, Rev. 21:3, Rev. 22:2-3)

God separated the waters of the Red Sea and dry land appeared. (Ex. 14:21-22)

They crossed the Jordan River on dry ground as they entered the Promised Land. (Num. 14:30, Heb. 3:10-11, Jos. 3:13, 17)

We are to enter God's rest. (Heb. 4:11, 14)

Yeshua passed through the heavens. (Isa. 43:2)

There will be no more sea. (Rev. 21:1-2)

Hebrew word picture

The earth: הארץ

Hey: ה = ⊞ = behold, window, "the" (as a prefix), lattice

Aleph: א = 𐤀 = ox, bull, strength, leader

Resh: ר = 𐤓 = a head, person, highest

Tsadik: ץ = 𐤑 = fish hook, harvest, need

The earth: Behold the strong man's harvest.

The harvest is the end of the age. (Mat. 13:36-43, Rev. 14:14-16)

Back to the beginning (1Cor. 15:22-23, Rev. 21:6-7)

New beginnings: What is the eighth word in Genesis 1?

V'ha'eretz והארץ means "and the earth." And so we continue with a New Earth.

> Isa 65:17-18 "For behold, I create new heavens and a new earth; And the former shall not be remembered or come to mind. 18 But be glad and rejoice forever in what I create; For behold, I create Jerusalem as a rejoicing, And her people a joy. (NKJV)

Discussion questions for the End is Declared from the Beginning

1. Creation is the house of firstfruits created through and for Yeshua. Read Revelation 21:1-4. Who is the new heaven and earth created for?

2. The first two letters of the Bible are בר which is one of two Hebrew words for son. בר also means grain (Strong's Dictionary #1250). Read John 12:23-24. How do these first two letters of the Bible reveal the death of the Son?

2. Read Luke 11:16-23 and John 17:20-21. How do these verses apply to the "strong man in creation?"

3. We have said that the aleph-tav, את, as the first and last letters of the Hebrew alphabet represent all of creation. Read Isaiah 41:6, 44:6-7, and 48:12-13. In all these passages God refers to Himself as the First and the Last. How do these passages reinforce the idea that the aleph-tav represents all of creation?

4. The sixth word, ואת, v'eth connects the heavens and the earth. How does Paul say Yeshua connects heaven and earth (Rom 10:5-10)? How does this agree with Deuteronomy 30:11-14?

5. Reread 1 Samuel 3:2-3. God called out to Samuel when Eli's eyes began to grow dim and the lamp of God had not yet gone out in the Tabernacle. Discuss how this has a deeper meaning when applied to the spiritual state of Israel at the time. How does this also apply to 1 John 3:17-21?

6. We read of another connection between heaven and earth in Jacob's dream about angels descending on a ladder in Genesis 28:10-15. There is no neutral pronoun in the Hebrew language so verse 12 would read that angels ascended and descended on "him" not on "it." Yeshua references this event in John 1:51 implying that He is that ladder. Discuss how Yeshua will fulfill the words the LORD spoke at the top of the ladder in Jacob's dream.

Appendix A: The Hebrew Alphabet

The Hebrew alphabet started out in the form of pictographs with each character representing a specific picture. Words were constructed by putting pictures together illustrating a characteristic of a word. An example is the word "father." The Hebrew word for father is spelled "ab" in English. In Hebrew it consists of the letters aleph, א, and bet, ב written from right to left, אב. From the Hebrew alphabet chart we see that the aleph represents an ox for strength or leadership and the bet represents a family or house. A father, therefore, is the strength and leader of his house and family.

The Hebrew letters also stand for numbers. There weren't different symbols for numbers. Many numbers have significance in scripture. We see numbers repeated over and over. For example, one is the number for God; seven is the number of completion, eight is the number of new beginnings; and forty is the number of testing or trial.

Even as the shape of the letters changed and became more abstract, the connection to the original picture language remains. Moses would have written in the pictograph or early ancient Hebrew form; David in the mid ancient Hebrew; and Yeshua would have written in the late ancient Hebrew form. The Modern Hebrew script was not established until the 15th century A.D. and was strongly influenced by the Aramaic form of the letters.

When we read the Old Testament of the Bible, we need to realize that it was originally written in ancient Hebrew and each of the letters in the words represents a picture. Many words and names carry extra, deeper meaning by examining the word picture presented by the original pictographs. Yeshua said that "not one jot or tittle" would pass away from the word of God.

> Mt 5:18 "For assuredly, I say to you, till heaven and earth pass away, one jot or one tittle will by no means pass from the law till all is fulfilled. (NKJV)

The jot refers to the smallest Hebrew letter the yad or yood, י. A tittle is a variation in how a letter is written. Some examples of a "tittle" would be a letter that is written larger or smaller than normal, a gap in the text, a word spelled with an additional letter or a letter left out, as well as embellishments of a letter. All those variations in text are for a purpose with the ultimate purpose to further reveal the character of God.

> 2Ti 2:15 Study to shew thyself approved unto God, a workman that needeth not to be ashamed, rightly dividing the word of truth. (KJV)

> Pr 25:2 It is the glory of God to conceal a matter, But the glory of kings is to search out a matter. (NKJV)

> 2Ti 3:16 All Scripture is given by inspiration of God, and is profitable for doctrine, for reproof, for correction, for instruction in righteousness, (NKJV)

Hebrew Alphabet Chart

Ancient Hebrew Early	Mid	Late	Sound	Name	Literal and symbolic meaning	Modern Script	End of Word	Numeric value
			silent	aleph	ox, bull – strength, leader, first			1
			b, bh, v	beyt (bet)	tent, house – household, into, family			2
			g	gimel	camel – pride, to lift up, animal			3
			d	dalet	door – pathway, enter			4
			h, e	hey	window, lattice – "the", to reveal			5
			w, o, u	vav	nail – "and", to secure, to add			6
			z	zayin	weapon – cut, to cut off			7
			h	het	fence, a chamber – private, to separate			8
			th	tet	to twist, a snake – to surround			9
			y, i	yad (yood)	hand, closed hand – a deed, to make, work			10
			k, kh	kaph	arm, open hand – to cover, to allow, to open		ך	20 / 500
			l	lamed	cattle goad, staff – prod, toward, control, authority			30
			m	Mem	water – massive, chaos, liquid		ם	40 / 600
			n	nun (noon)	fish (moving) – activity, life		ן	50 / 700
			s	samech	a prop – support, turn			60
			silent	ayin	eye – to see, know, experience			70
			p, ph	pey	mouth – to speak, to open, a word		ף	80 / 800
			ts	tsadik	fish hook – harvest, need, desire		ץ	90 / 900
			q	quph (koof)	back of the head – behind, the last, the least			100
			r	resh	head – a person, highest, the head			200
			sh	shin	teeth – consume, destroy			300
			t	tav	a sign, a cross – to covenant, to seal			400

Appendix B: The Biblical Calendar

Events in prophecy are frequently tied to specific times of the year. We need to understand and be on the Biblical Calendar to truly understand and recognize the fulfillment of these prophecies. God tells us that one of the ways Satan will try to deceive the Saints is by changing the "appointed times."

> Da 7:25 And he shall speak great words against the most High, and shall wear out the saints of the most High, and **think to change times** and laws: and they shall be given into his hand until a time and times and the dividing of time. (KJV)

He has successfully done this by getting the whole world on the Gregorian calendar which observes only a solar year. God created both the sun and the moon as signs of the appointed times.

> Ge 1:14 And God said, Let there be lights in the firmament of the heaven to divide the day from the night; and let them be for signs, and for seasons, and for days, and years: (KJV)

The word translated as seasons is mo'ed meaning a fixed or set time, an appointed time. From the very beginning, God set up both the sun and the moon to mark His calendar.

The **Biblical Calendar** is based on the combined solar and lunar cycles. The months are determined by the lunar cycles and the length of the year by the solar cycles. The cycle of the moon is 29 and ½ days long. So, the months in the Jewish calendar mostly alternate between 29 and 30 days long. Twelve months adds up to only 354 days. This is where the solar cycle comes in. The solar cycle is 365 and ¼ days long, just over 11 days longer than a strictly lunar year. To compensate for the extra length needed to make a complete year, the Biblical Calendar, like the Gregorian calendar, has leap years. Instead of having leap years that add a day, the Biblical calendar inserts whole months as "leap months." These occur on a 19- year cycle. A leap month is inserted every 3rd 6th, 8th, 11th, 14th 17th and 19th year before Adar, the last month of the religious calendar. Visually, the cycle is shown in the following chart. The year number in the cycle is in the top row. In the second row, R stands for a regular year and **L** stands for a leap year.

1	2	3	4	5	6	7	8	9	10	11	12	13	14	15	16	17	18	19
R	R	L	R	R	L	R	L	R	R	L	R	R	L	R	R	L	R	L

Today we simply look at a printed (or digital) calendar to determine what month it is. How did Israel determine months before printing or computers? Until the 4th century A.D. each new month had to be declared by the Sanhedrin (or the court of Israel). Witnesses would be stationed around Judea to watch for the new moon. The "new moon" in Biblical terms is not the total shadow, but the first sliver of the waxing moon. When the moon was sighted, the witnesses ran back to the Sanhedrin. Upon the arrival of the two witnesses and their testimony, the Sanhedrin would officially declare the beginning of the new month.

There are actually two Biblical Calendars that we are concerned with, a civil calendar and a religious calendar.

Civil calendar: This is the calendar used by modern day Jews. The first month, Tishrei begins in the fall. Jewish tradition believes that Tirhrei 1 is the day that God created Adam. The change in year number occurs at this time. Tishrei is referred to in scripture as the end of the year.

> De 31:10 And Moses commanded them, saying: "At the **end of every seven years**, at the appointed time in the year of release, at the Feast of Tabernacles… (NKJV)

Religious calendar: The First month is Nisan which is in the early spring. This is because Moses led the Israelites out of Egypt in the month of Nisan. It symbolizes new beginnings or new birth.

> Ex 12:1 And the LORD spake unto Moses and Aaron in the land of Egypt, saying, 2 This month shall be unto you the beginning of months: it shall be the first month of the year to you. (KJV)

You can think of these two ways of counting within the Biblical Calendar as the difference between our own traditional calendar year and the school year. A school year begins in August or September and ends in May or June whereas the traditional year begins with January and ends with December. The months are all the same but the beginning and ends change. See the chart below for how the Biblical Calendar is counted.

Biblical Calendar

Hebrew Name	Civil sequence#	Redemption sequence#	Gregorian equivalent
Tishrei	1	7	Sept-Oct
Chesvan	2	8	Oct-Nov
Kislev	3	9	Nov-Dec
Tevet	4	10	Dec-Jan
Shvat	5	11	Jan-Feb
Adar (I and II)	6	12	Feb-Mar
Nisan	7	1	Mar-Apr
Iyyar	8	2	Apr-May
Sivan	9	3	May-Jun
Tammuz	10	4	Jun-Jul
Av	11	5	Jul-Aug
Elul	12	6	Aug-Sep

Lastly, a few additional items about the Biblical Calendar are worth mentioning:

- Yom Kippur does not fall next to a Saturday.

- Hoshana Rabba (the seventh day of the Feast of Tabernacles) does not fall on a Saturday.
- Tishrei 1 is always on a Monday, Tuesday, Thursday or Saturday.
- The period between Nisan 1 and Tishrei 1 is always the same length.
- The period from Nisan 15 to Tishrei 22 (which encompasses all the Feasts of the LORD) is always 185 days. Incidentally, this is also the length of time between the spring and fall equinoxes.
- Years are counted from the beginning of creation so as of this writing it is 5769 (versus 2009)
- Days are counted from sunset to sunset rather than from midnight to midnight.

Appendix C: Sabbath Blessings

There are many ways to begin the Sabbath. The following two options are ways that we have opened the Sabbath. The first option uses the traditional Jewish blessing for lighting the Shabbat Candles. The second option uses a blessing for lighting the candles which incorporates Yeshua. Feel free to mix and match and write your own; there is no single right way to begin the Sabbath. The important thing is that one set it aside as a day of rest.

Option 1:

Welcome to our home and the Erev Shabbat, or the "evening of" Sabbath. Isn't it strange that man's way is always at odds with God's way? In Genesis1, we are continuously reminded that "the evening and the morning made" a day, where the first through the sixth days are described. God has us begin each and every new day in darkness and then He brings light to it, just as it was when He founded this creation. Shabbat begins at dusk *after* the daylight that ends Friday. This is a reminder regarding God's sovereignty and the source of all enlightenment.

At our weekly Sabbath celebration with our Heavenly Father, we dim the other lights of the room and kindle the Sabbath lights. We leave the candles burning until they go out on their own or put them out at bedtime. The woman of the house will usually light the candles but if she is not available, Dad can light the candles and recite the blessings. After the candles are lit, she will focus on the glowing warmth of the lights and recite the blessing. This sets the tone for the remainder of the Sabbath. Covering her eyes lightly with her finger tips, then with an outward sweeping motion she encircles the flames three times bringing her fingertips back briefly to cover her eyes; she will then lift up her arms in praise and recite the words of the blessing:

The Blessing of the Sabbath Lights

Baruch atah Adonai Eloheynu
melech ha-olam asher kidshanu
b'mitzvotav v'tzivanu l'hadlik ner shel Shabbat.

BLESSED ARE YOU, LORD OUR GOD,
King of the universe, who has made us holy
By giving us his commandments, and has
Commanded us to kindle the Sabbath lights.

The Lord is our light and our salvation. In His name we kindle these Sabbath lights.
May the Sabbath lights bring into our home the beauty of truth and the radiance of God's love. May the Lord bless us with Sabbath joy.
May the Lord bless us with Sabbath Holiness.
May the Lord bless us with Sabbath peace.

We look forward to this day because it is our Heavenly Father's gift of respite from the things we deal with daily. The Sabbath is our opportunity to reflect on who made us, to take stock of who we are today, and evaluate if we are in "His perfect will."

A special cup of wine is shared around the Sabbath table and the blessing of the fruit of the vine is offered. Usually, Dad says the blessing, but a son or anyone else might say it for him. Wine or juice can be used for this blessing. It is your choice. The purpose is not the form, but the opportunity to connect with past and future blessings from our Father.

The Blessing of the Wine

Baruch atah Adonai Eloheynu
Melech ha'olam,
Boray pri ha'gafen.

BLESSED ARE YOU, LORD OUR GOD,
King of the universe,
Who creates the fruit of the vine.

(Drink the wine)

Two loaves of bread, called Challah are baked together, covered and put on the Erev Shabbat table, until the blessings are said and the meal is about to start. The two loaves remind us of the double portion of manna that the LORD provided on that first Sabbath coming out of Egypt and that He will provide for our every need today as well. We are, also, reminded of Yeshua who was born in Bethlehem, which in Hebrew means "house of bread." He told us that He is the "Bread of Life" and we will never hunger when we allow Him to feed our spirit. The blessings over the wine and Challah are an appropriate time to remember his payment of our penalty for sin.

The Blessing of the Bread

Baruch atah Adonai Eloheynu
melech ha-olam
ha-motzi lechen min ha-eretz.

BLESSED ARE YOU, LORD OUR GOD,
King of the universe,
Who brings forth bread from the earth.

(Eat a piece of bread)

In your family setting, other blessings can be said at this time, blessings over the sons and daughters, the husband blessing the wife, sharing any special prayers or blessings from other family members, etc.

The Blessing for the Meal

Blessed are you, LORD our God,
King of the Universe
Bless this time together with family and friends
As we gather here on your Sabbath, the first of your Moedim, your divine appointments.
May your blessings be on this food, on the fellowship and on the study of your word, your Torah, in Yeshua's name. Amen.

Option 2:

Welcome to our home on this Erev Shabbat, the evening of the Sabbath. What is the Sabbath? It says in Exodus 31:16-17

> Exodus 31:16-17 NKJV 16 'Therefore the children of Israel shall keep the Sabbath, to observe the Sabbath throughout their generations as a perpetual covenant. 17 'It is a sign between Me and the children of Israel forever; for in six days the LORD made the heavens and the earth, and on the seventh day He rested and was refreshed."

The Sabbath is not just for the Children of Israel but for all who call upon the name of the LORD.

> Isaiah 56:6-7 NKJV 6 "Also the sons of the foreigner Who join themselves to the LORD, to serve Him, And to love the name of the LORD, to be His servants- Everyone who keeps from defiling the Sabbath, And holds fast My covenant- 7 Even them I will bring to My holy mountain, And make them joyful in My house of prayer. Their burnt offerings and their sacrifices will be accepted on My altar; For My house shall be called a house of prayer for all nations."

The Sabbath was given to the Jew and Gentile alike and it is to be a delight. In Isaiah 58:13 it says "You shall call the Sabbath a delight." The Hebrew word translated as delight is "Oneg." Oneg implies celebration, sharing time with loved ones, leisurely meals, hospitality and relaxation.

The Sabbath is a time of spiritual and physical rest and refreshment. It is more than just refraining from work; it is a rejuvenation of body and spirit. In Jewish tradition, the Sabbath is called "a foretaste of the days of Messiah."

A poem written in the 16th century by Rabbai Shlomo HaLevi Alkabetz emphasizes remembering God and His creation on the Sabbath, as well as the coming of the promised Messiah and the final redemption of Israel. Listen to these words.

> ***Come my beloved to welcome the bride, the presence of Shabbat we receive.***
> ***"Observe and Remember" in one divine utterance, we heard from the One and***

Only God, the LORD is One and His name is One, for renown, for splendor, and for praise. Come my beloved...

Shake off the dust and arise! Dress in garments of Glory, my people, through the son of Jesse, the Bethlehemite, redemption draws near to my soul. Come my beloved...

Wake up, wake up! For your light has come, awaken, awaken, sing a song, for the glory of the LORD is revealed to you! Come my beloved...

As we enter the Sabbath rest tonight, let it be a reminder that we are to be a light to the world. The lighting of the Shabbat candles marks the beginning of the Sabbath and, traditionally, is done eighteen minutes before local sunset. The honored woman of the house is the one who usually lights the candles and recites the blessing.

(The woman of the house recites the following)

Ba-rooch ah-ta Adonai Eh-lo-hay-noo
Meh-lech ha-oh-lahm ah-sher keed-sha-noo beed-va-reh-cha v'na-tahn
la-noo et Yeshua m'she-chay-noo, v'tzee-va-noo
l'he-oat oar la-oh-lahm. Ah-main.

Blessed are you, LORD our God,
King of the universe, who has sanctified us in Your Word,
and given us Yeshua our Messiah,
and commanded us to be a light to the world. Amen.

(The man of the house follows with this prayer)

The Lord is our light and our salvation. In His name we kindle these Sabbath lights. May the Sabbath lights bring into our home the beauty of truth and the radiance of God's love. May the Lord bless us with Sabbath joy. May the Lord bless us with Sabbath Holiness. May the Lord bless us with Sabbath peace. Amen.

Before the meal, a special cup of wine is shared around the Sabbath table and the blessing of the fruit of the vine is offered. Wine or juice can be used for this blessing. The purpose is not ritual form, but the opportunity to connect with past and future blessings from our Father.

The Blessing of the Wine (Recited by the man of the house)

Ba-rooch ah-ta Adonai Eh-lo-hay-noo
Meh-lech ha-oh-lahm,
Boo-ray pa-ree hah-gah-fen.

**Blessed are You, LORD our God,
King of the universe,
who creates the fruit of the vine.**

(Drink the wine)

Two loaves of bread, called Challah are baked together, covered, and put on the Erev Shabbat table. The two loaves remind us of the double portion of manna that the LORD provided on that first Sabbath as the Children of Israel came out of Egypt, and that the LORD will provide for our every need today as well. We are also reminded of Yeshua who was born in Bethlehem, which in Hebrew means "house of bread." Yeshua told us that He is the "Bread of Life" and we will never hunger when we allow Him to feed our spirit.

The blessings over the wine and Challah are an appropriate time to remember his payment of our penalty for sin.

The Blessing of the Bread (Recited by the man of the house)

**Ba-rooch ah-ta Adonai Eh-lo-hay-noo
Meh-lech ha-oh-lahm,
ha-mot-zee le-chem min ha-eretz.**

**Blessed are You, LORD our God,
King of the universe,
who brings forth bread from the earth.**

(Eat a piece of bread)

In your family setting, in your own homes, other blessings, prayers and songs can be shared that add to the richness of a family Shabbat celebration. Traditionally, blessings over children are recited, the husband will say a blessing over his wife, and any special prayers or blessings from other family members are shared as well.

As we prepare to share our Shabbat meal together, I will say this blessing.

The Blessing for the Meal (The man of the house recites this blessing)

Blessed are you, LORD our God,
King of the Universe
Bless this time together with family and friends
As we gather here on your Sabbath, the first of your Moedim, your divine appointments.
May your blessings be on this food, on the fellowship and on the study of your word, your Torah, in Yeshua's name. Amen.

Appendix D:THE THIRTEEN ATTRIBUTES OF GOD Ex 34:6,7				
1	יהוה	YHVH	The LORD	His Covenant Keeping Unchanging Nature
2	יהוה	YHVH	The LORD	Emphasizes His Unchanging Character and His Mercy
3	אל	EL	GOD	The Creator/King Underscoring His Capacity For Mercy
4	רחום	RACHUM	Compassionate	As For a Child in the Womb
5	חנון	CHANAN	Gracious	Showers Grace and Favor to the Undeserving
6	ארך אפים	EREK APAYIM	Slow to Anger	Patiently Waits For You To Repent
7	רב חסד	RAV CHESED	Abounding in Lovinkindness	To Both the Righteous and the Unrighteous
8	אמת	EMET	Truth	He's Fair and Equitable in His Justice
9	נצר חסד לאלפים	NOTZEIR CHESED L'ALAFIM	Keeps Lovinkindness for Thousands	His Generational Covenant Devotion is Boundless
10	נשא עון	NOSEI AVON	Forgives Iniquity	Intentional Sins
11	נשא פשע	NOSEI PESHA	Forgives Transgression	Rebellious Sins
12	נשא חטאה	NOSEI CHATAAH	Forgives Sin	Inadvertant Sins
13	נקה	NAKEH	Who Cleanses	He Cleanses Sin

Glossary

Brit Chadashah: New covenant, renewed covenant, the New Testament

Gemara: Written commentary on the Oral Law. Part of the Talmud

Ketuvim: The part of the Tanakh consisting of the writings. In our Protestant Bibles, these are the books of Joshua through The Song of Solomon.

Meshiach: Messiah, anointed one, Christ

Miqra: Convocation, assembly, dress rehearsal

Mincha: gift, offering, present, voluntary offering

Mishna: the written collection of the Oral Law. Part of the Talmud

Moed: appointed time or place, appointment, festival. Plural: Moedim

Navi'im: The books of the Prophets

Olah: to ascend or go up, a burnt offering

Owth: sign, signal, as an appearing

Talmud: A record of rabbinic discussions pertaining to Jewish law, ethics, customs, and history. It consists of two parts, the Mishnah and the Gemara.

Tanakh: An acronym for the Hebrew Scriptures. The T stands for the Torah which consists of the Books of Moses, the N stands for Navi'im which are the books of the prophets, and the K stands for the Ketuvim which are the writings.

Tallit: cloak, prayer shawl

Targum: Aramaic translation and interpretation of the Tanakh.

Torah: a precept or statute, especially the Decalogue or Pentateuch, teaching, law.

Year of Jubilee: Observed every 50th year. All the land in Israel was returned to its original tribe and family. All Israelite slaves were set free.

Yehoshua: Joshua. God (Yah) will save.

Yeshua: Given Hebrew name of Jesus. It means he will save.

Additional recommended resources

This is not intended to be an exhaustive list but it is some of the primary research resources that we have used and it will give you a good place to start.

Online resources:
>   www.biblestudytools.com
>   Multiple Bible versions, commentaries and other on-line reference tools.
>   www.elshaddaiministries.us
>   Weekly Torah teachings and other teaching sessions available free on-line.
>   www.jewishencyclopedia.com

CD and DVD's by Pastor Mark Biltz
>   The Feasts of the LORD
>   Song of Solomon
>   Spots, Wrinkles and Blemishes
>   Hebrew Roots, Volumes 1 and 2

Computer software

Power Bible
>   Available at www.powerbible.com

E-Sword
>   www.e-sword.net

Printed books or ebooks
E. W. Bullinger:
>   Numbers in Scripture
>   The Witness of the Stars
>   Figures of Speech Used in the Bible

Alfred Edersheim:
>   The Temple – Its Ministry and Services
>   The Bible History: Old Testament
>   Sketches of Jewish Social life in the Time of Christ
>   The Life and Times of Jesus the Messiah

Daniel Gruber
>   The Separation of Church and Faith, Volume 1—Copernicus and the Jews

Dr. Frank Seekins:
>   Hebrew Word Pictures
>   The Gospel in Ancient Hebrew
>   The Ten Commandments

Strong's Exhaustive Concordance and Dictionary

Made in the USA
Coppell, TX
11 November 2023

24101481R00122